The Global Economy and International Financing

The Global Economy and International Financing

HENRI L. BEENHAKKER

Q

QUORUM BOOKS
Westport, Connecticut • London

Library of Congress Cataloging-in-Publication Data

Beenhakker, Henri L.
    The global economy and international financing / Henri L. Beenhakker.
      p. cm.
    Includes bibliographical references and index.
    ISBN 1–56720–401–5 (alk. paper)
    1. International finance. 2. Foreign exchange. 3. International trade. 4. International
business enterprises—Management. I. Title.
HG3881.B42 2001
658.15'99—dc21   00–037265

British Library Cataloguing in Publication Data is available.

Library of Congress Catalog Card Number: 00–037265
ISBN: 1–56720–401–5

First published in 2001

Quorum Books, 88 Post Road West, Westport, CT 06881
An imprint of Greenwood Publishing Group, Inc.
www.quorumbooks.com

Printed in the United States of America

The paper used in this book complies with the
Permanent Paper Standard issued by the National
Information Standards Organization (Z39.48–1984).

10 9 8 7 6 5 4 3 2 1

Copyright Acknowledgment

Appendixes 2 and 6 are reprinted from Henri L. Beenhakker, *Risk Management in Project Finance
and Implementation* (Westport, CT: Quorum Books, 1997). Copyright © 1997 by Henri L.
Beenhakker. Reproduced with permission of Greenwood Publishing Group, Inc., Westport, CT.

To

Caroline, Barbara, Mark and Britta

Contents

Figures and Tables

FIGURES

TABLES

Preface

The world economy of the 2000s will experience a further growth of international business opportunities. As markets become more internationally integrated, foreign markets will have more influence on corporate performance. A good understanding of the characteristics of a new global economy and international finance is, therefore, becoming critical to a company's success. The main purpose of this book is to familiarize the reader with a multifaceted approach to decision making in an international context involving the interactions between the private and public sectors in a rapidly changing global economy. These interactions revolve around the forces of global competition and global governance and require a good perception of how macroeconomic issues affecting the global economy interact with issues in international financing.

Today's analysis of investment decisions draws from a wide range of sources such as economics, finance, accounting and statistics. This book is self-contained since no prior knowledge of these disciplines is assumed. Analytical techniques help translate the often vague rules of thumb used by international financial executives into specific decision criteria. Many of these criteria require an understanding of how strategic management, national government policies and the international public sector are related in, sometimes, subtle ways. A conceptual framework is provided for analyzing, predicting and responding to changes in the financial environment and global trade.

Naturally, an understanding of international financial management and trade is crucial for multinational corporations (MNCs). Such an understanding is also important for companies that have no intention of engaging in international business, since they must recognize how their foreign competitors will be affected by movements in exchange rates, foreign interest rates, labor costs, availability of skills and inflation. These economic characteristics can affect the foreign competitors' cost of production and pricing policy. In addition, it behooves companies to recognize how domestic competitors who obtain foreign supplies or foreign financing will be affected by economic conditions in foreign countries. These domestic companies may be able to reduce their costs by capitalizing on opportunities in international markets and, consequently, they may be able to reduce their prices without reducing their profit margins. This could enable them to increase their market share at the expense of the purely domestic companies.

The book should be of particular interest to investment bankers, capital market professionals, corporate finance staff, venture capital professionals, project finance managers and advisors and professionals who are concerned about the designation of policy prescriptions to meet current and future challenges in the world economy. Concepts that are likely to be new to many readers have been explained carefully, and many numerical examples have been included. The book can, therefore, also be used as a text in business schools and departments of economics. It is particularly recommended for those educators who wish to bridge the gap between the worlds of practice and education, and enhance the connection between what a student learns in school and what he or she will need to solve problems experienced by real managers. The chapters are written in a modular, self-contained manner so that they may be read in any order.

The book is organized as follows. Chapter 1 gives a brief history of the international monetary system and discusses the advantages and disadvantages of different foreign exchange policies. It also explains how transactions in the interbank market are executed and the role of international parity conditions. The last part of Chapter 1 examines foreign currency options or contracts which give the option purchaser the right, but not the obligation, to buy or sell a given amount of foreign exchange at a fixed rate per unit of domestic currency for a specified period of time.

Chapter 2 reviews the sources of comparative advantage in international trade, the role of targeted export subsidies and import tariffs, import quotas and voluntary export restraints. The formation of regional trade blocks such as the European Union (EU) and the North American Free Trade Agreement (NAFTA) is seen as an area of increasing concern in view of the implications that regionalism and preferential trade arrangements may have for the normative economics of trade. Differences between the General Agreement on Tariffs and Trade (GATT) and the World Trade Organization (WTO) are explored. Finally, the system of import and export financing and its benefits are discussed.

Chapter 3 starts with a discussion of the causes of international flows of capital and their economic and financial consequences. Next, different corporate strategies for direct foreign investment and various forms of political risk are examined. Deregulation of financial institutions in the United States, combined with an increase in international trade, led to the introduction of financial futures contracts, securitization, interest rate swaps, currency swaps and "junk" bonds in the mid- and late 1970s. The chapter ends with a review of these instruments and the effect of this deregulation on banking regulations.

Rapid changes in international monetary conditions make balance-of-payments (BOP) problems a major concern for governments and the management of MNCs alike. Chapter 4 discusses short-term and long-term monetary and fiscal policies governments can use to correct BOP deficits, and how these policies can affect an MNC's operation. Next, a review of how central banks implement these policies is presented. Finally, the potential conflicts between an MNC's operations and government policies are analyzed together with the best approach to avoiding conceivable areas of potential conflict.

Chapter 5 gives an in-depth examination of the determinants of interest rates. It commences with an exposition of the classical theory which prevailed until the 1930s, and the subsequent loanable funds approach. These approaches were followed by the monetarist view of interest rates and the neo-Keynesian approach. The monetarists focus on the growth rate of the money supply, while the neo-Keynesians emphasize the importance of the level of interest rates. In the United States, the Federal Reserve tended to follow the neo-Keynesian approach by monitoring closely the levels of interest rates during the 1950s and 1960s. In the 1970s and 1980s the Federal Reserve's focus was on the growth of the money supply, thus following more of a monetarist approach, although not completely ignoring the level of interest rates. In the 1990s, more of a focus on interest rates returned. Having a good understanding of the determinants of interest rates will assist the management of corporations with the determination of their future cost of capital.

In mid-1997 the East Asian countries suffered from a simultaneous onset of a banking crisis and a currency crisis. These countries were not the first to suffer from such crises. Why is it that policymakers don't seem to learn from past economic catastrophes? Chapter 6 sketches out a framework for learning from the East Asian crisis. A number of indicators such as the incremental capital-output ratio, the ratio of net domestic credit to GDP, the unhedged foreign exchange exposure of the financial structure of banks and firms, are suggested to foretell the beginning of a financial crisis. Similarities and dissimilarities between the East Asian crisis and the financial crises in Chile in 1982, in Mexico in 1994 and in Brazil in 1997 are also examined. Finally, the importance of matching liabilities with assets and the use of coverage ratios are discussed.

Chapter 7 explains how to manage three types of foreign exchange exposure: transaction exposure, operating exposure and accounting exposure. Transaction exposure measures changes in the value of outstanding financial obligations incurred prior to a change in exchange rates but not due to be settled until after the exchange rates change. In other words, transaction exposure deals with changes in cash flows that result from existing contractual obligations. Operating exposure measures the change in the net present value of a firm as a result from any change in the future operating cash flows of the firm caused by an unexpected change in the exchange rates. The change in value depends on the impact of the exchange rate change on future costs, prices and/or sales volume. Accounting exposure is the potential for accounting-derived changes in owners' equity that occur because of the need to "translate" foreign currency financial statements of foreign affiliates into a single reporting currency to prepare worldwide consolidated statements. This chapter also proposes an approach to determining the optimal financial structure of an MNC and its affiliates.

Chapter 8 starts with a review of sourcing equity and debt internationally. Next, various instruments or techniques to reduce gap risk are discussed. Gap risk is defined as the risk arising from mismatched timing in repricing interest-rate-sensitive assets and liabilities. It is typical of nonfinancial firms as opposed to financial institutions where the basis risk plays a role. The instruments/techniques reviewed include mismatched maturities, foreign exchange forward mismatching, forward rate agreements, interest rate futures, interest rate caps and floors, interest rate collars and swaptions.

To show real-world applications and issues on current multinational topics, four case studies have been included in annex form. Appendix 1 reviews the secured financing of a water supply project and the related issues of limited recourse, security and insurance. Appendix 3 explains how to establish the value of a government-owned company to be privatized. The appendix on Cash Flow Analysis demonstrates the establishment of cash flows of a direct foreign investment and how to deal with issues of taxation and inflation. The purpose of the appendix on the Development of a New Subsidiary is to show a capital budgeting analysis which starts with simplifying assumptions and, subsequently, relaxes them in order to demonstrate the potential complexity of such an analysis. Appendix 8 provides a more rigorous presentation of a number of topics introduced in the text.

Students in my courses at the New York Institute of Finance and the International Institute of USDA's Graduate School have made many useful suggestions for improving the book from the students' perspective. I am also most grateful for the comments on an earlier version of this text that I received from teachers and private and public investment planners. Finally, I wish to thank my wife, Caroline, for her forbearance and tireless support.

The Global Economy and International Financing

Chapter 1

Foreign Exchange Markets

THE INTERNATIONAL MONETARY SYSTEM

The international monetary system refers to the structure within which foreign exchange rates are determined, international trade and capital flows are accommodated and balance-of-payments adjustments are made. It also includes the institutions, instruments and agreements that link together the world's currency and money markets. Decision makers in both the private and public sectors need a better understanding of the international monetary system and the forces of global economic change. These forces are commonly summarized as constituting an intensified process of "internationalization" or "globalization." A better understanding of "globalization" will lead to the realization that it is shortsighted to maintain that national economies are completely subordinated by the globalization processes and that national policy making is powerless before global forces.

With the growth of Eurocurrency markets, international syndication of loans, government loans and foreign direct investment, the international movement of capital has increased significantly. The dismantling of restrictions on financial flows across borders, the deregulation of financial institutions and international financial innovations have also led to a rapid growth of the international linkage of national money and capital markets. Competition for capital is worldwide and long-term interest rates are increasingly determined by the integration of world capital markets.

The increased international flow of capital is reflected on the foreign exchange market, the most liquid of markets. Worldwide foreign exchange transactions increased from a gross turnover of $200 billion a day in the mid-1980s to $1.3 trillion a day in the mid-1990s. Assuming 240 business days in a year, the $1.3

trillion translates into an annual amount of $312 trillion. By comparison, the mid-1990s annual global trade in goods and services and annual global turnover in equity markets amounted to $4.3 trillion and $21 trillion, respectively.

To be successful, today's business executives can no longer limit the striving for a competitive advantage to maximizing internal efficiency (efficient performance in the functional activities of a firm—production, finance, marketing and organization). They also need to understand the international context in which their firm operates in order to achieve external efficiency. External efficiency means that the firm adapts to the ever-changing international environment with an appropriate response and in a timely fashion. Competitive advantage depends on achieving the proper mix of internal and external efficiencies.

In fact, there are two dimensions to external efficiency: adjusting to external shocks and taking advantage of new opportunities. International economic and political developments that are continually changing a firm's external environment include (but are not necessarily limited to) the establishment of a regional common market; rapid development in a newly industrializing country; the appearance of a foreign competitor; policies to remedy a country's balance-of-payments deficit; rescheduling a country's external debt; the policies of international organizations such as the World Trade Organization (WTO), the United Nations Conference on Trade and Development (UNCTAD), the World Bank and the International Monetary Fund (IMF).

EXCHANGE RATES

A foreign currency exchange rate is the price of one country's currency in units of another currency or commodity (gold or silver). There are two ways of quoting exchange rates. First, the exchange rate can be expressed as the number of units of domestic currency per unit of foreign currency. For instance, if $0.50 of US currency is required to buy one Swiss franc, the exchange rate would be quoted as 0.50 dollars per Swiss franc. This method is called *American terms* or a *direct quote*. Second, the exchange rate can be expressed as the number of units of foreign currency per unit of domestic currency. Using the same numbers, the exchange rate would be quoted as 2.00 Swiss francs per dollar. This method is called *European terms* or an *indirect quote*. As a matter of custom, some exchange rates are quoted one way (e.g., the US dollar/British pound exchange rate as dollars per pound) and some are quoted the other way (e.g., the US dollar/Japanese yen exchange rate as yen per dollar). A currency declines in value or depreciates if more units of that currency are required to buy the same number of units of the foreign currency. For instance, if market conditions would change the 1.5 US dollars per British pound exchange rate to 2 US dollars per pound, the dollar would depreciate relative to the pound and the pound would appreciate.

One of the two following formulas can be used to measure a change in the exchange rate.

With direct quotes:

Percentage change = [(ending rate − beginning rate)/beginning rate] × 100%

With indirect quotes:

Percentage change = [(beginning rate − ending rate)/ending rate] × 100%

Let us, for instance, compute the percentage increase in the dollar value of the German mark (or the value of mark-denominated accounts receivable or payable from the dollar perspective) if a recent quote of DM1.5535/$ suddenly strengthens to DM1.2755/$. With the direct quote:

[($0.7840/DM − $0.6437/DM)/$0.6437/DM] × 100% = 21.80%

With the indirect quote:

[(DM1.5535/$ − DM1.2755/$)/DM1.2755/$] × 100% = 21.80%

An exchange rate between countries B and C is implied by the exchange rates between countries A and B and countries A and C. It is called the *cross exchange rate*. For instance, if one dollar can be exchanged for 120 yen or 50 pesos, then 120 yen = 50 pesos, or one yen = 50/120 pesos. The general case can be defined as follows:

If $X(1,2)$ = the exchange rate between countries 1 and 2,
    $X(1,3)$ = the exchange rate between countries 1 and 3,
    $X(2,3)$ = the exchange rate between countries 2 and 3

then

$$[X(1,2)][X(2,3)] = X(1,3)$$

or

$$X(2,3) = [X(1,3)]/[X(1,2)]$$

Cross rates can be used to check on opportunities for intermarket arbitrage. Suppose the following exchange rates are available:

Dutch guilders (symbol fl) per US dollar fl1.9025/US$
Canadian dollars per US dollar   C$1.2646/US$
Dutch guilders per Canadian dollar fl1.5214/C$

The cross rate between Dutch guilders and Canadian dollars is:

$$[fl1.9025/US\$]/[C\$1.2646/US\$] = fl1.5044/C\$$$

Since this cross rate is not the same as the actual quotation of fl1.5214/C$, an opportunity for profit from arbitrage between these markets (*triangular arbitrage*) exists. A Dutch trader with fl1,000,000 can sell that sum in the spot market for US$525,624; simultaneously, he can sell the US dollars for C$664,704 and exchange the Canadian dollars for fl1,011,281, making a risk-free profit of fl11,281 before transaction costs. Such intermarket arbitrage should continue until the exchange rate equilibrium is reestablished or until the calculated cross rate equals the actual quotation less a margin for transaction costs.

If the government of a country regulates the rate at which its currency is exchanged for other currencies, the system or regime is classified as a fixed or managed exchange regime. The rate at which the currency is fixed, or pegged, is referred to as its *par value*. If the government of a country does not intervene in the exchange or valuation of its currency in any way, it is classified as *floating* or *flexible*.

Under a fixed exchange rate system, the government fixes the rate in one of two ways. First, the government can require all currency exchange to go through the government at the government-established exchange rate. Second, the government can buy and sell in the open market in sufficient quantity to fix the price. If people want to sell the domestic currency, the government buys it and sells the foreign currency. The foreign currency may come from government reserves, from sales of precious metals or from borrowings. Conversely, if holders of foreign currency want to buy the domestic currency, the government sells it and buys the foreign currency, thereby accumulating foreign currency reserves.

The advantages of fixed exchange rates are:

- they provide stability in international prices for the conduct of trade while stable prices aid in the growth of international trade; and
- they are anti-inflationary, requiring the country to follow restrictive monetary and fiscal policies; it is noted, however, that such restrictiveness may limit the country in ways to alleviate internal problems such as slow economic growth and high unemployment.

The disadvantages of fixed rates are:

- over time, as the structure of a country's economy changes due to the evolvement of its trade relationships and balances, they may become inconsistent with economic fundamentals; whereas flexible rates allow this to happen gradually and efficiently, fixed rates must be changed administratively (often too late); and

• they require central banks to maintain large quantities of international reserves (other hard currencies and gold) to be used in the occasional defense of their fixed rate; this has become a significant burden for many countries due to rapid growth in size and volume of the international currency markets.

If a government sets the fixed exchange rate at the wrong level, some transactions are discouraged and others are encouraged. A severely mispriced exchange rate creates a balance-of-payments surplus or deficit and makes a later exchange rate adjustment likely. Businessmen who include information about the balance of payments in their business decisions—as they should do—may be discouraged from committing themselves to international transactions if an exchange rate change appears likely. Alternatively, they can reduce risk of such a change by the use of forward contracts, futures contracts, options or swaps.

Many developing countries have pursued, or are pursuing, policies resulting in overvalued exchange rates. A currency is overvalued when the price of foreign exchange is lower than it would be under free trade equilibrium. Overvaluation makes imports inexpensive and exports expensive and, therefore, requires either that import duties be imposed on some or all imports or that imports be rationed by allocating foreign exchange according to import quotas. Although both measures are often used simultaneously, developing countries have often tended to rely more on quantitative restrictions. The two main arguments advanced to support the maintenance of overvalued exchange rates are closely interlinked. One is the belief that the foreign demand for traditional exports of developing countries is income inelastic and that the growth in demand is sluggish. Consequently, the other argument has been that the best way to achieve economic growth is to promote industrial development through substituting domestic manufactured goods for imported ones. Foreign exchange control regimes have thus aimed at promoting primarily the industrial sectors of developing countries. The substitution has been promoted by imposing import duties or quantitative import restrictions on goods to be substituted, while duties have been low or nonexistent on the inputs required by the emerging industries. Another argument sometimes advanced to support the maintenance of overvalued exchange rates is that they curb inflation. There is, however, sufficient evidence that, in the long run, this is not the case.

In retrospect, protectionist policies have proved to be ineffective and their economic costs have been substantial. One reason is that an overvalued exchange rate prevents a country from exploiting its comparative advantage as determined by world market prices. Protected industries often have monopolistic positions and operate in an environment that lacks incentives to operate efficiently, to innovate or to modernize in order to stay in tune with global progress. In addition, the small size of the domestic market often prevents such industries from exploiting economies of scale. The economic costs of these industrial policies have resulted in lower economic growth.

Experience shows that the demand for exports of developing countries is not as inelastic as claimed. Several empirical studies also show that countries that have pursued export-promoting policies have been more successful in achieving economic growth than those that have not. However, several developing countries have been reluctant to devaluate their currencies in order to reduce or eliminate overvaluation for fear that eliminating overvaluation will give rise to inflation and undermine the financial viability of many companies. In the short run, an adjustment of the exchange rate may well have such consequences, but in the long run, overvaluation means that many imports and potential exports consumed locally are being provided at artificially low prices, below the real cost to the country.

A BRIEF HISTORY OF THE INTERNATIONAL MONETARY SYSTEM

During 1876–1913, Western Europe had the gold standard as an international monetary system; the United States accepted it in 1879. According to the gold standard, each country set the rate at which its currency—paper or coin—could be converted to a weight of gold. For instance, the United States declared the dollar to be convertible to gold at the rate of $20.67/ounce of gold, the par value of gold. The British pound was pegged at 4.2474 pounds/ounce of gold. As long as both currencies were freely convertible into gold, the dollar/pound exchange rate was:

($20.67/ounce of gold)/(4.2474 pounds/ounce of gold) = $4.86651/pound

The gold standard worked adequately until the beginning of World War I when trade flows and the free movement of gold were interrupted. During World War I and the early 1920s, currencies were allowed to fluctuate over fairly wide ranges in terms of gold and each other, and exchange rates were increasingly unstable. The United States returned to gold in 1919, followed by the United Kingdom in 1925 and France in 1928. However, the problem of finding new and reasonable stable parity values for gold was never solved before the collapse of the Austrian banking system in 1931, when most trading nations abandoned the gold standard once again.

In 1934 the United States returned to the gold standard at $35.00/ounce of gold; however, gold was only traded with foreign central banks, not private citizens. From 1934 to the end of World War II, exchange rates were theoretically established by each currency's value in terms of gold. During World War II and its immediate aftermath, many of the world's major currencies lost their convertibility and the dollar was the only major trading currency.

Toward the end of World War II (1944) the Allied Powers adopted a so-called gold exchange standard at Bretton Woods, New Hampshire. In essence, the agreement established a dollar-based international monetary system and provided for two new institutions: the International Monetary Fund (IMF), for aiding countries with balance-of-payments and exchange rate problems; and the International Bank for Reconstruction and Development (World Bank), for postwar reconstruction and general economic development. The agreement required all countries to fix the value of their currency in terms of gold but they were not required to exchange their currencies for gold. Only the dollar remained convertible into gold (at $35.00 per ounce). Consequently, each country decided what it wanted its exchange rate to be vis-à-vis the dollar. Participating countries agreed to maintain their currencies within 1% of par value by buying or selling foreign exchange or gold as needed. If a currency became too weak to defend, a devaluation of up to 10 percent was allowed without formal approval by the IMF; larger devaluations required IMF approval.

To allow domestic autonomy for the pursuit of full employment, countries at Bretton Woods established the IMF with a pool of currencies as a source of additional official liquidity for its member countries. In other words, a central bank's limitation on the outflow of foreign reserves is, to some extent, relaxed. At Bretton Woods the countries established the basic principle that national gold and currency reserves were to be augmented so that they need not be forced to meet short-run balance-of-payments deficits by suffering deflation and unemployment. This should be in the form of prescribed "drawing rights" by a member country on its "quota" at the IMF. The amount of a member's subscription to the fund is equal to its quota. The financial resources subscribed to the fund by all of its members constitute an international reserve pool of currencies against which a member can draw for short-term financial assistance.

A member's right to buy other currencies from the IMF with its own currency is subject to complex rules. It has "drawing rights" up to a given percentage of its quota, divided into five equal tranches. The first tranche of 25 percent of a member's quota can be drawn upon automatically and unconditionally to achieve international liquidity; however, beyond the first tranche the IMF establishes under which conditions of national economic management the member country can exercise its drawing rights. In addition, a drawing country must repurchase its own currency from the IMF within a certain number of years by payment to the fund in the foreign currency previously acquired, or in any currency acceptable to the IMF. This temporary access to the fund's financial resources offers short-term financing to help ease the adjustment process for short-term balance-of-payments deficits. The adjustable peg came into force for a more fundamental disequilibrium.

The most important features of the IMF turned out to be its system of pegged-but-adjustable rates and provisions for liquidity. Following the suspension of gold convertibility by the United States, the Bretton Woods system gave way to a hybrid exchange rate regime of pegged exchange rates, nationally managed floats and joint floats. Today the IMF classifies currency arrangements into seven categories:

- *Pegged to another country.* About 50 countries peg their currency to some other currency. The French franc is the base for currencies in 14 former French colonies in Africa. The US dollar is the base for currencies in 24 countries ranging from the Bahamas to Djibouti. Six of the new countries created by the breakup of the Soviet Union peg their currencies to the Russian ruble; another six peg their currencies to an important neighbor (e.g., Bhutan's currency is pegged to the Indian rupee).

- *Pegged to a basket.* About 34 countries peg their currencies to a composite "basket" of currencies, where the basket consists of a portfolio of currencies of major trading partners. The base value of such a basket is more stable than any single currency. Examples of such countries are Austria, Hungary, Kuwait and Morocco. Four of these countries peg their currencies to Special Drawing Rights (SDRs).

- *Flexible against a single currency.* Four countries in the Persian Gulf area maintain their currencies within a limited range of flexibility vis-à-vis the US dollar.

- *Joint float.* The members of the European Union maintain their currencies within a flexible range against other members of their group. This structure, called the European Monetary System (EMS), pegs each member's currency to all the other members' currencies, with a joint float against non-EMS currencies.

- *Adjusted according to indicators.* Three countries (Chile, Colombia and Madagascar) adjust their currencies more or less automatically against changes in a particular indicator. One indicator is the real effective exchange rate, which reflects inflation-adjusted changes in a country's currency vis-à-vis the currencies of its major trading partners.

- *Managed float.* Some 23 countries maintain what is officially called a "managed float." Each central bank sets the nation's exchange rate against a predetermined goal, but allows it to vary. Central bank's support of the rate, which is not automatic, depends on each bank's view of an appropriate rate in the context of the country's balance-of-payments position, foreign exchange reserves and rates quoted outside the official market. Intervention may be taken to smooth out daily fluctuations and create an orderly pattern of exchange rate changes, or to "lean against the wind" by delaying, but not resisting, a fundamental exchange rate change.

- *Independently floating.* About 44 countries, including those with the most important currencies in the world (outside the EMS), allow full flexibility through an independent float. Their central banks allow exchange rates to be determined by market forces alone, although some central banks may intervene in the market from time to time, usually in an attempt to counter speculative pressures on their currency. However, they intervene only as one of many anonymous participants in the free market. They do not peg the currency by heavy or continued intervention. Since the late 1980s the number of countries belonging to this group has increased by 15 percent.

Throughout the 1950s and 1960s, the IMF was successful in increasing international liquidity through periodic increases in the quotas of its members. In 1969, the IMF introduced new reserve certificates—Special Drawing Rights (SDRs)—which were allocated to members in proportion to their IMF quotas in return for their payment of a convertible currency. The SDR is a standard currency basket created as a type of foreign exchange reserve. Originally, the SDR was the weighted average of 16 currencies; it was redesigned in 1981 to approximate the weighted value of the five IMF members with the largest exports of goods and services (the United States, Germany, Japan, the United Kingdom, and France). The basic purpose of the SDR is to be a reserve currency that members may use in transactions among themselves and with the IMF. The interest rate on the SDR, a weighted average of the yields on short-term obligations of the five currencies, is used to pay or charge interest to IMF members whose holdings of SDRs exceed or are below their required reserve allocation.

However, pressure on exchange rates became more extensive in the late 1960s and large devaluations became necessary, especially for the pound sterling. In November 1967, the British pound sterling was devalued from $2.80 to $2.40. Those holding sterling reserves took a 14.3 percent capital loss in dollar terms. This raised the question of the exchange rate of the other reserve assets: if the dollar was devalued with respect to gold, a capital gain in dollar terms could be made by holding gold. Therefore, demand for gold rose and, as it did, gold pool sales in the private market to hold down the price were so large that month that the US Air Force made an emergency airlift of gold from Fort Knox to London, and the floor of the weighing room at the Bank of England collapsed from the accumulated tonnage of gold bars.

Strains were also placed on the system by having it become increasingly dollar centered, but the dollar still had to coexist with gold. America's basic balance went into deficit between 1950 and 1970 as the outflow of private long-term capital and government grants and capital transactions exceeded the US surplus in the balance on current account. The persistent basic balance deficit was financed by a fall in the US gold stock and an increase in foreign holdings of dollar assets. While the deficit in the US balance of payments served to provide additional liquidity to the international monetary system, the very creation of the deficit also undermined confidence in the future exchange rate of the dollar. The persistent deficit and piling up of short-term indebtedness of the United States were bound to undermine the confidence of other countries in the ability of the United States to honor its commitment to redeem dollar holdings in gold. In 1971, with the "Nixon shock," the US Treasury closed the gold window and made the dollar inconvertible into gold.

TRANSACTIONS IN THE INTERBANK MARKET

Transactions in the foreign exchange market can be executed as on a "spot," "forward" or "swap" basis. A spot transaction in the interbank market is the purchase of foreign exchange with delivery and payment between banks to take place, normally, on the second following business day. The date of settlement is called the *value date*. Most dollar transactions are settled through the computerized Clearing House Interbank Payments Systems (CHIPS) in New York, which provides for the calculation of net balances owed by any one bank to another and for payment by 6:00 P.M. that same day in Federal Reserve Bank of New York funds.

An outright forward transaction (or "forward") requires delivery at a future date of a specified amount of one currency for a specified amount of another currency. Thus, the exchange rate is determined at the time of the agreement, but payment and delivery are not required until maturity. Forwards are normally quoted for value dates of one, two, three, six and twelve months. Actual contracts can be arranged for other numbers of months and for periods of more than one year. Payment is on the second business day after the even-month anniversary of the trade. Thus, a three-months forward contract entered into on April 20 will be for a value date of July 22, or the next business day if July 22 falls on a weekend or holiday. A contract to deliver dollars for Austrian shillings in three months is both "buying shillings forward for dollars" and "selling dollars forward for shillings."

A swap in the interbank market is the simultaneous purchase and sale of a given amount of foreign exchange for two different value dates. The purchase and the sale are with the same counterpart. With a "spot against forward" swap, the dealer buys a currency in the spot market and simultaneously sells the same amount back to the same bank in the forward market. The dealer incurs no unexpected foreign exchange risk since the transaction is executed as a single one with one counterpart. With a "forward-forward" swap, a dealer sells, for instance, DM30,000,000 forward for dollars for delivery in, say, two months at $0.78125/DM and simultaneously buys DM30,000,000 forward for delivery in three months at $0.6400/DM. The difference between the buying price and selling price is equivalent to the interest differential between the two currencies. Thus, a swap can be viewed as a technique for borrowing another currency on a fully collateralized basis.

Interbank quotations are given as a *bid* and *offer* (or *ask*). A bid is the exchange rate in one currency at which a dealer will buy another currency. An offer is the exchange rate at which a dealer will sell the other currency. Dealers bid (buy) at one price and offer (sell) at a slightly higher price, making their profit from the spread between the buying and selling prices. Assume a bank makes the quotations of Table 1.1 under the heading "European terms."

The spot quotations of the table indicate that the bank's foreign exchange trader will buy dollars (i.e., sell marks) at the bid price of DM1.4625 per dollar and sell dollars (i.e., buy marks) at the offer price of DM1.4635 per dollar. The heading "Outright Quotations" means the full price to all of its decimal points is given. Traders often abbreviate when talking on the phone or putting quotations on a video screen. The first term, the bid, of a spot quotation is given in full or "1.4625." The offer is, however, expressed as the digits that differ from the bid. Thus, the bid and offer for spot marks is printed as "1.4625 − 35" on a video screen. On the telephone the trader may say "1.4625 to 35" or simply "25 to 35," assuming the leading digits, called the *big*

Table 1.1
Spot and Forward Quotations for the German Mark (DM)

	Quotations as given in interbank market		Reciprocals calculated for convenience of retail customers	
	European Terms		American Terms	
	Bid	*Offer*	*Bid*	*Offer*
OUTRIGHT QUOTATIONS				
Spot	1.4625	1.4635	0.6838	0.6833
One month forward	1.4567	1.4579	0.6865	0.6859
Three months forward	1.4450	1.4466	0.6920	0.6913
Six months forward	1.4283	1.4301	0.7001	0.6993
POINTS QUOTATIONS				
One month forward	58 - 56			
Three months forward	175 - 169			
Six months forward	342 - 334			

figure, are known. The last two digits used by themselves are called the *small figure*.

Among themselves foreign exchange traders often quote forward rates in terms of *points*. A quotation in points is not a foreign exchange rate as such; it is the difference between the forward rate and the spot rate. The bottom part of Table 1.1 shows forward quotations given on a points basis. In the mark/dollar quotations, the forward dollar is at a discount relative to the spot dollar. Consequently, points must be subtracted from the spot quotation to obtain the lower forward quotation. The three-months forward outright mark/dollar quotation is derived as follows:

	Bid	*Offer*
Outright spot	1.4625	1.4635
Less points	175	169
Outright forward	1.4450	1.4466

When the bid in points is larger than the offer in points, as in Table 1.1, the points should be subtracted and the forward quotation is at a discount. If the bid in points is smaller than the offer in points, the points should be added and the forward quotation is at a premium.

A forward bid and offer quotation expressed in points is often called a *swap rate*. It enables a person to borrow one currency for a limited time while giving up the use of another currency for the same time. In other words, it is a short-term borrowing of one currency combined with a short-term loan of an equivalent amount of another currency. If they wanted, the two parties could charge each other interest at the going rate for each of the currencies. However, it is easier for the party with the higher interest currency to simply pay the net interest differential to the other. The swap rate expresses this differential on a points basis rather than as an interest rate.

In order to facilitate the comparison of premiums or discounts in the forward market with interest rate differentials, forward quotations are sometimes expressed in terms of the percent-per-annum deviation from the spot rate. Using direct quotes, the percent-per-annum premium or discount is:

Forward premium or discount = [(Forward − Spot)/Spot](360/n)100%

where:

n = the number of days in the contract.

With indirect quotes the expression is:

Forward premium or discount = [(Spot − Forward)/Forward](360/n)100%

As an example, let us assume the following quotations where the dollar is the home currency:

	Indirect Quote	Direct Quote
Spot rate	yen 103.55/$	$0.0096571/yen
Three months forward	yen 103.04/$	$0.0097049/yen

The annualized three-months forward premium/discount on the yen from a dollar perspective is as follows:

Using direct quotes: [(0.0097049 − 0.0096571)/0.0096571](360/90)100%
= +1.98%
Using indirect quotes: [(103.55 − 103.04)/103.04](360/90)100% = +1.98%

The forward yen is selling at a premium since the premium value is positive.

INTERNATIONAL PARITY CONDITIONS

No single theory is available to forecast exchange rate movements since the international monetary system consists of a mix of freely floating, managed floating and fixed exchange rates. Nevertheless, certain basic economic relationships which help to explain exchange rate movements exist; these relationships are called parity conditions.

A basic principle of competitive markets is that prices will equalize across markets if frictions or costs of moving the products or services between the markets do not exist. Under these conditions the prices of an identical product or service in two different markets should be the same. This is called the *law of one price*. If the two markets are two different countries, the price of the product, although expressed in different currencies, should still be the same. Comparison of prices would only require a conversion from one currency to the other:

$$P(\$) \times S = P(yen)$$

where:

P(\$)   = the price of the product in US dollars,
S   = the spot exchange rate (yen per US dollar),
P(yen) = the price of the product in Japanese yen.

If the law of one price were true for all goods and services, the *purchasing power parity* (PPP) exchange rate could be found from any individual set of prices. A less extreme version of this principle is to work with a basket of goods. This is called the *absolute version of the theory of PPP*. Absolute PPP states that the spot exchange rate is determined by the relative prices of similar baskets of goods.

In practice, the absolute version of PPP theory is not particularly helpful in determining what the spot rate is today. It has, therefore, been suggested to work with *relative purchasing power parity*. Accordingly, the relative change in prices between two countries over a period of time determines the change in the exchange rate over that period. More specifically, if the spot exchange rate between two countries starts in equilibrium, any change in the differential rate of inflation between them tends to be offset over the long run by an equal but opposite change in the spot exchange rate. Figure 1.1 shows the general case of relative PPP. The horizontal axis shows the percentage higher or lower rate of inflation in the foreign country relative to the home country, and the vertical axis shows the percentage appreciation or depreciation of the foreign currency relative to the home currency.

The diagonal PPP line indicates the equilibrium position between a change in the exchange rate and relative inflation rate. For example, point P represents an equilibrium point where inflation in the foreign country, say Germany, is 4 percent lower than in the home country, say the United States. The relative PPP predicts that the German mark would appreciate by 4 percent per annum with respect to the US dollar. The justification of relative PPP is that if a country experiences inflation rates higher than those of its main trading partners, and its exchange rate does not change, its exports will become less competitive with comparable products and services produced elsewhere. In addition, im-

Figure 1.1
Purchasing Power Parity

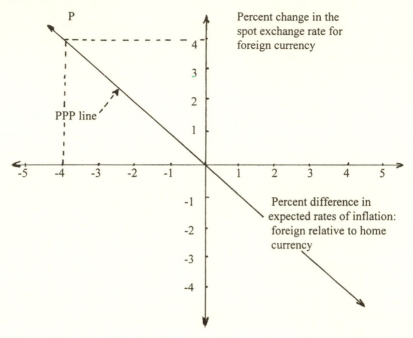

ports will also become more price competitive with higher priced domestic products.

The accuracy in predicting future exchange rates with the absolute and relative versions of PPP has been extensively tested and the results are poor, because (a) goods and services do not in reality move at zero costs between countries, (b) many goods/services (e.g., housing and medical services) are not tradable and (c) many goods and services are not of the same quality across countries. Nevertheless, some tests appear to indicate that (1) PPP holds better for countries with relative high rates of inflation and underdeveloped capital markets and (2) PPP holds up reasonably well over the very long run. Whether these conclusions are valid or not is questionable, since there are a number of problems with the tests (how to take care of differences in taste, level of development and income; government interference in the trade process; and the establishment of future inflation rates).

It seems reasonable to state, however, that given normal trade between two countries A and B, a certain exchange rate will establish itself between them, and, apart from slight fluctuations, this rate will remain unaltered so long as no variations take place in either of the currencies' purchasing power, and no obstacles are placed in the way of trade. In addition, when the currencies of A and B have undergone inflation, the normal rate of exchange will be equal to the old rate multiplied by the quotient of the degree of inflation in the one country and in the other. Naturally, deviations from this new normal rate will always be found, and during the transition period these deviations may be expected to be fairly wide. But the rate that has been calculated by the above method must be regarded as the new parity between the currencies, the point of balance toward which, in spite of all temporary fluctuations, the exchange rates will tend.

Let us now discuss the relationship between exchange rates and interest rates. The relationship between the percentage change in the spot exchange rate over time and the differential between comparable interest rates in different national capital markets is called the *international Fisher effect*. *Fisher-open*, as it is often termed, states that the spot exchange rate should change in an equal amount but in the opposite direction to the difference in interest rates between two countries. More formally, and using indirect quotes for the spot exchange rates, it states:

$$[S_1 - S_2]/S_2 = [i_h - i_f]/[1 + i_f]$$

where:

S_1 = spot exchange rate at the beginning of the period,
S_2 = spot exchange rate at the end of the period,
i_h = interest rate in the home country, and
i_f = interest rate in the foreign country.

The mathematical derivation of the above formula is beyond the scope of the present text. In principle, the Fisher effect states that investors must be rewarded or penalized to offset the expected change in exchange rates. For instance, if a dollar-based investor buys a 10-year guilder bond earning 4 percent interest, compared to 6 percent interest available on dollars, the investor must be expecting the guilder to appreciate relative to the dollar by at least 2 percent per year during the 10 years. If not, the investor would be better off remaining in dollars. If the guilder appreciates by 3 percent during the 10-year period, the dollar-based investor would earn a bonus of 1 percent higher return. The Fisher effect predicts, however, that with unrestricted capital flows, an investor should be indifferent between investing in dollar or guilder bonds, since investors worldwide would be aware of the same bonus opportunity and compete it away. Recent studies suggest that a foreign exchange risk premium exists for most major currencies; consequently, the expected change in exchange rates may not be consistently equal to the difference in interest rates. The theory of *interest rate parity* (IRP) gives the linkage between the foreign exchange markets and the international money markets: The difference in the national interest rates for securities of similar risk and maturity should be equal to, but opposite in sign to, the forward rate discount or premium for the foreign currency, except for

Figure 1.2
Interest Rate Parity

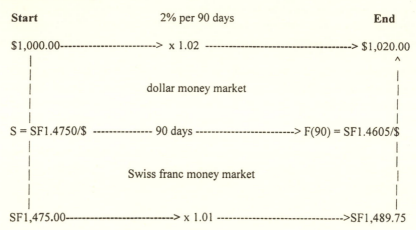

transaction costs. The theory applies only to securities with maturities of one year or less, since forward contracts are not routinely available for periods longer than one year. Figure 1.2 illustrates the theory. A dollar-based investor who has $1,000 available may choose to invest in a 90-day dollar money market instrument with an annual interest rate of 8 percent (2% per 90 days). He or she may, however, choose to invest in a Swiss franc money market instrument of identical risk and maturity for the same period and with an annual interest rate of 4 percent (1% for 90 days). If so, the investor would have to exchange dollars for Swiss francs at the spot rate of exchange, invest the Swiss franks in a money market instrument, and at the end of the 90 days convert the resulting proceeds back to dollars.

A dollar-based investor examines the relative returns by starting in the top left corner of Figure 1.2 and investing in the dollars (going to the top right corner) compared to investing in the Swiss franc market (going to the left lower corner, the right lower corner and the right top corner). The comparison of returns are:

$$[1 + i_s] = S[1 + i_{SF}][1/F]$$

where:

i_s = interest rate in the dollar money market,
i_{SF} = interest rate in the Swiss franc money market,
S = the spot rate of exchange, and
F = the forward rate of exchange.

Substituting in the spot rate (SF1.4750/$), the forward rate (SF1.4605/$) and the respective interest rates [i_s = 2% and i_{SF} = 1%] from Figure 1.2, gives the interest rate parity condition:

$$(1 + .02) = 1.4750(1 + .01)(1/1.4605)$$

The left-hand side of the equation is the gross return the investor earns by investing in dollars and the right-hand side is the return the investor earns by exchanging dollars for Swiss francs at the spot rate, investing the Swiss franc proceeds in the Swiss franc money market, and simultaneously selling the principal plus interest in Swiss francs forward for dollars at the current 90-day forward rate. Ignoring transaction costs, if the returns in dollars are equal between the two alternatives, the spot and forward rates are considered at interest rate parity. The transaction is "covered" since the exchange rate back to dollars is guaranteed at the end of the 90 days. The two alternatives will be equal if the difference in interest rates is offset by the difference between the spot and forward exchange rates:

$$F/S = [1 + i_{SF}]/[1 + i_s] \text{ or}$$
$$[SF1.4605/\$]/SF1.4750/\$] = 0.9902 = 1.01/1.02 = 0.9902$$

The IRP assumes that the spot and forward exchange markets and interest rates are in constant equilibrium, which is not always the case. The potential for arbitrage ("riskless") profit exists if these parameters are not in equilibrium. The arbitrageur who recognizes such an imbalance will move to take advantage of the disequilibrium by investing in whichever currency offers the higher return on a covered basis. This is called *covered interest arbitrage* (CIA). For instance, if the forward rate of Figure 1.2 were SF1.4500/$ instead of SF1.4605/$, the investor would get $1,027.41 by investing in the Swiss franc money market, or $7.41 more compared with the alternative of investing in the dollar money market. These types of imbalances exist for very short times (a few minutes) since the process of CIA drives the international currency and money markets toward the equilibrium described by IRP. Slight deviations from equilibrium provide opportunities for arbitrageurs to make small, riskless profits. Such deviations provide the supply and demand forces that will move the market back toward parity (equilibrium).

Figure 1.3 shows an example of the equilibrium between interest rates and exchange rates. The vertical axis represents the percentage difference between foreign and domestic interest rates, and the horizontal axis shows the forward premium or discount of foreign currency. The *interest rate parity line* indicates the equilibrium state; however, the line is a band due to transaction costs arising from foreign exchange and investment brokerage costs on buying and selling securities. Transaction costs are in the range of 0.20 percent to 0.25 percent on an annual basis.

Figure 1.3
Interest Rate Parity and Equilibrium

Percent difference between
foreign and domestic
interest rates

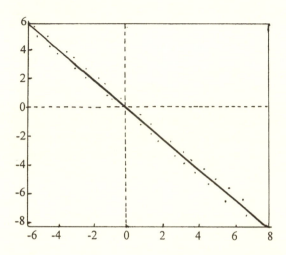

Percentage premium
on foreign currency

In the figure above, we introduced the forward exchange rate, which is based on forward contracts or agreements to buy or sell an asset at a fixed price (called the delivery price) at a specific date in the future. Currency futures are based on the principle of futures contracts. Futures contracts are similar to forward contracts; the difference is that they are standardized. That is, the size of the contract is standardized (for instance, the Chicago Mercantile Exchange contract for German marks is in terms of 125,000 marks), the expiration date is fixed (generally, March 15, June 15, September 15 or December 15), and the credit risk is standardized. By a standardized risk we mean that each of the two parties of the futures contract are exposed, not to each other's risk of default, but rather to the risk of a *clearing house*. A clearing house is an adjunct of the exchange and acts as an intermediary in futures transactions by guaranteeing the performance of the parties to each transaction. Unlike forward contracts, futures contracts are normally traded on an exchange such as the Chicago Board of Trade and the Chicago Mercantile Exchange. As the two parties to the contract may not necessarily know each other, the exchange provides the clearing house mechanism to guarantee that the contract will be honored. Futures contracts are fungible since they are standardized; this means that they can be sold or liquidated before the expiration date, which is impossible with forward contracts. It is estimated that about 90 percent of the futures contracts in the United States are sold before expiration.

Futures contracts call for:

- the investor to deposit funds (referred to as the *initial margin*) in what is called the *margin account* at the time the contract is first entered into (the initial margin is like a performance bond in the construction industry);
- the broker to adjust the margin account at the end of each trading day, which is known as *marking the account*;
- the broker to give the investor a *margin call* if the investor's equity, as determined by the initial margin and the market value of the contract, falls below the *maintenance level*; and
- the investor to pay an amount to reestablish the initial margin.

The following example elucidates this procedure. Suppose an investor contacts his or her broker on June 1 to buy three December (same year) gold futures contracts and that the current futures price is $355 per ounce. Since the contract size is standardized in 100 ounces, the investor has contracted to buy a total of 300 ounces at this price. The broker requires the investor to deposit an initial margin equal to $2,000 per contract, or $6,000 in total, on June 1; this initial margin is determined by the broker. The broker also requires the investor to maintain a maintenance level of $4,000.

Now suppose that at the end of the day of June 1, June 2 and June 3, the futures prices of gold are $360, $350 and $338 per ounce, respectively. Thus, at the end of each of these days, the margin account has to be adjusted to reflect the investor's gain or loss. By the end of June 1, the investor's equity increases to $6,000 plus the investor's gain of 300 × $5, or $7,500, which means that he or she can withdraw $1,500 from the margin account. By the end of June 2, the investor's equity drops to $6,000 minus a loss of 300 × $5, or $4,500, which is still above the maintenance level of $4,000. However, by the end of June 3, the equity drops to $6,000 minus a loss of 300 × $17, or $900, which is below the maintenance level. The broker gives the investor a margin call with the request to deposit $6,000 minus $900 or $5,100 in the margin account. If the investor is unable to receive the call or unable to deposit the $5,100, the broker will liquidate the long position in order to minimize the risk to the clearing house. This process is repeated at the end of each day until the futures contract is executed on its expiration date to ensure that there will always be enough funds available to cover losses. It is noted that the investor normally receives interest on the amount deposited in the margin account.

Like forward contracts, futures contracts allow businesses to protect themselves against changes in the exchange rate. Consider, for instance, a retail firm in the United States which plans to buy 125,000 German marks of merchandise in Germany three months from now. At the current exchange rate of 0.6150 dollars per mark, the dollar cost is $76,875. The firm expects to sell the merchandise for $82,000 or to make a profit of $5,125 at the current exchange rate. The firm's management is concerned about a possible rise in the exchange rate to 0.6750 dollars per mark when the merchandise is purchased in three months. At this exchange rate, the dollar cost of the merchandise is $84,375 and the firm would not make a profit. It therefore buys a 90-day futures contract at 0.6100 per mark, locking in the purchase of 125,000 marks for $76,250. Regardless of the value of the exchange rate in 90 days, the firm is guaranteed a profit.

FOREIGN CURRENCY OPTIONS

A *foreign currency option* is a contract giving the option purchaser the right, but not the obligation, to buy or sell a given amount of foreign exchange at a fixed rate per unit of domestic currency for a specified period of time. The buyer of an option is called the *holder* and the seller of an option is referred to as the *writer* or *grantor*. There are two basic types of options: a *call* is an option to buy foreign currency and a *put* is an option to sell foreign currency. The distinction between an *American option* and a *European option* has nothing to do with the location of issue. American options can be bought in Europe (and in the United States) and European options can be bought in the United States (and in Europe). An American option gives the buyer the right to exercise the option at any time between the date of writing and the expiration or maturity date. European options can only be exercised on their expiration date, not before.

The *premium* or *option price* (sometimes also referred to as the *value* or *cost* of the option) is the cost of the option. It is usually paid in advance by the buyer to the seller. In organized exchanges like the Philadelphia Stock Exchange, premiums are quoted as a domestic currency amount per unit of foreign currency. In the over-the-counter market (options offered by banks), premiums are quoted as a percentage of the transaction amount. The *exercise price* or *strike price* is the exchange rate at which the foreign currency can be purchased (call) or sold (put). An option whose exercise price is the same as the spot price of the underlying currencies is said to be *at-the-money* (ATM). An option which would not be profitable if exercised immediately is referred to as *out-of-the-money* (OTM). An option which would be profitable if exercised immediately is said to be *in-the-money* (ITM).

Over-the-counter options have the advantage that they are tailored to the specific needs of a firm. Banks are willing to write or buy options that vary by amount (notional principal), strike price and maturity. Exchange traded options are traded in standardized amounts per option contract. For instance, on the Philadelphia Stock Exchange each option on German marks is for DM62,500. Foreign currency options are for trading with one, two, three, six, nine and twelve months to run until expiration. Expiration months are March, June, September and December, with trading also available in two additional near-term consecutive months. For example, in November, trading would occur in November, December, January, March, June and September maturities. Finally, each mid-month option contract expires at 11:59 P.M. on the Friday preceding the third Wednesday of the expiration month. All end-of-month options expire at 11:59 P.M. on the last Friday of the expiration month.

The following is an example of how newspapers typically quote foreign currency options:

Option and Underlying	Strike Price	Calls—Last			Puts—Last		
		July	*Aug.*	*Sept.*	*July*	*Aug.*	*Sept.*
62,500 German marks–cents per unit							
52.51	52 1/2	0.50	—	—	0.60	0.89	—

The *Option and Underlying* means that 52.51 cents, or $0.5251, is the spot dollar price of one German mark at the close of trading on the preceding day. The *Strike Price* is the price per mark that must be paid if the option is exercised. The July call option on marks of 52½ means $0.5250/DM. The price of the July call option on German marks is 0.50 cents per mark, or $0.0050/DM. There was no trading of the August and September 52½ call on that day. The July 52½ put's premium is 0.60 cents per mark. Since one option contract on the Philadelphia Stock Exchange consists of 62,500 marks, the total cost of one option contract for the call is DM62,500 × $0.0050/DM = $312.50. The total cost of one option contract for the put is DM62,500 × $0.0060/DM = $375.00.

The upper half of Figure 1.4 illustrates the position of a buyer of a call option on German marks with a strike price of 58.00 cents ($0.580/DM) and a premium of $0.005/DM. The vertical axis measures profit or loss for the option buyer, at each of several different spot prices for the mark up to the time of maturity. The buyer would choose not to exercise his option at all spot rates below the strike price of $0.580 since the price of the mark would be lower on the spot market. He/she would exercise the option if the spot rate is between the strike price and the *break-even price* of $0.585/DM, which is the price at which the buyer neither gains nor loses on exercising the option. The premium cost of $0.005 plus the cost of exercising the option of $0.580 is exactly equal to the proceeds from selling the marks in the spot market at $0.585. The buyer would still exercise the option at the break-even price because by doing so he/she at least recovers the premium paid for the option. He/she would also exercise the option at spot rates between the strike price and the break-even price since the gross profit earned on exercising the option and selling the underlying currency covers part of the premium cost.

At spot prices above the break-even price, the buyer would make a profit. For instance, if the spot rate were $0.597 per mark at maturity, the buyer would

Figure 1.4
**Profit and Loss for the Buyer and Writer of a Call Option on German Marks
with a Premium of $0.005/DM**

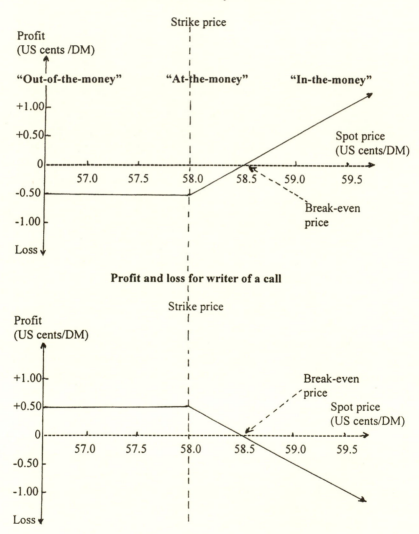

exercise his call option, buying German marks for $0.580 each instead of buying them on the spot market at $0.597 each. He/she could sell the marks in the spot market for $0.597 each, pocketing a gross profit of $0.017/DM, or a net profit of $0.012/DM after deducting the original cost of the option of $0.005/DM. The buyer could also realize the profit through executing an offsetting contract on the options exchange rather than taking delivery of the currency if he/she expects the dollar price of the mark to rise. In other words, the buyer of a call option has a limited loss and an unlimited profit option.

The bottom part of Figure 1.4 illustrates the position of the writer (seller) of the same call option. If the option expires when the spot price of the underlying currency is below the exercise price of $0.580, the option holder does not exercise. What the holder loses, the writer gains. The writer keeps as profit the premium of $0.005/DM. Above the strike price of $0.580, the writer of the call must deliver the underlying currency for $0.580/DM at a time when the value of the mark is above $0.580 and, therefore, has a loss. The amount of the loss increases as the price of the underlying currency rises and is unlimited. Once again, what the holder gains, the writer loses, and vice versa. The writer of a call option has a rather unattractive combination of potential outcomes: limited profit potential and unlimited loss potential. However, there are ways to limit such losses through other techniques.

Figure 1.5 illustrates the position of a buyer of a put with basic terms similar to those used to illustrate a call. The buyer of a put option, however, wants to be able to sell the underlying currency at the exercise price when the market price of that currency drops (rather than rises as with a call option). For instance, if the spot price of the mark drops to $0.570/DM, the buyer of the put will deliver the marks to the writer and receive $0.580/DM. The marks can now be purchased on the spot market for $0.570 each. If the cost of the option was $0.005/DM, the buyer of the put has a net gain of $0.005/DM. The break-even price of the put option is the strike price less the premium, or $0.575 in our example. The profit potential increases as the spot rate falls further below the strike price. At any exchange rate above the strike price, the buyer of the put would not exercise his option and lose the $0.005/DM premium paid for the put option. Like the buyer of a call, the buyer of a put can never lose more than the premium paid up front.

The lower half of Figure 1.5 shows the position of the writer of the above-mentioned put. Below a price of $0.580/DM the writer will lose more than the premium ($0.005/DM) received for writing the option, falling below break-even. Between $0.580/DM and $0.585/DM the writer will lose part of the premium received. If the spot price is above $0.585/DM, the option will not be exercised, and the option writer gains the premium of $0.005/DM. Note the symmetry of profit/loss, strike price and the break-even price between the buyer and the writer of the put and call options.

Figure 1.5
**Profit and Loss for the Buyer and Writer of a Put Option on German Marks
with a Premium of $0.005/DM**

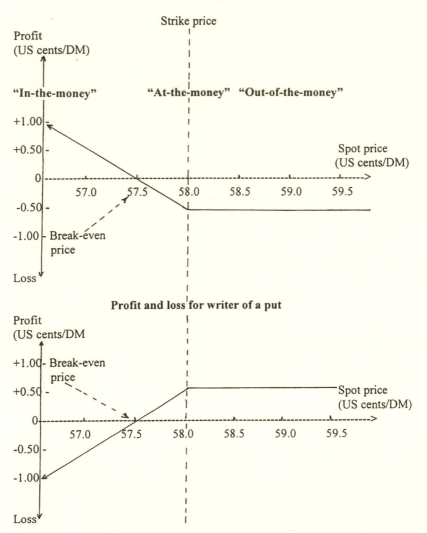

Profit and loss for buyer of a put

Strike price

Profit
(US cents/DM)

"In-the-money"   "At-the-money" "Out-of-the-money"

+1.00 -

+0.50 -   Spot price
                                                (US cents/DM)
0
          57.0   57.5   58.0   58.5   59.0   59.5
-0.50 -

-1.00 - Break-even
         price

Loss

Profit and loss for writer of a put

Profit
(US cents/DM

+1.00 - Break-even
         price
+0.50 -   Spot price
                                                (US cents/DM)
0
          57.0   57.5   58.0   58.5   59.0   59.5
-0.50 -

-1.00

Loss

SUGGESTIONS FOR FURTHER READING

Bodurtha, James N., Jr., and George R. Courtadon. "Efficiency Tests of the Foreign Currency Options Market." *Journal of Finance* (March 1986): 151–161.

Bordo, Michel David. "The Classical Gold Standard: Some Lessons for Today." *Federal Reserve Bank of St. Louis Review* (May 1981): 2–17.

Conix, Raymond G. F. *Foreign Exchange Dealer's Handbook*, 2nd ed. Homewood, IL: Dow Jones–Irwin, 1986.

Fama, Eugene. "Forward and Spot Exchange Rates." *Journal of Monetary Economics* (November 1984): 319–383.

Goodhart, Charles A.E., and Thomas Hesse. "Central Bank Forex Intervention Assessed in Continuous Time." *Journal of International Securities Markets* (August 1993): 368–389.

Chapter 2

International Trade

SOURCES OF COMPARATIVE ADVANTAGE

Changes in the volume, composition and terms of international trade play a crucial role in changes in the fundamentals of the world economy. To understand why these changes take place and their significance, one needs to understand the concept of "comparative advantage." Comparative advantage has a significant impact on the commodities and services a country will export or import as well as the competitiveness of a firm with a global strategy.

In 1776, Adam Smith advised, in his *Wealth of Nations*, "never to attempt to make at home what it will cost more to make than to buy." About 40 years later David Ricardo, another English economist, refined this insight into the logical principle of comparative advantage which still plays an important role in today's economic theory. In a simple illustration of what, under free trade, would determine trade between England and Portugal in wine and cloth, Ricardo focused on the relative differences in labor productivity (output per hour) in producing wine and cloth in England and Portugal. Ricardo wanted to "pierce the monetary veil" and concentrate instead on the nonmonetary forces that determine trade. The focus is on the allocation of resources rather than the balance of payments, which is adjusted through changes in wages or foreign exchange rates.

In the Ricardo model, even though Portugal is more productive ("better") than England in both wine and cloth, giving Portugal absolute advantage in both wine and cloth, its labor is relatively more productive ("more better") in wine than cloth. Portugal therefore has a comparative advantage in wine. England is less productive in both wine and cloth (absolute disadvantage) but has the lesser disadvantage (or comparative advantage) in cloth. In other words, technological differences in production functions between England and Portugal give relative productivity differences that allow a basis for mutually profitable trade between the countries. In a free market-price system, Portugal will export its comparative advantage commodity wine and import cloth, while England does the reverse. As a result, both countries can consume their importable commodity at a lower cost than if each country tried to produce each commodity for itself.

Exports may be viewed as the intermediate goods used for the "production" of the importables. The cost of "indirectly producing" imports through direct specialization on exports is less than if the country produced the importables directly at home. Foreign trade is thus like an industry that uses exports as inputs to produce imports as output. The principle of comparative advantage becomes an efficiency rule for *maximizing output (imports) per unit of input (exports)*. This explanation of comparative costs can be applied to a variety of problems of resource allocation—whether for a country, for a group of countries, for a multiproduct enterprise or for an individual. Its logic is institution-free.

Ricardo established a basis for international trade according to relative productivity differentials or differences in the countries' comparative cost ratios. Naturally, it is necessary to translate these differences in comparative cost ratios into absolute differences in money prices. It is clear that a buyer of imports will only purchase imports if their absolute money price is less than the price of a domestic substitute good. Provided the relative wage differentials are within the relative productivity differentials, the translation into absolute differences in money price will follow. For instance, if labor is three times more productive in country A than in country B, the absolute money price of the exports from A will be less than the absolute money price of the substitute commodity in B, provided the money wage rate is not more than three times higher in A than in B. This can be illustrated as follows:

Case	Country	Amount of labor required for producing 1 unit of X	Y	Wage rate per labor unit at existing foreign currency exchange rate	Money price of X	Y
(i)	A	5	10	$2	$10	$20
	B	7	30	$1	$7	$30
(ii)	A	5	10	$4	$20	$40
	B	7	30	$1	$7	$30

The comparison of the above case (i) with case (ii) shows that under competitive conditions, the wage differences must be within the productivity differences, or else only one country [country B in case (ii)] would be able to export, and its wage rates would be bid up to compensate for this; or the exchange rate would have to be altered to preserve the condition of balanced trade.

It is easier to understand how comparative cost ratios become translated into differences in absolute money prices if one appreciates the relationships between productivity, wage rates, foreign currency exchange rates and the resultant changes in absolute prices. Suppose country B is more productive than country A in every commodity, and that B can, therefore, readily export to A, but A cannot export to B. However, when the demand for B's exports increases, its wages will also increase, thereby raising its absolute prices and reducing its competitive position. At the same time, the fall in demand for A's products will lower wage rates and absolute prices in A, thereby enabling A to acquire a comparative advantage in another commodity; or as the demand for B's currency rises on foreign exchange markets, the price of B's currency in terms of A's currency will rise (B's currency will appreciate) and, consequently, the demand for B's exports will decline and its demand for imports will rise. In other words, through wage changes or foreign exchange rate movements (or both), the goods of country B will rise in price and those of country A will fall. Similarly, even if one industry in country B is so competitive that it dominates the world export market, the resulting exchange rate appreciation in B will make other export industries in that country less competitive.

Two Swedish economists, Eli Heckscher and Nobel laureate Bertil Ohlin, have generalized the theory of comparative advantage to modern conditions. Recognizing all factors of production that may be inputs, the Heckscher-Ohlin (H-O) theory of comparative advantage focuses on factor proportions in the production of different products in different countries. A country's comparative advantage is then determined by its relative factor endowment (i.e., the country's relative factor supplies of labor, capital and natural resources or the inputs necessary for production). In other words, the H-O model expanded the Ricardian differences in labor productivity to differences in factor endowments. As long as there are relative resource differences—with some countries being relatively abundant in labor, while others are relatively abundant in capital or natural resources—there will be a difference in relative costs and prices, thereby giving the foundation for trade based on comparative advantage.

Whereas the usual application of the H-O model emphasizes relative endowments of capital, labor and natural resources, recent variations of the model focus increasingly on the importance of skills in the trade equation. In fact, over time an industrializing country tends to proceed up a ladder of comparative advantage—from initially exporting commodities that are natural resource-intensive (coffee or rice) to commodities that are unskilled labor-intensive (textiles) to semiskilled and skilled labor-intensive (electronics) to capital-intensive (machinery) and finally to the export of knowledge-intensive commodities (computers, control equipment). Thus the H-O model could include factors of endowment such as unskilled labor, semiskilled labor, skilled labor, highly educated and skilled personnel and research and development (R&D) activities. The basic factors are passively inherited, representing natural or historical comparative advantage based on differences in labor productivity (Ricardo-type goods) or in labor, capital and natural resources endowments (H-O-type goods).

The basic factors dominate only the lower rungs of the aforementioned ladder. As a country develops, the advanced factors dominate the top rungs of the ladder and they are upgraded over time through investment in human and physical capital to enable the country to acquire comparative advantage in differentiated products and propriety production technology. This results in a product-based advantage derived from differentiated products and/or increasing returns to scale. (Increasing returns to scale exist when output increases in greater proportion than inputs—for instance, a doubling of expenditure on inputs results in a more than double expansion of output). These conditions explain *intraindustry* trade as, for example, the exchange of automobiles for automobiles or office machines for office machines. Trade involving Ricardo-type or H-O-type goods is referred to as *interindustry* trade.

When early-comers climb the ladder of comparative advantage, late-comers can occupy the vacant rungs. For example, as Japan has proceeded up the ladder, South Korea has come behind it—first exporting primary goods in the late 1950s, subsequently moving upscale to textiles and plywood in the 1960s and then iron and steel products and electrical machinery in the 1970s. By 1995, Korea's top three semiconductor makers were expanded to take away most of the global memory chip market from Japan. While the Asian NICs (Taiwan, South Korea, Hong Kong and Singapore) moved up the ladder of comparative advantage, their former positions are taken by those behind them in the "queue": Indonesia, Malaysia, the Philippines and Thailand. In the years prior to the start of the East Asian crisis in 1997, Malaysia and Thailand, in particular, gained impressive footholds in export markets for manufactures. The changing pattern of the Asia Pacific trade has also carried over to changes in trade patterns between the OECD (Organization for Economic Cooperation and Development) countries (North America, Japan and the European Union) and Asia Pacific. Capital-intensive and technology-intensive goods are exchanged for labor-intensive and lower-technology consumer goods. To a lesser extent, the same is true for the OECD area and Latin America. Since sub-Saharan African countries have not yet become exporters of manufactures, OECD countries' trade with Africa has remained of the more traditional type of manufactures for primary commodities. Japan's trade is the most complementary and integrated with the Asian countries. The major destination of American exports is Latin America.

So far, the discussion has emphasized the static gains from trade—the increase in each country's real income based on efficient international resource allocation. In addition to these static gains there are indirect, dynamic benefits stemming from trade in ideas and the educative effect of trade. Trade widens the extent of the market and generally enables the trading country to enjoy increasing returns and further growth.

How do the sources of and changes in a country's comparative advantage relate to the competitive advantage of a firm? The competitive advantage of a firm with a global strategy depends on where the firm locates its various activities. If the global competitor locates its different activities in different countries according to each country's comparative advantage, it will then, at the same time, achieve competitive advantage. For instance, components can be made in South Korea, software written in India and basic R&D performed in Silicon Valley.

Intrafirm trade (imports from a firm's own subsidiaries abroad) is typical for many MNCs. Beyond horizontal international specialization among different final products, MNCs are important in promoting vertical international specialization among different intermediate stages of production. Thus, to be competitive the MNC should seek corporate advantage in conformity with the comparative advantages of the countries in which it operates by:

- decomposing the production process into different activities that are located in various countries according to factor endowments;
- undertaking worldwide sourcing for inputs and commodities;
- realization of increasing returns to scale in R&D and marketing;
- investing in R&D in order to maintain its competitive advantage over time or achieve higher-order competitive advantages; and
- continually anticipating changes in the comparative advantages of nations and being prepared to respond to these changes.

The last point is important since, over time, a country's comparative advantage in the production of different products may widen or narrow, according to changes in factor supplies, factor quality, factor prices, the opening and closing of technological gaps, variations in learning curves, innovations, and so on.

PROTECTION

Economists no longer question the logical validity of the principle of comparative advantage on which rests the case of free trade. Why is it that more than two centuries after Adam Smith there is still much disagreement over free trade? Disagreement persists because governments still intervene with mercantilistic policies to protect particular industries and because of special interests with political influence. The demand for protection is expressed by special interests through lobbying, contributions to candidates who support their position, and filing at administrative and regulatory hearings. Those demanding protection are normally special interest groups who face losses because of imports. Their losses are concentrated within a small group and come immediately with the market disruption from imports.

Although small in number, the 12,000 domestic sugar growers in the United States have become one of the most powerful lobbying groups in Washington. They are joined by the producers of corn syrup, who benefit from the higher prices for all sweeteners that result from inflated sugar prices. It is estimated that sugar quotas add about $3 billion annually to American consumers' grocery bills. The US government does not only maintain a peanut quota system that allows only 1.7 million pounds of imports, it also limits the number of farmers who can sell peanuts in the United States; and it sees to it that the minimum selling price for their so-called quota peanuts is about 50 percent higher than the world price! The program costs the American consumers about $370 million a year. In addition to the loss to the consumers, there is a deadweight loss of economic efficiency resulting from the distortion of producer decisions and consumer decisions. High cost resources are allocated to the production of goods that can be imported at a lower cost. Consumer choice is restricted and there is too little consumption of the good.

One way of achieving protection is through subsidies. Some arguments for protection are stimulated by game theory or the notion of strategic behavior by competitors in a zero sum game. The techniques of game theory establish the conditions under which trade policy targeted to particular industries facing foreign competition might result in more profits for "us" in world markets. The theory indicates that export subsidies can affect the structure of the game among a small number of firms (oligopoly) that are domestic and foreign competitors so as to allow "our" domestic firms to achieve extra profits from exports at the expense of foreign competitors. In the United States there is also the popular belief that if Japan, France, Korea or other countries are "targeting" profitable industries, why shouldn't the United States do so?

Proponents of targeted export subsidies argue that a subsidy to domestic firms, by deterring investment and production by foreign competitors, can increase the profits of domestic firms by more than the subsidy, thereby raising national income. Following such a policy is, however, dangerous since:

• a favorable outcome to strategic trade policy based on the principles of game theory rests on some narrow assumptions which are likely going to be violated in real-life situations;

• if the increased output of the protected firm draws resources away from other industries in the home country, then costs will rise, in turn, for these adversely affected industries;

• the gain is probably overstated if it is not recognized that in reality there are substantial costs to raising revenue to finance subsidy schemes;

• the gain will be offset if other governments retaliate (which is likely to happen); and

• it is not likely to have a sound basis for identifying strategic industries.

Agricultural subsidies are widespread in the United States, Japan and the European Union (EU). For political reasons, these have not been subjected to countervailing action. The Subsidies Code of the General Agreement on Tariffs and Trade (GATT) permits subsidies on agricultural products as long as the subsidies do not result in the exporter obtaining "more than an equitable share of the world market." Since the equitable share has not been defined in quantitative terms, this provision has had little bite in practice.

Other forms of export subsidies include cheap bank loans for exporters, the remission of indirect taxes on inputs into exports and on the exports themselves, exemption from corporate income taxes on a part of export earnings, preferential rates for services of public utilities, accelerated depreciation on the assets of exporters, cash subsidies to exporters and, in case foreign exchange is not freely available, permission for exporters to use their export earnings on the purchase of imports.

Protection can also be achieved by imposing import tariffs on, and/or import quotas for goods produced by foreign competitors. When a tariff is imposed, producers in a tariff-imposing country are in essence subsidized, and consumers are in essence taxed. The high cost and inefficient firm can now meet foreign competition and the inframarginal firms make more profit. Consumers pay a higher price and buy a smaller quantity. Tariff revenue goes to the government. In the case of a quota there is no government revenue unless the government decides to auction off import licenses. Trade restrictions in the form of tariffs or quotas by one country are very likely to have larger costs than benefits no matter what any other country does.

With regard to tariffs, GATT does not adopt the pure free trader's position of unilateral free trade but instead bases negotiations to reduce tariffs on the principle of reciprocity—a country negotiates to reduce tariffs on the principle that other countries reciprocate. The reciprocity principle is applied to multilateral negotiations with all members of GATT, and reciprocity is sought in terms of a broad balance of concessions on a group of products considered together.

Protection can also be achieved by voluntary export restraints (VERs). For instance, in 1998 Japan had a VER in order to restrict the import of Japanese cars in the United States. To diminish opposition, it is politically astute to adopt policy measures that are indirect and opaque—VERs rather than tariffs.

From the above discussion it is clear that, in principle, the exceptions to free trade should be extremely limited. They arise when (a) a noneconomic objective receives priority and (b) there is a domestic market failure in which prices do not equal the future social benefit from the industry. National defense is an example of a noneconomic objective receiving priority. Adam Smith expressed this by "Defense before opulence." For instance, it would not be in the interest of the US defense system to let the shipping industry go bankrupt.

An example of the aforementioned domestic market failure would be an "infant industry" conferring a social benefit outside its own production but not being paid for this external benefit. For instance, by training labor an industry provides experienced labor to other industries at no cost; or by introducing technology that can be used by other firms, it confers an external benefit for which it is not paid. In short, the social gain is greater than the private profit, and more output should be encouraged.

Dumping is price discrimination which can be a common practice for maximizing profits when a firm faces a more elastic demand in foreign markets than at home, and realizes economies of scale. The traditional definition of dumping is selling at a lower price in one national market than in another. In other words, dumping is price discrimination between national markets. Dumping tests include foreign price less than home price for goods, foreign price less than cost of production, or selling to country *A* at an export price FOB (free on board) lower than in country *B*. These tests may call for complicated calculations. In comparing the US price and foreign market value, American legislation specifies adjustment for a "constructed value of the exported product." "Less than fair value" is constructed by comparing the price in the imported country with (i) cost of materials and fabrication plus (ii) general expenses that must be calculated as not less than 10 percent of (i) plus profits equivalent to not less than 8 percent of [(i) plus (ii) plus interest]. It is noted that if firms are highly levered, as in Japan, the "profit" calculation can be unusually high.

Anti-dumping duties are a major weapon against this unfair trade. The threat of dumping was a rationale for the adoption of the first US protective tariff in 1816. The difference between countervailing duties/tariffs on dumped exports and countervailing duties/tariffs on subsidized exports is that the former ones respond to the action of a firm and the latter ones to the action of a foreign government. During periods of slack demand, a firm that has high fixed costs and low variable costs will, in the short run, rationally produce if it can sell at any price above the variable costs. In that situation it may export to countries where firms have higher variable costs. However, persistent sales at a loss tend to indicate a lack of comparative advantage, and if they continue over the longer run the firm will go bankrupt unless it receives some assistance from the government.

Imposing countervailing and anti-dumping duties calls for discipline and transparency if the truly unfair cases are to be resolved without being protectionist for high-cost firms competing against importers. Thus, these measures should not be used in trivial cases, nor as harassment of successful foreign competitors. Fair trade does not mean equal market shares since this would result in less gain from trade. Neither does it mean that all countries should play according to US rules, because doing so would lose the gains from trade that arise due to different environments.

The formation of regional trade blocks such as the EU and NAFTA are of increasing concern in view of the implications that regionalism and preferential trade arrangements (PTAs) may have for the normative economics of trade policy. Under specified conditions, GATT's Article XXIV allows a preferential trading arrangement as an exemption to its basic principles of nondiscrimination and most-favored-nation treatment. Thus, a trade block in the form of a customs union or free trade agreement is permitted, provided that the member countries that discriminate in favor of one another eliminate all restrictions on a substantial part of all their trade, and that the formation of the block not result in an increase of barriers for states outside the block. In a customs union, trade barriers among the member countries are eliminated, but a common external tariff—no higher than the previous average of the members—exists on imports to the union. In a free trade area, members also remove trade barriers against another, but can retain individual country tariffs instead of a common tariff against outside countries.

The rationale behind Article XXIV appears to be that half a step toward free trade (i.e., within the customs union or free trade area) is better than no step at all. In addition, one can ask oneself whether a trade block is a building block or a step in the right direction (i.e., multilateral free trade), or whether it is a stumbling block that threatens to fragment the world economy. The movement to free trade within the block may or may not be desirable when there are still trade restrictions for nonmembers, because a trade block can lead to "trade creation," which improves international resource allocation, or to "trade diversion," which worsens the international allocation of resources. Trade creation occurs when a member country in a trade block imports from another member country that is a low-cost producer and, previously, the former country did not import at all because of a duty on the foreign product. When the duty is removed and the other country is a lower-cost source, the international division of labor is enhanced when resources shift into more efficient production. If, however, a member country now imports from another member that is a higher-cost producer than an outside country from which it formerly imported but no longer does so since the outside country now faces a discriminatory tariff, then the block is diverting trade. In this case, there is an uneconomic diversion of production from the low-cost outside source to the high-cost supplier within the block.

The following factors have to be examined in considering whether trade creation or trade diversion is likely to dominate in a particular union:

- pre-union level of tariff rates among the members,
- the level of the post-union external tariffs compared with the pre-union tariff levels of each member country,
- the elasticities of demand for the imports on which duties are reduced, and
- the elasticities of supply of exports from the members and foreign sources.

Naturally, the number of trade creations and the number of trade diversions may differ among the members of a trade block so that some may benefit/lose more than others.

Regional integration may be beneficial in encouraging competition among the member countries. As a consequence, technical efficiency in existing industries may be enhanced as marginal firms are forced to reduce their costs, resources are reallocated from less efficient to more efficient firms and monopolies which had previously been established behind tariff walls are no longer in a sheltered position. Regional integration could also lead to an improvement in the region's commodity terms of trade if the demand for imports from outside by the members of the union is reduced or if the members' bargaining power in trade negotiations is strengthened. The members of the union are, however, unlikely to be able to exercise sufficient monopolistic or monopsonistic power to influence their terms of trade (by inducing outsiders to supply their goods more cheaply or by raising duties on their trade with the outside world), unless they are the major buyers on the world market for their imports or the chief suppliers of their exports. In addition, when confining free trade to a region, there is a risk of retaliation through the formation of other economic blocks. A union may thereby inhibit the realization of more significant gains from the universal approach to free trade.

The effects of a regional trade organization may differ according to whether it is a North-South type of integration as in NAFTA, or a type of integration involving two or more developing countries, as in the Association of Southeast Asian Nations (ASEAN). In fact, a number of economic objections to a union among developing countries could be raised: The case for an economic union is weak when the constituent countries have not yet established a number of industries; limitations on the supply side may be more of a deterrent to the creation of an industry than is the narrow market on the side of demand; when manufacturing industry is only at a rudimentary stage in the member countries, there is not much scope for eliminating high-cost manufacturers within the region.

The case for a union is strongest among countries that have little foreign trade in proportion to their domestic production, with countries outside the union, but conduct a high proportion of the foreign trade with another. When these conditions prevail, there is less possibility for introducing, within each member country, a distortion of the price relationships between goods from other member countries and from outside the union, and more of a possibility for eliminating any distortion by tariffs of the price relations between domestic goods and imports from other member countries. Naturally, one could question the need for a union when the aforementioned conditions prevail, since the end result would probably not differ much from a situation of nondiscriminatory, multilateral free trade.

THE WORLD TRADE ORGANIZATION

The World Trade Organization (WTO) was established on January 1, 1995 to take charge of administering the new global trade rules, agreed in the Uruguay Round, which took effect on the same day. These rules—achieved after seven years of negotiations among more than 120 countries—establish the rule of law in international trade, which for goods and services together are estimated to have approached about $5 trillion in 1995. Through the WTO agreements and market access commitments, world income is expected to rise by over $500 billion annually by the year 2005, and annual global trade growth will be as much as a quarter higher by the same year than it would otherwise have been. The difference between GATT and WTO is that the latter organization

- is more global in its membership than GATT;
- has a far wider scope than its predecessor, bringing into the multilateral trading system, for the first time, trade in services, intellectual property protection and investment;
- is a full-fledged international organization in its own right while GATT was basically a provisional treaty serviced by an ad hoc Secretariat;
- administers a unified package of agreements to which all members are committed, whereas the GATT framework included many important side agreements among a few countries (e.g., anti-dumping measures and subsidies);
- contains a much improved version of the original GATT rules plus a lot more; and
- reverses policies of protection in certain "sensitive" areas (e.g., trade in agricultural products and textiles) which were more or less tolerated in the GATT framework.

The WTO administers, through various councils and committees, the many agreements contained in the Final Act of the Uruguay Round, plus a number of plurilateral agreements, notably on government procurement and civil aircraft. It also oversees the implementation of the significant tariff cuts (averaging 40%) and reduction of nontariff measures agreed to in the negotiations.

It is a watchdog of international trade, regularly examining the trade regimes of individual members. In its various bodies, members flag proposed or draft measures by others that can cause trade conflicts. Members are also required to notify the WTO of various trade measures and statistics, which are maintained by the WTO in a large data base.

As in any partnership, conflicts can arise among members. The WTO, from the very start of these conflicts, provides several conciliation mechanisms for finding an amicable solution. Trade disputes that cannot be solved through bilateral talks are adjudicated under the WTO dispute settlement court. Panels of independent experts are established to examine disputes in the light of WTO rules, and provide rulings. This tougher, streamlined procedure ensures equal treatment for all trading partners and encourages members to live up to their obligations.

The WTO is also a management consultant for world trade. Its economists keep a close watch on the pulse of the global economy and provide studies on the main trade issues of the day. It is also a forum where countries continuously negotiate exchanges of trade concessions to further lower trade barriers all over the world.

The WTO Secretariat services all meetings of the WTO bodies at its headquarters in Geneva. The Secretariat works with developing countries and countries undertaking economic reform to help them negotiate accession and draw maximum benefit from the WTO.

IMPORT AND EXPORT FINANCING

The importer prefers to pay after the goods have been received since then all risk is shifted to the exporter. The exporter, however, prefers exactly the opposite, which of course shifts all risk to the importer. The dilemma of not trusting a stranger in a foreign land is solved by using a respected bank as intermediary. Thus, the importer obtains a bank's promise to pay on its behalf, knowing the exporter will trust the bank. The bank's promise to pay is called a *letter of credit*. The exporter ships the merchandise to the importer's country; title to the merchandise is given to the bank on a document called an *order bill of lading*. Upon the exporter's request, the bank pays for the merchandise. The document to request payment is called a *draft*. After having paid for the goods, the bank passes title to the importer, whom the bank trusts. At that time or later, depending on their agreement, the importer reimburses the bank.

The three key trade documents—letter of credit, order bill of lading and draft—are part of a carefully constructed system to determine who bears the financial loss if one of the parties defaults at any time. In addition, they assure the amount, currency and time of payment, and thus lay the groundwork for effective currency hedging. The remaining part of this section discusses the three documents.

A letter of credit, abbreviated L/C, is an instrument issued by a bank at the request of an importer, in which the bank promises to pay a beneficiary upon presentation of documents specified in the L/C. In international trade an L/C is sometimes called a *commercial letter of credit*, a *documentary letter of credit* or simply a *credit*. An L/C reduces the risk of noncompletion because the bank agrees to pay against documents rather than actual merchandise.

A typical transaction is as follows. An importer and exporter agree on a transaction and the importer applies to its local bank for the issuance of an L/C. Based on its assessment of the importer's creditworthiness, the bank may require a cash deposit or other collateral from the importer and issues the L/C. The bank wants to know the type of transaction, the amount of money and currency involved and which documents must accompany the draft that will be drawn against the L/C. Examples of such documents are a commercial invoice, a packing list issued by the beneficiary, an insurance certificate and a full set of original shipped "on board" ocean bills of lading issued by the shipping company. At this point in time the credit of the importer's bank has been substituted for that of the importer and the L/C becomes a financial contract between the importer's bank and the designated beneficiary, the exporter. This financial contract is a separate transaction from the sale of the goods. If the terms of the L/C are met, any payment problems that develop at a later date are of concern only to the importer and the issuing bank. All other parties to the transaction may rely on the bank's credit without concern about the financial status of the importer.

The importer's bank which issued the L/C sends it to an *advising bank* in the exporter's country, which will advise the beneficiary (the exporter) of the establishment of an L/C in the beneficiary's name. After shipping the goods, the exporter draws a draft against the issuing bank in accordance with the terms of the L/C, attaches the required documents and presents the draft to its own bank for payment. The exporter's bank will forward the L/C and documents to the importer's bank that issued the L/C. If all the terms and conditions expressed on the L/C have been complied with and the required documents are attached, the importer's bank will honor the draft and pay the exporter's bank. When the exporter's bank receives the funds, it passes them on to the exporter.

The importer's bank, in turn, collects from the importer in accordance with the terms agreed upon at the time the L/C was opened. The importer might pay at once and receive the documents, including the order bill of lading that is needed to obtain physical possession of the goods. Alternatively, the bank may release the documents to the importer who promises to pay later, usually under a trust receipt arrangement.

The essence of an L/C is the promise of the issuing bank to pay against specified documents, which must accompany any draft drawn against the credit. The L/C is a separate transaction from the sales or other contracts on which it might be based. To constitute a true L/C, the following conditions must be satisfied:

- the issuing bank must receive a fee or other valid business consideration for issuing the L/C,
- the L/C must contain a specified expiration date or a definite maturity,
- the bank's commitment must have a stated maximum amount of money,
- the bank's obligation to pay must arise only on the presentation of specific documents,
- the bank cannot be called on to determine disputed questions of fact or law, and
- the bank's customer must have an unqualified obligation to reimburse the bank on the same condition as the bank has paid.

The main advantages of an L/C are:

- the exporter can sell against a bank's promise to pay rather than the promise of a commercial firm,
- the importer need not pay out funds until the goods have arrived at a local port, and
- the exporter is in a more secure position as to the availability of foreign exchange to pay for the sale, since banks are more likely to be aware of foreign exchange conditions and rules than is the importing firm.

The main disadvantages are the fee charged by the importer's bank for issuing the L/C and the possibility that the L/C reduces the importer's borrowing line of credit from its bank.

A draft, sometimes called a *bill of exchange* (B/E) or *first of exchange*, is the instrument normally used in international trade to effect payment. In other words, a draft is simply an order written by an exporter (seller) instructing an importer (buyer) or its agent to pay a specified amount of money at a specific time. The person or business initiating the draft is known as the *maker, drawer* or *originator*. Normally, this is the exporter. The party to whom the draft is addressed is the *drawee*, who is asked to honor the draft, that is, to pay the amount requested according to the stated terms. The drawee could be either the buyer, in which case the draft is called a *trade draft*, or the buyer's bank, in which case the draft is called a *bank draft*. A draft may be drawn as a bearer instrument, or it may designate a person to whom payment is to be made. This person, known as the *payee*, may be the drawer itself or it may be some other party such as the drawer's bank. It is of interest to note that a personal check is another type of draft; the drawer writes an order to a bank to pay a specified amount of money on demand to the order of a designated beneficiary.

If properly drawn, drafts can become *negotiable instruments*. As such, they provide a convenient instrument for financing the international movement of merchandise. In accordance with the Uniform Commercial Code, Section 3104(1), a draft must conform to the following requirements in order to become a negotiable instrument:

- it must be in writing and signed by the drawer,
- it must contain an unconditional promise or order to pay a definite sum of money,
- it must be payable on demand or at a fixed or determinable future date, and
- it must be payable to order or to bearer.

If a draft is drawn in conformity with the above requirements, a person receiving it with proper endorsements becomes a *holder in due course*. This is a privileged legal status that enables the holder to receive payment despite any personal disagreements between him and the drawee because of controversy over the underlying commercial transaction.

There are two types of drafts: *sight drafts* and *time drafts*. A sight draft is payable on presentation to the drawee. A time draft, sometimes called a *usance draft*, allows a delay in payment. The drawee accepts the time draft by writing or stamping a notice of acceptance on its face. Once accepted, the time draft becomes a promise to pay by the accepting party. When a time draft is drawn on and accepted by a business firm, it becomes a *trade acceptance*. When it is drawn on and accepted by a bank, it becomes a *banker's acceptance*. The time period of the time draft is called its *tenor* or *usance*.

Drafts are also classified as *clean* or *documentary*. A clean draft is an order to pay unaccompanied by any other documents. When used in trade, the seller has usually sent the shipping documents directly to the buyer, who can obtain possession of the goods independent of its payment (on a clean sight draft) or acceptance (on a clean time draft). MNCs frequently use clean drafts when shipping to their affiliates because matters of trust and credit are not involved.

Most drafts in international trade are documentary, which means that shipping documents are attached to it. Payment (for sight drafts) or acceptance (for time drafts) is required in order to obtain possession of those documents, which are in turn needed to obtain the merchandise involved in the transaction. The draft is called a *D/P draft* if the documents are to be delivered to the buyer on payment of the draft. If the documents are delivered on acceptance, the draft is called a *D/A draft*.

When a draft is accepted by a bank, it becomes a banker's acceptance and as such it is the unconditional promise of that bank to make payment on the draft when it matures. The holder of a banker's acceptance does not need to wait until maturity to liquidate the investment since he/she may sell the acceptance in the money market, where constant trading in such instruments occurs. In fact, the quality of a banker's acceptance is practically identical to a marketable bank certificate of deposit. The exporter is the first owner of the banker's acceptance created from an international trade transaction; he/she receives the accepted draft back after the bank has stamped it "accepted." The exporter may either hold the acceptance until maturity and then collect, or *discount*—that is, sell at a reduced price—it to his/her bank in order to receive the funds immediately. If the exporter collects at maturity an acceptance of, for instance, $100,000 for six months, he/she would receive the face amount less the bank's commission of 1.5 percent per year. Thus, the exporter would receive:

Face amount of the acceptance	$100,000
Less 1.5% per year commission for six months	− 750
Amount received by exporter in six months	$99,250

If the exporter discounts the acceptance, he/she will receive the face amount of the acceptance less both the acceptance fee and the going market rate of discount for bankers' acceptances. If the discount rate were 6 percent per year, the exporter would receive the following:

Face amount of the acceptance	$100,000
Less 1.5% per year commission for six months	− 750
Less 6% per year discount rate for six months	− 3,000
Amount received by exporter at once	$95,750

The discounting bank may hold the acceptance in its portfolio, earning the 6% per year discount, or the acceptance may be resold in the acceptance market to portfolio investors. The investors who buy bankers' acceptances provide the funds that finance the underlying commercial transaction.

The third key document for financing international trade is the bill of lading, or B/L, which is issued to the exporter by a common carrier transporting the merchandise. The B/L serves three purposes: a receipt, a contract and a document of title. As a receipt, the B/L indicates that the carrier has received the goods described on the face of the document. It is not the carrier's responsibility to ascertain that the containers hold what is alleged to be their contents. The B/L is stamped "freight paid" or "freight prepaid" if shipping charges are paid in advance. If merchandise is shipped collect, the carrier maintains a lien on the goods until freight is paid. As a contract, the B/L indicates the carrier's responsibility to provide certain transportation in return for certain charges. Common carriers cannot disclaim responsibility for their negligence through inserting special clauses in a B/L. As a document of title, the B/L is used to obtain payment or a written promise of payment before the merchandise is released to the importer. It can also be used as collateral against which funds may be advanced to the exporter by its local bank prior to or during shipment and before final payment by the importer.

Bills of lading are either *straight* or *to order*. A straight B/L stipulates that the carrier deliver the merchandise to the designated consignee; it is not title to the goods and, therefore, not good collateral for loans. The straight B/L is not required to obtain possession of the goods and is, therefore, used when the goods have been paid for in advance, when the transaction is being financed by the exporter or when the shipment is to an affiliate. An order B/L directs the carrier to deliver the merchandise to the order of a designated party. It grants title to the merchandise only to the person to whom the document is addressed, and surrender of the order B/L is required to obtain the shipment. The order B/L is typically made payable to the order of the exporter, who thus retains title to the merchandise after it has been handed to the carrier. Title to the goods remains with the exporter until payment is received, at which time the exporter endorses the B/L (which is negotiable) in blank or to the party making the payment, usually a bank. Most frequently, payment is advanced against a documentary draft accompanied by the endorsed order B/L. After paying the draft, the exporter's bank sends the documents to the bank of the importer. The importer's bank, in turn, releases the documents to the importer after payment (sight drafts), after acceptance (time drafts addressed to the importer and marked D/A), or after payment terms have been agreed (drafts drawn on the importer's bank under provisions of a letter of credit).

A *clean* B/L indicates the goods were received by the carrier in apparently good condition. It is not the carrier's responsibility to inspect the goods' condition beyond external visual appearance. A *foul* B/L indicates that the goods appeared to have suffered some damage before being received for shipment; it lacks complete negotiability.

As mentioned earlier, the letter of credit, the draft and the B/L are the principal documents required in most international transactions. Some or all of the following documents are sometimes needed as a condition of the letter of credit for honoring a draft: an *insurance document*, a *commercial invoice*, a *certificate of analysis*, a *consular invoice*, an *export declaration* and a *packing list*.

The insurance document must be as specified in the letter of credit and is issued by an insurance company or its agents. The insurance may be issued in the name of the importer or it may be issued to the exporter, who subsequently endorses the policy to the importer. The document is normally expressed in the same currency as the credit and must not be dated later than the date of the shipment.

A commercial invoice is issued by the seller and contains a description of the merchandise. In addition, the commercial invoice may give unit prices, financial terms of sale, amount due from the buyer and shipping conditions related to charges such as FAS (*free alongside*), FOB (*free on board*), C&F (*cost and freight*) or CIF (*cost, insurance and freight*).

A certificate of analysis may be required to ascertain that certain specifications such as weight, purity and sanitation have been met. It may be issued by a government or a private organization, as specified in the letter of credit. These certificates may be required by health or other officials of the importing country or by the importer as assurance that goods are received as ordered.

The consular invoice is issued by the consulate of the importing country to provide customs information and statistics for that country and to help prevent false declarations. It may be combined with a *certificate of origin* of the goods.

An export declaration is a document prepared by the exporter to assist the government with the preparation of export statistics.

A packing list may be required so that the contents of containers can be identified, either for customs purposes or for importer identification of the contents of separate containers.

CHALLENGES TO PRIVATE AND PUBLIC MANAGEMENT

Today's business executive must not only strive for internal efficiency, he/she should also strive for external efficiency. Internal efficiency is obtained by the efficient performance in the functional activities of the firm—production, finance, marketing and organization. External efficiency is obtained by adjusting to external shocks and taking advantage of new opportunities. External shocks may relate to the appearance of a foreign competitor, the establishment of a regional common market, policies to remedy a country's balance of payments, appreciation or depreciation of currencies, policies of the IMF, and so on. In other words, there are a host of international economic and political developments that are continually changing a firm's external environment. These changes can have more effect on a firm's profit-and-loss statement than can its internal efficiency.

Managers who understand the international context in which their firm operates are not only better prepared to adjust to external shocks, they may also be able to create new opportunities as a result of these shocks. Among the most significant changes in the world economy that directly affect a firm through international market forces are changes in the volume of international trade, the commodity composition of foreign trade and movements of import and export prices. Changes in the flow of international capital, which are commonly linked to changes in the volume and pattern of international trade, are also important. Private foreign investment is of increasing significance—both portfolio and direct investment (equity control of the enterprise). Attention should also be given to the role of public movements from the World Bank, regional development banks (such as the Interamerican Development Bank) and the IMF. Finally, the modern manager should be familiar with forward, futures and option contracts in order to eliminate the risk of variations in exchange rates.

It is clear that firms operating in international markets can be affected by the changing world economy; what may not be clear is that firms operating domestically may feel the impact of the changing world economy through the indirect effect of government policies. For instance, a country's balance-of-payments position may dictate whether domestic monetary policy will be easy or tight. To reduce the country's balance-of-payments deficit, the national government may decrease its expenditure or increase taxes in order to cut private spending; the change in the amount and composition of national expenditure will then affect domestic firms. A national central bank may adopt tight money policies and raise domestic interest rates to attract short-term capital from abroad in an effort to stabilize the country's foreign exchange; or a rise in the world demand for savings may cause central banks to raise interest rates, thereby affecting the volume and the pattern of domestic investment and consumer spending on the "big" items (automobiles, houses, etc.). Monetary, fiscal and trade policies are the most important policy areas in which governments respond to international developments.

Globalization is often troubling to a national policymaker since it heightens the vulnerability of a nation to external developments, and domestic autonomy in policy making may be subordinated to international policy considerations. In addition, international tension and conflict may arise when the domestic economic objectives of different countries clash. These conflicts then give rise to governmental policies that have an impact on industries and business firms. Conflicts may arise, since each nation:

- wishes to exercise national economic autonomy over its own fiscal and monetary policies in order to maintain full employment with stable prices;
- attempts to minimize the cost of adjustment to a balance-of-payments problem by avoiding remedial policies or by trying to place some of the burden of adjustment on other countries (because for every country that has a deficit in its balance of payments there is a country that has a surplus);
- wishes to raise the return of foreign investment in its economy by, for instance, having high license fees or taxes, whereas the foreign investor would like to raise the return for its own enterprise; and

- would like to have free access for its exports and try to preserve domestic markets by resorting to import tariffs and/or quotas, and/or export subsidies.

In order to resolve these potential conflicts, it is crucial that government policymakers understand the forces of the new global economy and the impact of government policies introduced by them as a result of changes in the global economy.

SUGGESTIONS FOR FURTHER READING

Cavusgil, S. Tamer, Shaoming Zou, and G. M. Naidu. "Product and Promotion Adaption in Export Ventures: An Empirical Investigation." *Journal of International Business Studies* (Third Quarter 1993): 497–506.

Celi, Louis J., and I. James Czechowicz. *Export Financing: A Handbook of Sources and Techniques*. Morristown, NJ: Financial Executives Research Foundation, 1985.

Francis, Dick. *The Countertrade Handbook*. Westport, CT: Quorum Books, 1987.

Hennart, Jean-Francois. "Some Empirical Dimensions of Countertrade." *Journal of International Business Studies* (Second Quarter 1990): 243–270.

Korth, Christopher M., ed. *International Countertrade*. Westport, CT: Quorum Books, 1987.

Chapter 3

International Capital Flows

TYPES OF CAPITAL FLOWS

Capital flows across countries are typically classified in terms of maturity, short term and long term. Short-term capital flows respond primarily to interest rate differentials and expectations of interest rate changes across countries. Long-term capital is typically attracted to economic and business environments expected to provide significant long-run stability and economic growth. Examples of short-term debt instruments are US Treasury bills with maturities of 13, 26 or 52 weeks. Their relatively high yields during the early 1980s, combined with the "safe haven" argument that the United States constituted one of the most stable political and economic environments, induced significant capital flows from abroad. During the Reagan administration, this portfolio investment from abroad was the subject of much debate over foreign financing of the US budget deficit. Long-term capital flows play a significant role in the balance-of-payments structure of many countries.

International capital flows are also classified according to the degree of control over a target investment by a foreign investor. In the United States, a 10 percent or more acquisition of the equity of a US enterprise is considered sufficient for a foreign investor to exercise some influence on the firm's management and operations. Such investment is then categorized as *direct foreign investment* (DFI) and the firm itself is reclassified as the US affiliate of a foreign company. The definitional requirement of DFI varies across countries: it is 25 percent in Germany and 20 percent in France and the United Kingdom. All investment transactions between parent organizations and their foreign affiliates are direct foreign investment flows. An investment is classified as portfolio investment if ownership is less than the DFI threshold level or the investment is a debt instrument. Portfolio investments primarily refer to the ownership of financial securities, broadly defined to include sales and purchases of securities and amounts of outstanding claims and liabilities reported by banks and nonbanking concerns.

Sometimes the DFI is further subdivided into the nature of the investment:

- *acquisition* investments that are the purchase of preexisting enterprises or operations, and

- *Greenfield* projects in which the capital is used for the construction of new production, sales or commercial facilities.

Normally, governments consider Greenfield investments as a strong potential contributor to economic welfare and they are, therefore, often encouraged. Acquisitions, on the other hand, are increasingly becoming the topic of emotional "sovereignty" as citizens of the countries receiving these capital inflows worry over the potential loss of home control.

Finally, capital flow transactions are also classified as *official* or *private*. US official capital flows include changes in the reserves of US monetary authorities in monetary gold, foreign exchange, SDRs at the IMF and loans and credits to foreigners by US government agencies. Changes in foreign official assets in the United States occur through the transactions in United States Treasury securities, other US government obligations, bank deposits and US corporate stocks and bonds. Private capital flows include direct foreign investment and portfolio investment undertaken by both American residents abroad and foreigners in the United States.

In Chapter 4 we will see that incomes on direct and portfolio investment are reported in the *current account* while exchanges in financial assets between US and foreign residents are measured in the *capital account*. The US Department of Commerce compiles the value of accumulated stocks of US assets abroad and of foreign assets in the United States (resulting from capital flows in and out of the United States) in a summary statement of the US international investment position as follows:

Summary Components of the US Net International Investment Position ($ Billions)

	1994	1995
Net position		
At current cost	−580.1	−814.0
At current stock-market value	−492.5	−773.7
US government and foreign official assets	−301.3	−420.3
Direct investment		
At current cost	199.5	241.6
At market value	287.0	281.9
US and foreign securities	−463.2	−665.8
Bank- and nonbank-reported claims and liabilities	−15.0	30.5

The formation of the Eurocurrency market in the 1960s was a significant contribution to the evolution of international capital markets. *Eurocurrencies* are sometimes viewed as another kind of money, although in reality they are domestic currencies of one country on deposit in another country. Their value is identical to that of the same currency at "home." For instance, a Eurodollar is a US dollar-denominated interest-bearing deposit in a bank outside the United States. The bank may be a foreign bank or the overseas branch of a US bank. Any convertible currency can exist in "Euro-" form. For instance, the Eurocurrency market includes Eurosterling (British pounds deposited outside the United Kingdom), Euromarks (German marks deposited outside Germany), Euroyen (Japanese yen deposited outside Japan), and so on. To escape the regulations of national monetary authorities, holders of dollars—and later holders of other strong currencies—deposited them in Eurocurrency markets or money markets outside the borders of the national currencies. Today, the Eurocurrency market is the major international currency market. Transactions in the Eurocurrency market involve mainly short-term capital movements since the dominant instruments are certificates of deposit, time deposits and bank loans.

In the 1970s, after OPEC countries invested their petrodollars in Euromarket bank deposits, international banks had considerable amounts of liquidity to recycle through syndicated bank loans from the Euromarkets to developing countries. Official bank lending rose in the early 1980s to partially offset the decline in private lending. In the 1990s, private flows to developing countries increased, making foreign private investment and portfolio investment in developing countries a growing share of global capital movements.

The foreign exchange market is the major international money market and involves primarily short-term capital flows. Foreign exchange can be considered as an asset since the demand for a foreign currency bank deposit or a foreign short-term security is determined by the same factors as for any other asset, namely, its expected rate of return, the asset's degree of liquidity and the risk involved. Individuals and institutional investors balance their portfolio holdings according to their estimates of expected rates of return on various assets and their degree of aversion to risk. The changes in portfolio balance result into financial capital movements. In determining a portfolio balance, a prospective lender of financial capital will estimate the range of possible yields on a foreign security after converting the payments of interest into domestic currency, allowing for the possibility of depreciation in the foreign currency during the period until maturity of the security. To hedge against the risk of depreciation, the lender can buy forward cover on the forward exchange market against the risk that a future change in the exchange rate may affect the capital value of the investor's holdings of foreign assets. By selling expected foreign exchange rate forward, the lender can be assured of the amount of domestic currency that will be received upon maturity.

The Eurobond market is the long-term counterpart of the Eurocurrency market. Thus, the Eurobond market is the long-term (normally 10- or 20-year maturities) market for bonds denominated in a currency other than that of the country where the market is located. Between 1981 and 1995, the size of the Eurobond market has grown by more than tenfold.

Until the 1970s, the growth of international trading in securities, bonds and other debt instruments was closely related to the growth of international trade in goods and services, since multinational enterprises in the global marketplace do not only gain a competitive advantage through exports, but through foreign investment as well. Since the 1970s, the rate of growth in lending and investing across national borders has been more rapid than the rate of growth in world trade, as countries have liberalized their financial markets by eliminating capital controls, and transaction costs fell with advances in telecommunications and computers. Cross-border financial transactions in most industrial countries expanded from less than 10 percent of GDP in 1980 to in excess of 100 percent of GDP by the early 1990s. Today, the capital flows generated by investment institutions and large corporations that trade currencies for their own books are far greater than those of banks.

The large US trade deficit and the large amount of borrowing by the US (especially by the federal government) are two other factors that have contributed to the increase in international capital flows. The trade deficit is the difference between exports and imports. In the 1980s and 1990s, imports greatly exceeded exports, resulting in a large trade deficit which has been financed by capital inflows. Since savings within the United States have been insufficient to finance total borrowing needs, international borrowing has made up for the shortfall.

Significant potential exists for an increase in supply of funds into emerging countries since the percentage of institutional money (mutual funds, pension funds and insurance companies' investable surplus) in developing markets is low (less than 1 percent for US institutional investors and 5 percent for UK investors). Increased inflow of external finance into developing markets would be beneficial to developing countries since they would rely less on external debt, thereby making them less vulnerable to increases in international interest rates and to problems of debt servicing. It is noted, however, that large portfolio inflows may be volatile and potentially destabilizing in financial markets and the economy of developing countries.

Increasing the inflow of external finance into developing countries may be difficult since many European, Japanese and American investors became reluctant to invest in these countries after the financial crises in East Asia, Brazil and Russia. In addition, many developing countries have one or more of the following obstacles toward the realization of further gains from the integration of their emerging stock markets: exchange rate controls, high and variable inflation, poor credit ratings and lack of a high-quality regulatory and accounting framework.

COUNTRY RISK

The risks involved in international bank lending may be classified as *commercial risk* and *country risk*. Commercial risk is the same risk which exists in domestic bank lending and requires the assessment of the likelihood that a client will be unable to repay its debt because of business reasons. However, in the case of international bank lending, cultural differences and lack of information may inhibit an assessment of the firm's management and differing accounting standards and disclosure practices may preclude the type of financial analysis common in the home country. In addition, a bank may find it difficult to evaluate foreign economic conditions that may affect the client firm and may need legal advice to determine its position in any bankruptcy proceedings. For instance, in many countries firms cannot easily dismiss workers whose jobs have been rendered redundant. The magnitude of payments to be made to redundant workers may have a significant effect on a firm's ability to repay any bank loans.

Country risk refers to the possibility that unexpected events within a host country will influence a client firm's or a government's ability to repay a loan. It is usually divided into *sovereign risk* and *currency risk*. Sovereign risk, also called *political risk*, arises because a host government may exercise its sovereign power to unilaterally repudiate foreign obligations, or may prevent local firms from honoring their foreign obligations. The risk may be the result of direct government action or the result of indirect consequences of ineffective government (for instance, a government being unable to maintain law and order). Currency risk, also called foreign exchange risk, arises from the possibility that an unexpected change in foreign exchange rates will alter the home currency value of repayment of loans by foreign clients. Naturally, if the debt is denominated in the home currency, say, the US dollar, the risk is shifted to the borrower. However, the bank still runs the risk that the borrower is unable to obtain dollars to repay the loan. A bank may partially avoid this possibility by sourcing funds for foreign clients in local currencies. Although the repayment of principal will not be subject to a currency risk, in this case, the profit margin between the lending rate and the local cost of sourcing the funds remains subject to currency risk since this margin is of value to the parent bank only in terms of its home currency value.

Sovereign risk analysis should focus on probable future willingness or ability of a government to honor past obligations or to allow firms and banks within the country to honor their obligations. Variables considered include:

- expected trends in the country's balance of payments (BOP),
- the country's magnitude of the foreign exchange obligations,
- the country's political stability, and
- present and likely future holdings of foreign exchange reserves of the country.

Expected trends in the BOP are important because the ability to generate foreign exchange depends on either a favorable current account or a favorable capital account. Naturally, a country risk is higher when its magnitude of the foreign exchange obligations, in particular relative to its GNP and international trade, is higher. Political stability is important since a new government may

abrogate obligations incurred by its predecessor. Present and likely future holdings of foreign exchange reserves are considered in sovereign risk analysis since
they act as a buffer for a limited period of time in the country's ability to repay
foreign debt. These aforementioned factors, in turn, are influenced by differential
rates of domestic and foreign inflation and whether or not the country's
exchange rates are allowed to adjust to the differential. In this context, foreign
currency debt includes both government debt and the debt of private firms and
banks in the country.

In addition to analyzing the "stand-alone risk" of an individual country as
described above, banks often analyze country risk from a portfolio theory perspective. Thus, international loans are viewed as a portfolio of risky assets whose
returns will vary as a result of both commercial and country risks. The total risk
of the portfolio will be reduced if the bank successfully diversifies its assets
across countries. Portfolio diversification works best if default risk in each country is independent of that in every other country. Defaults can, however, be
closely correlated due to (a) geographical or ideological proximity resulting in
a common view of nationalism, (b) drought and starvation and (c) civil strife
with foreign intervention. International dependency complicates the assessment
of risk in an international portfolio, but it does not completely negate the advantages of international loan diversification.

Besides rescheduling the debts, the main strategies used by debtor countries
to survive a debt crisis are:

- austerity,
- overdevaluation of their currencies,
- encouraging direct foreign investment, and
- debt-for-equity swaps.

Countries have tried to reduce the demand for imports and free up capacity
for exports by following tighter monetary and fiscal policies. The IMF has usually taken the lead in suggesting austerity as a condition for further loans. Austerity is often not the only solution since some governments are too weak
politically to endure austerity policies for a prolonged period. It is also noted
that tighter monetary and fiscal policies may result in a slowing of growth rates
and a reduction in per capita consumption.

Some of the indebted countries have tried to become more competitive in
nontraditional exports by overdevaluating their currencies or having their real
effective exchange rates lie well below an index value of 100 on purpose. Creditor countries may be willing to tolerate such a policy in the interest of encouraging debt repayment.

Many of the debtor countries encourage more incoming direct foreign investment by removing barriers such as local ownership requirements, work permits for expatriates, local content requirements and other interferences with the

free market. In addition, these countries often try to create a more favorable environment for private enterprises in general and privatizing many of the in- efficient public enterprises.

A *debt-for-equity swap* is a technique to encourage a reversal of capital flight by local citizens and an encouragement to banks to convert from debt to equity claims (creditors are allowed to exchange their loans for equity in local firms). The success of this approach depends on the terms of the exchange, that is, how much the debt is discounted, and on the desirability of owning local firms. So far, the results have been modest relative to the size of external debt.

Many of the creditor international banks have reduced their burden of devel- oping country debt by increasing their equity capital base and their loan loss reserves and by reducing any new lending to the debtor countries. Banks have also quietly been selling off some of their exposed loans at big discounts to investors willing to take the risk. For example, in 1991 the debt of Chile was selling for 75 cents on the dollar and the debt of Brazil was selling for as little as 23 cents on the dollar.

A *political risk assessment function* has to be incorporated in an international firm in order to carry out a rigorous political risk analysis. The task of political risk analysis is not so much to identify social and political upheavals that may lead to the expropriation of most, if not all, foreign-owned firms, since these upheavals are rare. Instead, the task of political risk analysis is to identify the politically generated managerial contingencies in routine policy making by the government and to examine what can be done, if anything, to protect one's firm against the consequences. Political risks may include:

- a collapse of the existing political order in the borrower's country;
- changes in taxation;
- changes in tariffs and/or quotas;
- changes in the exchange rate regime;
- foreign exchange remittance restrictions;
- expropriation;
- the introduction of quotas or prohibitions on exports of the investment's production in cases of domestic shortages;
- labor law revisions;
- changes in local content rules;
- the introduction of controls to restrict the rate of depletion of the project's reserves;
- the use of preemption rights on the part of the host government to purchase the production from the project in certain circumstances;
- the introduction during the life of the project of more stringent environmental protection legislation, which could adversely affect planned production rates or operating costs;
- the introduction of restrictions on the repatriation of profits and debt service;
- the introduction of restrictions on access to supplies of raw materials or energy; and

- deregulation or the lifting of tariff barriers in cases where the project was planned on the assumption that fixed prices and a regulation of access to markets would continue.

Political risks may be mitigated through:

- Taking out insurance against political risks on a commercial basis or with official bodies, such as export credit departments or multilateral development agencies;
- Familiarization with the tax and tariff laws in the host country;
- Collecting, controlling, and, if necessary, retaining the project's cash flows offshore to generate hard currency through, for example, sales contracts;
- seeking assurances against expropriation or nationalization with guarantees that if these assurances were later proved false, proper compensation would be payable; and
- checking and clarifying any licenses granted to the project sponsors.

If financing is arranged in parallel with the World Bank or international aid agencies, a formal arrangement of the lending structure may reduce the risk that the host government will interfere with the lenders' interests. Similarly, if the financing is syndicated to lenders from different "friendly" countries, the risk of jeopardizing trade and other relations with these countries may deter the host government from taking actions that are detrimental to the lenders' or sponsors' interests.

Political risks can be insured against by project sponsors, lenders, suppliers and purchasers through private commercial agencies or multilateral or governmental agencies whose role is to promote exports, trade or development in the host country. Governmental agencies providing this coverage in the G-7 countries are as follows:

Canada	Export Development Corporation (EDC)
France	Compagnie Francaise d'Assurance pour le Commerce Exterieur (COFACE)
Germany	Hermes Kreditversicherungs AG und Treuarbeit AG Wirkschaftsprufungs-gesellschaft (Hermes)
Italy	Sezione Speciale per l'Assicurazione del Credito all' Esportazione (SACE)
Japan	Export-Import Insurance Division of the International Trade Administration Bureau of the Ministry of International Trade and Industry (EID/MTI)
UK	The Export Credit Guarantee Department
US	The Export-Import Bank (EXIM)

The available support differs from country to country; however, project sponsors, lenders and other interested parties can apply for some degree of protection against war, insurrection (rebellion) or revolution; expropriation, nationalization or requisition of assets; and the nonconversion of currency or the imposition of discriminatory exchange rates. In addition, the insuring agencies will often provide coverage to guarantee performance by contractors and exporters of essential suppliers to the project.

One multilateral agency that provides insurance against political risks is the World Bank's Multilateral Investment Guarantee Agency (MIGA). Policies may be purchased either individually or in combination against losses arising from:

- currency transfers resulting in the inability of investors or lenders to convert and transfer local currency into foreign exchange;
- expropriation, that is, acts by the host government that reduce or eliminate ownership of, control over, or rights to insured investment, whether the acts are direct or indirect;
- war and civil disturbance (including politically motivated acts of sabotage and terrorism) resulting in damage to, or destruction or disappearance of, tangible assets; and
- breach of contract by the host government, provided the investor obtains an arbitrated award or judicial sentence for damages and is unable, after a specified period, to enforce it.

The right to develop and operate a project is often based on a license or concession from the government of the country in which the project is situated. The license or concession is frequently issued under regulations that give the host government widely stated rights to revoke it should certain events occur. Where coventures are involved, there is also a risk to the lenders that the license may be revoked, not merely through an act of omission of the borrower with which the lender is concerned, but also through an act or omission of any other member of the consortium. In addition, a license may impose on the licensee obligations that must be performed by set dates, sometimes under the threat of forfeiture or revocation. Lenders/sponsors are advised to examine the following potential issues:

- assurances that the government will not seek to impose direct or indirect restrictions on production or depletion that risk affecting the projected cash flow adversely;
- the host government's approval of any plans for development and operation of the project;
- the host government's approval of the financing;
- whether the lenders will be allowed to take a security interest in the license or concession, and if so, whether that security will be enforceable without further approval;
- the lenders' ability to remedy breaches of the license before the government revokes it;
- the terms on which any new license will be granted in case the original one is revoked;
- the lenders' rights to take over and operate the project upon default and to transfer the license to another operator;

- assurances regarding the rate of royalties and other charges to be imposed by the government; and
- assurances regarding the tax treatment to be applied to the project.

Investments are often made in countries where the legal system is less sophisticated than in the United States or Western Europe. Thus, investors should be aware of potential legal risks pertaining to (a) the rudimentary protection of intellectual property rights (patents, trademarks, copyrights), (b) the inadequate regulation of fair trading and competition, (c) problematic dispute regulation (unequal access to courts, unenforceable foreign judgments, and the inability to refer disputes to arbitration) and (d) limited rights to appeal. Investors are well advised to become thoroughly familiar with the legal risks at an early stage by getting the relevant information from their local lawyers and to seek confirmation of the position from the host government's law agencies such as the ministry of justice and the attorney general's office, or equivalent. It is also noted that the local lawyers and judiciary may be unversed in the sorts of problems likely to be involved in project-related issues. In addition, the legal system may be slower, more expensive and less predictable than investors are accustomed to.

Foreign direct investors should also be aware of potential environmental risks. In addition to fines and penalties for pollution, environmental costs may include:

- costs of environmental impact assessments;
- fees payable to regulatory and licensing bodies;
- costs of taking out insurance to cover the risk on environmental damage;
- costs of environmental audit programs;
- costs of compliance with new packaging and labeling requirements;
- loss of profits arising from forced shutdowns of the plant;
- cleanup costs of polluted sites and civil liabilities for damage to property, health or the environment;
- costs of increased waste disposal, handling and transportation; and
- environmental taxes on the use of nonrenewable resources or the production of polluting products.

Some general steps that investors can take to protect themselves are: familiarization with the legal framework governing environmental liability in the host country; obtaining experts to evaluate the information that is gathered; and ongoing monitoring of the project to include environmental assessments. In case of lenders, they can make compliance with environmental standards a specific condition of financing and have the documentation contain representations, warranties and covenants on the borrower's part to ensure a focus on these issues and compliance with all applicable regulations and recommended practices.

To meet the risks of political and environmental policies that could have adverse impact on the firm, the investor should try to reduce exposure, share the risks with others or create deterrent structures. At the outset, the forestalling of political and environmental vulnerability is closely related to the bargaining power of the foreign investor. Experience shows that the bargaining power tends to be greater for:

- relatively large investments (compared with other investments in the host country);
- investments for high technical intensity of production;
- investments for high managerial intensity of production;
- investments for the production of goods or services for which the degree of competition in the host country is small;
- investments for the production of goods or services with well-known brand names and consumer loyalty; and
- investments with a demonstrated high return to the host country.

It is important that the analysis underlying a proposed investment shows the benefits to be had by the host country. In fact, it is necessary to continue to demonstrate a high return to the host government during the expected life of the investment. The protection of private foreign investment rests less in legal covenants than in the demonstration of its benefits to the host government concerned with its accelerated economic development.

Appendix 1 discusses the financing of a water supply project and the related issues of limited recourse, security and insurance; Appendix 2 presents interest tables for discrete compounding.

CORPORATE STRATEGY AND FOREIGN INVESTMENT

The decision on whether to invest abroad at all is driven by strategic motives that can be classified into five categories:

- *Market seekers* produce in foreign markets to either satisfy local demand or to export to markets other than their home market, such as Japanese automobile firms manufacturing in the United States;
- *Raw material seekers* extract raw materials wherever they can be found, either for export or for further processing and sale in the host country, such as firms in the oil, mining, plantation and forest industries;
- *Production efficiency seekers* produce in countries where one or more of the factors of production are underpriced relative to their productivity, such as labor-intensive production of electronic components in Malaysia;
- *Knowledge seekers* operate in foreign countries to gain access to technology or managerial expertise, such as Dutch and Japanese firms having purchased US-located electronics firms for their technology; and
- *Political safety seekers* acquire or establish new operations in countries that are con-

sidered unlikely to expropriate or interfere with private enterprise, such as Hong Kong firms having invested in manufacturing, real estate and services in the United States, Canada and Australia prior to China's takeover of the British colony in 1997.

It is noted that low direct labor costs are not of as much importance as is commonly believed, since in many industries direct labor costs account for only 10 to 15 percent of production costs. However, due to rising costs of white-collar and supervisory manpower in developed countries, it has become increasingly attractive to invest in countries that offer a well-educated pool of labor (e.g., the software industry in India). Foreign investors are also influenced by structural factors such as market size, the quality of infrastructure, the level of industrialization and the size of the existing stock of DFI. The degree of industrialization is especially important for investment in the more technical industries.

Before deciding whether to invest abroad, management must determine if the firm has some sustainable competitive advantage that enables it to compete effectively in the home market. The competitive advantage must be firm-specific, transferable and sufficiently powerful to compensate the firm for the potential disadvantages of operating abroad. Examples of competitive advantages enjoyed by MNCs are:

• economies of scale arising from their large size,
• managerial and marketing expertise,
• financial strength,
• superior technology owing to their heavy emphasis on research, and
• differentiated products which are difficult and costly for competitors to copy.

The following alternative modes of foreign involvement exist as opposed to a 100 percent–owned Greenfield (new) subsidiary abroad:

• a joint venture with one or more foreign partners,
• a merger with or acquisition of an existing foreign firm,
• licensing a foreign firm, and
• undertaking a management contract for a foreign firm.

A *joint venture* between an MNC and a host country partner is a viable strategy provided the right local partner can be found. Advantages of having a compatible local partner may include:

• the local partner's understanding of the institutions and customs of the local environment,
• possible enhancement of the access to the host country's capital markets by the local partner's contacts and reputation,

- the local partner's technology which is appropriate for the local environment, and
- improvement of sales possibilities due to the public image of a firm that is partially locally owned.

Despite these advantages, joint ventures are not as common as 100 percent–owned foreign subsidiaries because MNCs fear interference by the local partner in certain critical decision areas such as control of financing, the need for cash dividends, growth financed from retained earnings versus new financing, required rates of return and appropriate premiums for business risk.

A *cross-border merger* with or *acquisition* of an existing foreign firm has the following advantages:

- it is a much faster way of establishing an operating presence in a host country,
- foreign exchange operating exposure can be reduced by servicing a market with local manufacturing rather than through imports,
- it may be a cost-effective way to capture valuable technology rather than developing it internally, and
- economies of scale can be gained with a larger base (whether the acquisition is cross border or domestic).

As in the domestic acquisition case, cross-border acquisitions have potential pitfalls such as cultural differences inhibiting the melding of two organizations, unfavorable host country political reactions when an acquisition is by a foreign firm and labor troubles because of unequal union contracts, seniority, favoritism or other potential grievances. Appendix 3 explains how to establish the value of a government-owned company to be privatized.

In both domestic and cross-border acquisitions, the method of accounting for an acquisition affects net worth (book value), capital surplus, retained earnings and earnings per share (EPS). Financial analysts, stockholders, management and the stock market frequently pay much attention to these factors, although they should concentrate on the net present value (NPV) of an acquisition since this is the best indicator of profit-making ability. However, the NPV computation requires more time than the determination of the above factors. The accounting method may also affect the amount of taxes payable and, therefore, the NPV of the combined company (after the acquisition). Thus, the choice of the accounting method to be used is important from several viewpoints. The principal methods of accounting for an acquisition in the United States are the *pooling of interests* and the *purchase* methods. In *Accounting Research Bulletin No. 48*, the American Institute of Certified Public Accountants describes the pooling of interest as follows.

When a combination is deemed to be a pooling of interests, a new basis of accountability does not arise. The carrying amounts of the assets of the constituent corporations, if stated in conformity with generally accepted accounting principles and appropriately adjusted when deemed necessary to place them on a uniform basis, should be carried forward; and the combined earned surpluses and deficits, if any, of the constituent corporations should be carried forward, except to the extent otherwise required by law or appropriate corporate action. Adjustments of assets or of surplus which would be in conformity with generally accepted accounting principles in the absence of a combination are ordinarily equally appropriate if effected in connection with the pooling of interests; however, the pooling-of-interests concept implies a combining of surpluses and deficits of the constituent corporations, and it would be inappropriate and misleading in connection with a pooling of interests to eliminate the deficit of one constituent against its capital surplus and to carry forward the earnings surplus of another constituent.

The procedure applicable to accounting for purchase of assets is, according to the aforementioned institute: "when a combination is deemed to be a purchase, the assets acquired should be recorded on the books of the acquiring corporation at cost, measured in money, or in the event other consideration is given, at the fair value of the property acquired, whichever is more clearly evident."

The quotations indicate that accounting principles are not very well-defined. Who determines what the "fair value" is in case of a purchase? The description of the pooling of interests refers to "generally accepted accounting principles," which are vaguely defined. The requirements for an acquisition to qualify as a pooling of interests are also vague. In the case of a transaction involving listed securities, the Securities and Exchange Commission (SEC) makes the final decision. For unlisted companies, this decision hinges on the interpretation of the SEC rulings by accounting experts.

The two methods of accounting can best be described in terms of the hypothetical example of Table 3.1. Part A of this table gives the relevant information about the acquiring company and the one to be acquired, while parts B and C present the effects on the balance sheet and EPS of the purchase and pooling of interests methods, respectively. Notice that according to the purchase method, the retained earnings are equal to the earned surplus of the acquiring company ($3,500,000) and the capital surplus equals $40,000 \times (\$60 - \$2) = \$2,320,000$. The difference between the purchase price ($2,400,000) and the book value for the seller ($1,000,000) is recorded on the buyer's balance sheet as "good will." According to the pooling of interests method, the retained earnings are equal to the earned surpluses of the acquiring company and the one to be acquired ($3,5000,000 + \$880,000 = \$4,380,000$). The capital surplus amounts to only $40,000, while no good-will item is created if the combination is accounted for as a pooling of interests.

The pooling of interests method takes into account the results of the operations of the two companies during the preceding part of the fiscal period in which the acquisition takes place, as well as the results of the operation of the combined company during its existence over the remaining part of the fiscal period. For instance, if the acquisition takes place on the first day of the tenth

Table 3.1
Illustrative Differences in Net Worth, Capital Surplus, Retained Earnings and EPS Caused by Accounting Methods

A. Information about the acquiring company and the one to be acquired prior to the acquisition in December 1999:

Item	Acquiring Company	Company to be acquired
Net Assets	$4,500,000	$1,000,000
Common stock	$1,000,000	$ 120,000
Number of shares	500,000	120,000
Par value	$ 2.00	$ 1.00
Earned surplus	$3,500,000	$ 880,000
Book value	$4,500,000	$1,000,000
1999 Income Statement:		
Net income	$1,200,000	$ 240,000
EPS	$ 2.40	$ 2.00
Market Price per Share at Closing Date	$ 60.00	$ 20.00

B. Relevant items of the December 31, 1999, balance sheet and EPS of the combined company according to accounting for acquisition as a purchase:

Net Assets	$5,500,000	Common Stock (540,000	
Good will	1,400,000	@ $2.00)	$1,080,000
		Capital Surplus	2,320,000
		Retained Earnings	3,500,000
Total Net Assets	$6,900,000	Net Worth	$6,900,000

EPS = $2.40

C. Relevant items of the December 31, 1999, balance sheet and EPS of the combined company according to accounting for acquisition as a pooling of interests:

Net Assets	$5,500,000	Common Stock (540,000	
		@ $2.00)	$1,080,000
		Capital Surplus	40,000
		Retained Earnings	4,380,000
Total Net Assets	$5,500,000	Net Worth	$5,500,000

EPS = ($1,200,000 + $240,000)/540,000 = $2.67

month of the fiscal year for the purchasing company, the buyer can report its own earnings for the 10 months prior to the closing, the seller's 10-month earnings and the combined company's earnings on its income statement for the first two months of the combination. Clearly, this can affect the amount of taxes payable.

The company to be acquired in Table 3.1 is privately owned; the acquiring company issues 40,000 new shares of $2.00 per common stock to pay the owner $2,400,000 worth of its stock. The acquisition is assumed to be taking place in December, the last month of the fiscal year for the purchasing company. Consequently, the seller's earnings for the year are, according to the pooling of interests method, included in the buyer's combined earnings for the year. This results in an EPS of $2.67 as compared to an EPS of $2.40 in accordance with the purchase method.

Let us assume that in the year after the acquisition, the earnings of the combined company amount to $1,600,000 before amortization of good will. Good will is amortized over a period of 10 years. The EPS of the combined company the year after the acquisition would be ($1,600,000 − $140,000)/540,000 = $2.70 according to the purchase accounting, and $1,600,000/540,000 = $2.96 with the pooling of interests accounting.

Licensing is a popular method for nonmultinational firms to profit from foreign markets without the need to commit sizable funds. Political risk is minimal since the foreign producer is typically 100 percent–owned. MNCs have not typically used licensing of independent firms because most licensing arrangements have been with their own affiliates or joint ventures. Licensing fees have been a way to spread the corporate research and development costs among all operating units and a means of repatriating profits in a form typically more acceptable to some host countries than dividends. License fees are likely to be lower than direct investments profits. Other disadvantages include risk that the technology will be stolen, possible loss of quality control, the establishment of a potential competitor in foreign markets and possible loss of opportunity to enter the licensee's market with a direct investment later on.

Management contracts are similar to licensing insofar as they provide for some cash flow from a foreign source without significant foreign investment or exposure. International engineering and consulting firms often conduct their foreign business on the basis of a management contract.

INCREASE IN NUMBER OF DEBT INSTRUMENTS

Financial intermediaries such as commercial banks play a *fiduciary role*, by which we mean that they are perceived to be trustees of funds, not merely borrowers of funds. For instance, depositors in commercial banks are usually not perceived as creditors of the bank; the bank is typically considered as a guardian of their funds. Financial intermediaries are normally regulated by (a) restrictions on the amount of financial leverage, (b) restrictions on entry into banking, (c) examinations on nonbanking activities and, until recently, (e) limits on bank interest rates. To preserve confidence in the banking system, *deposit insurance* of up to $100,000 was instituted by the US government.

During the 1970s, the view that the financial intermediaries had been over-regulated in the US became popular with the result that in the late 1970s and the early 1980s the regulatory restraints were relaxed or *deregulation* took place. The elimination of the interest rate ceilings on deposits was a major element of the deregulation. Deregulation also (a) reduced the amount of bank examination, (b) allowed banks and savings and loans to invest in some highly risky ventures (some of which failed) and (c) allowed weak banks and thrifts to operate and incur even larger losses eventually covered by the government insurance funds. The deregulation resulted in a large number of failures of savings and loans and commercial banks. The response to these failures has been a tightening of regulation in the form of (a) an increase in the amount of bank equity capital required by regulators, (b) a more careful bank examination, (c) higher insurance premiums, (d) encouragement of larger, more diversified institutions and (e) closing of weak institutions sooner, before the insurance losses increase.

Deregulation of financial institutions in the United States combined with an increase in international trade led to the introduction of a number of new instruments in the security markets in the mid- and late 1970s. These instruments increased the choices available to borrowers and lenders. Perhaps the most important new instrument was the *variable interest rate* loan or loan with an interest rate tied to a short-term interest rate such as the prime interest rate or the Treasury bill rate. This type of loan enabled banks to shift the interest rate risk to borrowers.

The second major innovation in the marketplace was the expansion of *financial futures contracts* for debt instruments. This innovation enables security holders such as underwriters and mortgage bankers, who market initial offerings of securities to the public, to protect their net positions against rising interest rates. Security holders would find it difficult to operate in an environment of highly variable interest rates without futures contracts. The next innovation was the expansion of markets for *option contracts* on underlying securities and on futures contracts. As explained in detail in Chapter 1, an option enables a person to buy an "insurance contract" to protect the buyer from unfavorable market price changes.

The fourth type of innovation was the introduction of *securitization* whereby mortgage loans are sold as part of a pool of mortgages in the open market. The buyers get a *security* which is a claim on the pool. Prior to the introduction of securitization, commercial banks and thrifts made mortgage loans which they held for the duration of the mortgages and were, therefore, exposed to the risk of interest rate changes. With the new technique banks are able to pass on the interest rate risk to the buyer of the security. After initiating the mortgage, the bank is no longer involved except for channeling the interest payments between the parties. In other words, the bank plays the role of intermediary by matching up the borrower with the buyer.

The fifth type of innovative instrument was the introduction of swaps, which are an exchange of obligations by two parties. There are basically two types of swaps: *interest rate swaps* and *currency swaps*. In the case of interest rate swaps, one firm with a fixed-rate debt exchanges this debt for another firm's variable-rate debt. Each firm improves its position. In general, swap dealers serve as intermediaries, exchanging fixed-rate and variable-rate debt for their own account. Currency swaps involve exchanging principal and fixed-rate interest payments on a loan in one currency for the principal and fixed-rate interest payments on an approximately equivalent loan in another currency.

The sixth innovation was the original issue of the high-yield or "junk" bond, which is a trade name for a low-quality bond with a high risk of default. Many of the original junk bonds resulted from corporate takeovers. The growth of the original-issue junk bond market has opened up the capital market to a wider group of borrowers, who would have been unable to borrow under the older standards. Default risk is, however, an increasingly real prospect for many corporate bonds today, requiring much greater care on the part of bond investors. In a serious recession, default rates on junk bonds can be expected to be high.

The following is an example of selling mortgages as part of a pool of mortgages and the use of financial futures. Suppose a mortgage banker, Mr. Smith, promises to deliver mortgage loans to a financial institution before he lines up borrowers. Specifically, on April 1 his firm agrees to turn over 10 percent coupon mortgages with a face value of $1 million (M) to Insurance Company XYZ. The 10 percent coupon represents the going interest rate on mortgages at the time. Company XYZ is buying the mortgages at par; that is, it will pay Mr. Smith $1M on June 1. As of April 1, Smith had not yet signed up any borrowers; over the next one and a half to two months, he will seek out individuals who want mortgages beginning June 1. Mr. Smith realizes that changing interest rates will affect him. If interest rates fall before he signs up a borrower, the borrower will demand a premium on a 10 percent coupon loan. That is, the borrower will receive more than par on June 1. The alternative of the mortgage remaining at par and the coupon rate below 10 percent is not considered since the insurance company, XYZ, only wants to buy 10 percent mortgages. If the borrower receives more than par on June 1, Mr. Smith must make up the difference, since he received par from the insurance company. However, if interest rates rise, a 10 percent coupon loan will be made at a discount. That is, the borrower will receive less than par on June 1. In this case, the difference will be pure profit to Mr. Smith, who will still receive par from the insurance company.

Mr. Smith does not want to take the risk of having to make up the difference should interest rates fall. He therefore offsets his advance commitment with a transaction in the futures market (Chapter 1). He buys 10 June Treasury bond futures contracts to reduce the risk, since he would lose in the cash market when interest rates fall, in which case the value of his futures contracts would increase.

Table 3.2
Illustration of Advance Commitment for Mr. Smith, Mortgage Banker

	Cash Markets	Futures Markets
April 1	Mr. Smith makes a forward contract (advance commitment) to deliver $1M of mortgages to Insurance Company XYZ, which will pay par to Mr. Smith for the loans on June 1. The borrowers will receive their funding from Mr. Smith on June 1. The mortgages are to be 10% coupon loans for 20 years.	Mr. Smith buys ten June Treasury bond futures contracts (10 x $100,000 = $1M).
May 15	Mr. Smith signs up borrowers to 10% coupon, 20-year mortgages. He promises that the borrowers will receive funds on June 1.	Mr. Smith sells all futures contracts.
If interest rates rise:	Mr. Smith issues mortgages to borrowers at a discount. Mr. Smith gains because he receives par from the insurance company.	Futures contracts are sold at a price below purchase price, resulting in a loss. Mr. Smith's loss in the futures market offsets the gain in the cash market.
If interest rates fall:	Loans to borrowers are issued at a premium. Mr. Smith loses because he receives only par from the insurance company.	Futures contracts are sold at a price above purchase price, resulting in gain. Mr. Smith's gain offsets the loss in the cash market.

The gain in the futures market offsets the loss in the cash market. Conversely, the value of his futures contracts will decrease when interest rates rise, offsetting his gain in the cash markets. The details of Mr. Smith's transactions are given in Table 3.2. The column on the left is labeled "Cash markets" because the deal in the mortgage is transacted from an exchange.

Let us now consider another mortgage broker, Ms. Jones, whose company faces problems similar to those facing Mr. Smith's company. However, she tackles problems through a strategy that is the opposite of Mr. Smith's. That is, on April 1 she made a commitment to loan a total of $1M to various home-owners on June 1. The loans are 20-year mortgages carrying a 10 percent coupon. Thus, the mortgages are made at par and the homeowner is buying a forward contract on a mortgage (although he or she is not likely to use this term). Ms. Jones agrees on April 1 to give $1M to her borrowers on June 1 in exchange for principal and interest from them every month for the next 20 years.

Like most mortgage bankers, Ms. Jones does not intend to pay the $1M out of her own pocket. Instead, she intends to sell the mortgages to an insurance company, which will actually loan the funds and receive the principal and interest over the next 20 years. On April 1, Ms. Jones does not yet have an insurance company in mind, but she plans to visit the mortgage departments of insurance companies over the next two months to sell the mortgages to one or more of them. She sets May 31 as a deadline for making the sale because the borrowers expect the funds on the following day.

On May 15, Ms. Jones finds Insurance Company ABC interested in buying the mortgages; however, ABC agrees to pay only $950,000 since interest rates have risen. Since Ms. Jones agreed to loan a full $1M to the borrowers, she must pay the additional $50,000 out of her own pocket. Ms. Jones was aware of this risk, and to hedge it, she wrote ten June Treasury bond futures contracts on April 1. As with mortgages, Treasury bond futures contracts fall in value when interest rates rise. Because Jones writes the contracts, she makes money if they fall in value. Consequently, with a rise in the interest rate, the loss in the mortgages is offset by the gain in the futures market.

Treasury bond futures contracts rise in value if interest rates fall. Because Ms. Jones wrote the contracts, she would suffer a loss when rates fall. However, she would make a profit on the mortgages should the interest rate decrease. Table 3.3 gives the details of Ms. Jones' transactions. The risk of changing interest rates ends in the cash market, when the loans are sold. Thus, this risk must be terminated in the futures market at that time. Ms. Jones therefore nets out her position in the futures market as soon as the loan is sold to the Insurance Company ABC.

The following observations about the illustrations of Tables 3.2 and 3.3 are of interest:

- In these examples, 10 Treasury bond futures contracts are written because the deliverable instrument on each contract is $100,000 of Treasury bonds. The total is $1M, equal to the value of the mortgages.
- Although risk is clearly reduced via the offsetting transaction in the futures market, it is not likely to be eliminated because mortgages and Treasury bonds are not identical instruments. They are not identical since mortgages (a) may have different maturities than Treasury bonds, (b) require that a portion of the principal be paid every month, whereas the principal is only paid at maturity with Treasury bonds, (c) may be paid off early and therefore have a shorter expected maturity than Treasury bonds and (d) have a default risk whereas Treasury bonds do not.
- Since mortgages and Treasury bonds are not identical instruments, they are not identically affected by interest rates. If Treasury bonds are less volatile than mortgages, Ms. Jones may wish to write more than 10 Treasury bond futures contracts.

Table 3.3
Illustration of Hedging Strategy for Ms. Jones, Mortgage Banker

	Cash Markets	Futures Markets
April 1	Ms. Jones makes forward contract to loan $1M at 10% for 20 years. The loans are to be funded on June 1.	Ms. Jones writes ten June Treasury bond futures contracts (10 x $100,000 = $1M).
May 15	Loans are sold to Insurance Company ABC. Ms. Jones will receive sales price from ABC on the June 1 funding date.	Ms. Jones buys back all the futures contracts.
If interest rates rise:	Loans are sold at a price below $1M. Ms. Jones loses because she receives less than the $1M she must give to the borrowers.	Each futures contract is bought back at a price below the sales price, resulting in a profit. Ms. Jones' profit in the futures market offsets the loss in the cash market.
If interest rates fall:	Loans are sold at a price above $1M. Ms. Jones gains because she receives more than the $1M she must give to the borrowers.	Each futures contract is bought back at a price above the sales price, resulting in a loss. Ms. Jones' loss in the futures market offsets the gain in the cash market.

• Mortgage bankers like Ms. Jones and Mr. Smith are interested in selling mortgages, since in this way they get two fees. The first is an origination fee, which is paid to the mortgage banker by the insurance company on the date the loan is sold. This fee often amounts to 1 percent of the value of the loan (in the examples, 1 percent of $1M, or $10,000). The second fee pertains to the mortgage banker acting as a collection agent for the insurance company. For this service, he or she will receive a small portion of the outstanding balance of the loan each month. For instance, if Mr. Smith is paid .04 percent of the outstanding balance of the loan each month, he will receive $400 in the first month. Naturally, he will receive less as the outstanding balance of the loan declines.

SWAPS

The following example elucidates the manner in which interest rate swaps work. In an interest rate swap, one party, A, agrees to pay the other party, B, cash flows equal to interest at a predetermined floating rate on a notional principal for a number of years (normally 2 to 15). At the same time, party B *agrees* to pay party A cash flows equal to interest at a fixed rate on the same notional principal for the same number of years. The currencies of the two sets of cash flows are the same. The swap has the effect of transforming a fixed-rate loan into a floating-rate loan, or vice versa. The reason why two parties enter into a swap is that one has a comparative advantage in floating-rate markets and the other has a comparative advantage in fixed-rate markets. Naturally, it makes sense for a party to go to the market where it has a comparative advantage when obtaining a loan. By doing this, however, the party ends up borrowing at a fixed rate when it wants a floating rate or vice versa.

In many interest rate swaps, the floating rate is the London Inter-Bank Offered Rate (LIBOR), which is the rate of interest offered by banks on deposits from other banks in Eurocurrency markets. Similar to the US prime rate, which is often the reference rate of interest for floating-rate loans in the United States, LIBOR is frequently a reference rate of interest in international markets. To enhance our understanding of how LIBOR is used, consider a loan where the interest rate is specified as the three-month LIBOR plus .5 percent per year. The life of the loan is divided into three-month time periods. For each period, the interest rate is set at .5 percent per annum above the three-month LIBOR rate at the beginning of the period. Interest is paid at the end of the period.

Suppose that the two parties, A and B, both want to borrow $15M for a period of ten years and have been offered the following rates:

	Fixed Rate	*Floating Rate*
Party *A*	10.00%	six-month LIBOR + .35%
Party *B*	11.25%	six-month LIBOR + 1.00%

Assume that A wants to borrow floating funds at a rate linked to the six-month LIBOR, and B wants to borrow at a fixed interest rate. The above fixed and floating rates show that B has a lower credit rating than A since it pays a higher interest rate in both markets. Party A appears to have a comparative advantage in fixed-rate markets, while B appears to have a comparative advantage in floating-rate markets, since the extra amount that B pays over the amount paid by A is less in this market than in the fixed-rate markets. The fact that the difference between the two fixed rates is greater than the difference between the two floating rates (B pays 1.25% more than A in fixed-rate markets and only .65% more than A in floating-rate markets) allows a profitable swap to be negotiated as follows. A borrows fixed-rate funds at 10 percent per annum and B borrows floating-rate funds at the LIBOR plus 1 percent per annum. Next, the two parties enter into a swap to ensure that A ends up with floating-rate funds and B with fixed-rate funds.

Typically, a swap is carried out through the intermediary of a bank. To enhance our understanding of how a swap works, we first assume that A and B get in touch directly. The sort of swap that they might negotiate is as follows:

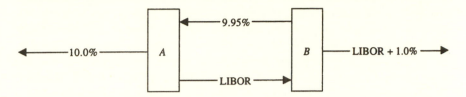

Party A agrees to pay party B interest at the six-month LIBOR on $15M, and B agrees to pay A interest at a fixed rate of 9.95 percent per year on $15M. Party A has three sets of interest-rate cash flows: (1) it pays 10 percent per annum to an outside lender, (2) it receives 9.95 percent per annum from B and (3) it pays the LIBOR to B. Cash flows (1) and (2) cost A .05 percent per annum. Thus, the net effect of the three cash flows is that A pays the LIBOR plus .05 percent per annum, or .30 percent per annum less than it would pay if it went directly to the floating-rate markets. Party B also has three sets of cash flows: (1) it pays the LIBOR + 1.00 percent per annum to an outside lender, (2) it receives the LIBOR from A and (3) it pays 9.95 percent per annum to A. The first two cash flows taken together cost B 1.00 per cent per annum. Consequently, the net effect of the three cash flows is that B pays 10.95 per cent per annum, or .30 percent per annum less than it would if it went directly to the fixed-rate markets.

From the discussion it is clear that the swap arrangement improves the position of both A and B by .30 percent or 30 basis points (a basis point is .01 percent) per annum. The total gain is, therefore, 60 basis points per annum. The total gain from an interest rate swap is always x-y where x is the difference between the interest rates facing the two parties in fixed-rate markets and y is the difference between the interest rates facing the two parties in the floating-rate markets. In our example, $x = 1.25$ percent and $y = .65$ percent.

Let us now consider the financial intermediary or the bank. The total gain of 60 basis points per annum has to be split three ways: among A, B and the bank. A possible arrangement is as follows:

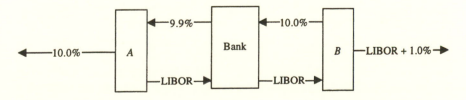

Now A has the following three sets of interest rate cash flows: (1) it pays 10 percent per year to an outside lender, (2) it receives 9.90 percent per year from the bank and (3) it pays LIBOR to the bank. The net effect of these three cash flows is that A pays the LIBOR plus .10 percent per annum, which is a .25 percent per annum improvement over the rate it could get by going directly to the floating-rate markets. The interest rate cash flows of B are: (1) it pays the LIBOR + 1.00 percent per year to an outside lender, (2) it receives the LIBOR from the bank and (3) it pays 10.00 percent per year to the bank. The net effect of these three cash flows is that B pays 11.00 percent per annum, a .25 percent per year improvement over the rate if it went directly to the fixed-rate markets. The bank's net gain is .10 percent per annum, since the fixed rate it receives is .10 percent higher than the fixed rate it pays, and the floating rate it receives is the same as the floating rate it pays. The total gain to all parties is 60 basis points.

Let us now examine currency swaps which involve exchanging principal and fixed-rate interest payments on a loan in one currency for the principal and fixed-rate interest payments on an approximately equivalent loan in another currency. As in the case of interest rate swaps, currency swaps are done to benefit from comparative advantage. Suppose that companies A and B are offered the following fixed rates in US dollars and British pound sterling:

	Dollars	*Pounds Sterling*
Company A	7.0%	11.0%
Company B	6.2%	10.6%

Company B is clearly more creditworthy than company A since it is offered a more favorable interest rate in both currencies. Company A wishes to borrow dollars, and company B pounds sterling. Since A has a comparative advantage in the pound market (the difference in the pound rates is smaller than the difference in the dollar rates), it borrows in the pound rate. For B it is advantageous to borrow in the dollar market. The two companies then use a currency swap to transform A's loan into a dollar loan and B's loan into a pound loan. There are many ways in which the swap can be arranged. One is as follows:

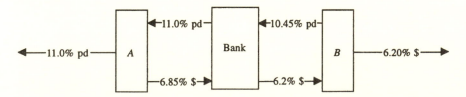

The swap's effect is to transform the sterling rate of 11.00 percent per annum to a dollar rate of 6.85 percent per annum for company A. Note that the advantage of the swap to A is 7.00 percent − 6.85 percent = .15 percent per year, and to B is 10.60 percent − 10.45 percent = .15 percent per year. The bank gains .65 percent per annum on its dollar cash flows and loses .55 percent per annum on its pound cash flows. Ignoring the difference between the two currencies (for the sake of simplification), the bank comes ahead with .10 percent per annum. The total gain to all parties is .40 percent per annum, which is equal to the difference between the dollar rates minus the difference between the pound rates.

Assume, for instance, that the principal amounts are $15 million and 10 million pounds. At the beginning of the swap in our example, *A* pays 10 million pounds and receives $15 million. Each year during the life of the swap, *A* receives 11.00 percent of 10 million pounds and pays 6.85 percent of $15 million. At the end of the swap's life, *A* pays a principal of $15 million and receives a principal of 10 million pounds. In our example the bank is exposed to foreign exchange risk. Each year it makes a gain of .65 percent of $15 million, or 97,500 dollars, and a loss of .55 percent of 10 million pounds or 55,000 pounds. The bank can avoid the foreign exchange risk by buying 55,000 pounds per annum in the forward market during each year of the swap's life. By doing so, the bank locks in a net gain in US dollars.

SUGGESTIONS FOR FURTHER READING

Baker, James C. *Foreign Direct Investment in Less Developed Countries: The Role of ICSID and MIGA*. Westport, CT: Quorum Books, 1999.

Beenhakker, H. L. *Investment Decision Making in the Private and Public Sectors*. Westport, CT: Quorum Books, 1996.

Harvey, Michael G. "A Survey of Corporate Programs for Managing Terrorist Threats." *Journal of International Business Studies* (Third Quarter 1993): 465–478.

Murphy, Austin. *Scientific Investment Analysis*. Westport, CT: Quorum Books, 2000.

Woodward, D., and D. Nigh. *Foreign Ownership and the Consequences of Direct Investment in the United States*. Westport, CT: Quorum Books, 1998.

Chapter 4

Balance-of-Payments Policy

BALANCE-OF-PAYMENTS ACCOUNTING

The balance of payments (BOP) is an accounting system that measures all economic transactions between residents of one country and residents of all other countries. Economic transactions include:

- imports and exports of goods and services,
- capital inflows and outflows,
- gifts and other transfer payments, and
- changes in a country's international reserves.

A foreign country's BOP may be important for international investors and managers since:

- it helps forecast a country's market potential because a country experiencing a serious BOP deficit is not likely to import as much as it would if it were running a surplus;
- it is an important indicator of pressure on a country's foreign exchange rate and thus an indicator for a company investing in or trading with that country to experience foreign exchange losses or gains;
- in view of a government's BOP deficit, it may use monetary policy (a rise in interest rates, or a decrease in the money supply) to attract foreign capital or to slow down domestic expansion and, hence, lower the demand for imports;
- a government may use fiscal policy (a decrease in government expenditure and/or an increase in taxes) to slow down domestic expansion and the demand for imports in times of a BOP deficit; and
- a government may impose foreign exchange controls and trade restrictions to alleviate BOP problems.

In dealing with the rest of the world, a country expends foreign exchange on some transactions and earns foreign exchange on others. Transactions earning foreign exchange are recorded in the BOP as a "credit" and are marked by a plus sign. Transactions that expend foreign exchange are recorded as "debits" and are marked with a minus sign. Thus, the BOP records the sources (receipts) and uses (payments) of funds for a country's external transactions; it is neither a balance sheet nor an income statement, but a form of a flow-of-funds statement that shows changes in assets, liabilities and net worth over time. The sources of funds are exports, investment income, transfer payments received and long-term and short-term borrowing. The uses of funds are imports, investment income paid abroad, transfer payments abroad, long-term and short-term lending and investing abroad.

It is also helpful to realize that a nation operates within an uneasy triangle of multiple objectives: freer trade, internal economic stability (full employment and stable prices) and external balance (the avoidance of BOP problems). External balance is sought not as an end in itself but to achieve the other two objectives.

The BOP can be divided into three broad accounts:

- the *current account* which records transactions in goods and services and transfer payments,
- the *capital account* which represents a change in a country's financial assets and liabilities, and
- the *official reserves account* which records transactions in monetary gold and other reserve assets such as convertible currencies, the country's reserve tranche at the IMF and its holdings of SDRs at the IMF.

Table 4.1 presents a consolidated BOP table. The summation of the net balances of the current account, capital account and official reserves equals zero. The balance on the current account must always equal the balance on the capital account plus official reserves (with sign reversed), because the BOP is constructed as an accounting identity. In terms of the economic transactions that are occurring, this means that if increases in claims on foreigners are to exceed increases in liabilities to foreigners by any amount—that is, if the country is able to invest abroad—exports must exceed imports. On the other hand, if the country is running a deficit on current account, this must be offset by investment from abroad and/or a loss of reserves. In Table 4.1 the deficit of 30 on the current account must be offset by a capital inflow of 25 and a reserve outflow of 5.

The right column of Table 4.1 indicates "Balance of Trade," "Current Account Balance" and "Basic Balance." The Balance of Trade is the net balance on merchandise trade. For instance, in 1992 the United States exported $440.14 billion of merchandise and imported $536.28 billion for a "trade deficit" of $96.14 billion. The Current Account Balance expands the trade balance concept

Table 4.1
Consolidated Balance of Payments

	Debits	Credits	Net Balance
Current Account	−110	+ 80	−30
A. Goods, Services & Income			
Merchandise exports		+	
Merchandise imports	−		
			Balance of Trade
Shipping payments	−		
Tourist expenditures	−		
Interest and dividends received		+	
B. Unilateral Transfers			
Private remittances received		+	
Government transfers abroad	−		
			Current Account Balance
Capital Account			+25
Long-term capital inflow		+	
Repayment on long-term loans	−		
			Basic Balance
Short-term capital outflow (net)	−		
Official Reserves			+5
Monetary gold inflow	−		
Official purchases of foreign currencies	−		
Allocation of SDRs received		+	
Reserve position in IMF		+	
			Sum = 0

to include earnings and expenditures on account of services and for investment income. Examples of services are airline transportation, tourism and banking. The investment income component is the flow of earnings from different forms of capital or portfolio investments made in prior years. For example, the income a US corporation currently earns on a manufacturing facility constructed in Germany in previous years falls into the current account. The initial investment of capital, however, was capital outflow recorded in the Capital Account back in the year when originally made. When the net effect of earnings and expenditures on account of services and investment income is added to the merchandise trade balance, the resultant balance on "goods, services and income" measures the net effect of both physical trade and what is sometimes called "invisible" trade in services, plus income payments.

The items in Group B of the Current Account of Table 4.1 measure the transactions not matched by a quid-pro-quo transaction. The remittances include sums of money sent home by migrant workers, parental payments to students studying abroad, Fulbright grants, private gifts, pension payments to retirees living abroad, and so on. Government transfers include gifts and grants. The net sum of all merchandise, service, income and unilateral transfers is the balance on Current Account, shown at the top of Table 4.1 (-30).

The Current Account Balance is the measure most frequently used in economic analysis because it comes closest to measuring the effect of current international payments on a nation's economy. Newspaper reporting on BOP focuses either on balance of trade or current account balance. The Basic Balance is the net result of the current account activities and the long-term capital inflow and repayment on long-term loans mentioned under Capital Account in Table 4.1. This balance is useful in evaluating long-term trends in the BOP because it does not include volatile, easily reversible, short-term capital flows.

The short-term capital outflow of Table 4.1 measures short-term capital movements such as transactions in money market instruments and bank deposits and changes in outstanding corporate account receivable and account payable balances. In one sense these are "autonomous" in that they are made by private parties. From another perspective, however, they are frequently induced by a country's monetary policies. For this reason short-term capital movements are sometimes regarded as volatile and readily reversible rather than as fundamental and stable in nature.

Because a country's current account balance can significantly affect its economy, it is important to identify and monitor the factors that influence it. The most influential factors are: inflation, national income, tax on imported goods and exchange rates. If a country's inflation rate increases relative to the other countries with which it trades, its current account is likely going to decrease, other things being equal. Consumers and businesses within the country would be expected to purchase more goods overseas, while the country's exports will decline. If a country's national income increases by a higher percentage than those of other countries, its current account is expected to decrease, other things being equal. The rise in the real income level (adjusted for inflation) will result in an increase in consumption of goods. A portion of that increase in consumption is likely to be an increased demand for foreign goods.

Prices of foreign goods to consumers are increased if a country's government imposes a tax (frequently referred to as a tariff) on imported goods. An increase in the use of tariffs is expected to increase a country's current account balance, unless other countries retaliate. If a country's currency begins to increase in value against other currencies, its current account balance should decrease, other things being equal. This is so since goods exported by the country will become more expensive to the importing countries if its currency strengthens and, as a consequence, the demand for such goods will decrease.

Since the factors that affect the balance of trade interact, their simultaneous influence on the balance of trade is difficult to estimate. For instance, as a country's high inflation rate reduces its current account, it places downward pressure on the value of its currency. Since a weaker currency can improve the current account, it may partially offset the impact of inflation on the current account.

The capital account (see Table 4.1) reflects changes in country ownership of long-term and short-term assets. Long-term foreign investments measures all capital investments made between two countries, including both DFI and purchases of securities with maturities exceeding one year. Short-term foreign investment measures flows of funds invested in securities with maturities of less than one year. As with trade flows, national governments have authority over capital flows that enter the country. For instance, a government may impose a special tax on income accrued by local investors who invested in foreign markets. Such a tax is likely to discourage people from sending their funds to foreign markets and could, therefore, increase the country's capital account. Naturally, other countries affected by this tax could retaliate by imposing a similar tax on their local people. The ultimate impact would be a reduction in foreign investing by investors across various countries. The capital account can also be affected by anticipated exchange rate movements by investors in securities. If a country's currency is expected to strengthen, foreign investors may be willing to invest in its securities to benefit from the currency movement.

Capital flows can also be affected by interest rates. As long as local currencies are not expected to weaken, money tends to flow to countries with high interest rates. Finally, capital flows can be influenced by capital controls enforced by countries. Some countries, such as Finland and Sweden, have commonly imposed restrictive controls on outflows of domestic currency. Typically, such an imposition is designed to deal with a structural weakness in the country's balance-of-payments position.

The following short-term policies are recommended for governments to react to sharp changes in capital flows and to buy time to examine more fundamental causes and cures (they should not be maintained for too long since they then can lead to distortions as bad as the ills they are supposed to cure):

- higher reserve requirements for banks on foreign or all transactions,
- limitations on open foreign exchange positions of financial institutions,
- foreign borrowing limits on classes of liabilities or public borrowers,
- taxes on short-term foreign borrowing,
- restrictions on foreign ownership of certain short-term assets, and
- restrictions on certain speculative transactions.

Sound macroeconomic policy encourages productive investment, minimizes distortions in transactions (both internal and external) and keeps inflation under control. Indirect instruments are generally more effective than direct ones and more consistent with overall liberalization programs. The following long-term policies are recommended for managing capital flows:

- liberalization of external and domestic trade,
- promotion of high domestic saving,
- positive investment climate with minimal restrictions on foreign ownership of assets,
- macroeconomic policy balance in support of relatively tighter fiscal policy and some-what more relaxed monetary policy,
- relatively wide intervention bands on the exchange rate, with periodic revisions if necessary,
- support for a strong financial sector with foreign participation,
- sound prudential regulation and enforcement in financial and capital markets,
- free capital movement (in both directions),
- dissemination of information by rating agencies and other means,
- reduction or elimination of government financial guaranties (like for bonds issued by parastatal organizations or organizations with 50 percent or more government owner-ship), and
- encouragement of private hedging markets, with adequate prudential regulation.

NATIONAL INCOME ACCOUNTS AND BALANCE OF PAYMENTS

The following notation is introduced in order to express the relationships between the BOP and national income accounts.

Y = the value of a country's national income
O = the value of a country's domestic output
E = the value of a country's national expenditure
C = the value of a country's consumption expenditure
I = the value of a country's investment expenditure
G = governmental expenditure on goods and services
X = the value of a country's exports
M = the value of a country's imports
D = receipts (+) or payments (−) of dividends and interest on foreign investment
U = unilateral transfers (gifts and grants) received (+) or given abroad (−).

For a closed economy the value of the economy's national income will be equal to the value of its domestic output and to the value of its national expenditure, or

$$Y = O = E = C + I + G \tag{1}$$

Now open the economy to foreign trade. The value of domestic output is then

$$O = C + I + G + X - M \tag{2}$$

National income for an open economy is

$$Y = O +/- (D +/- U) \tag{3}$$

Equation (3) shows that, unlike a closed economy, the national income of an open economy can exceed the value of domestic output if net income payments are being received from abroad. In an open economy, national expenditure, or the rate of total absorption of goods and services, can also exceed the value of domestic output by having imports exceed the country's exports. National expenditure is now

$$E = C + I + G = O - (X - M) \tag{4}$$

or

$$X - M = O - E \tag{5}$$

If $(D + U)$ are assumed to be zero, then $Y = O$, and

$$X - M = Y - E \tag{6}$$

and

$$(S + T) - (I_d + G) = X - M \tag{7}$$

where:

    S = household and business savings
    T = taxation revenue
    I_d = value of domestic investment expenditure

From equations (6) and (7) follows that a current account surplus $(X > M)$ in the BOP is equivalent to:

• national income $(Y) >$ national expenditure (E),
• household and business savings $(S) >$ domestic investment expenditure (I_d) and/or taxation revenue $(T) >$ government expenditure (G), and
• net foreign investment.

Conversely, a current account deficit $(M > X)$ is equivalent to:

• national expenditure $(E) >$ national income (Y),
• domestic investment expenditure $(I_d) >$ household and business savings (S), and/or government expenditure $(G) >$ tax revenue (T), and
• net foreign borrowing.

Thus, national expenditure is greater than the value of national output produced if a country is experiencing a current account deficit. The internal imbalance between expenditure and output spills over into the external imbalance of imports greater than exports on current account. To finance this excess spending, the nation must be disinvesting abroad or becoming more of a net debtor to pay for the extra net imports on current account.

From equation (6), it is clear that if E is greater than Y, then the excess absorption by consumption, investment and government expenditures can only be made possible by an excess of imports over exports. The external deficit reflects an excess of spending over income at home. Under a fixed exchange rate regime, the excess absorption must be supported by an induced capital inflow or loss of foreign reserve assets. A country borrows from abroad—that is, utilizes foreign savings—to the extent that its current account is in deficit. Under flexible exchange rates, the home country currency will depreciate when E > Y.

If, in contrast, Y is greater than E, then the excess savings under fixed exchange rates will flow overseas in the form of foreign investment (a capital outflow) or there will be an inflow of foreign reserves. A country saves and invests abroad to the extent that it has a surplus on current account (equal to a deficit on capital account). With flexible rates, the home currency would appreciate when Y > E.

From the above discussion it follows that to reduce a current account deficit, it is necessary to raise national output relative to national expenditure and to reduce the excess of domestic investment plus government expenditure over savings and taxation. A country can have a double deficit problem, that is, one in the trade balance (M > X) and one in the federal budget (G > T).

CORRECTING A BALANCE-OF-PAYMENTS DEFICIT

Ordinary supply and demand analysis applies to foreign exchange markets. Consider the exchange rate between the US dollar and the British pound sterling. In Figure 4.1, the price of the pound is expressed in terms of the dollar. The price of foreign exchange is on the vertical axis (number of dollars per pound) while the horizontal axis represents the volume of pounds traded for dollars. In other words, the figure is from the US point of view. Going up the vertical scale, the dollar depreciates (more dollars are offered per pound) and the pound appreciates. When the dollar depreciates, the prices of imports from England increase in terms of the dollar. Consequently, the demand for pounds decreases as the dollar depreciates. As the dollar appreciates, the prices of imports from England become lower in terms of the dollar. Hence, the demand for pounds increases. The demand curve for the pound, DD, therefore slopes down to the right, as in Figure 4.1. What lies behind DD are all the transactions that give rise to payments from the United States to England for the imports of goods, services and financial assets.

Figure 4.1
Policy Options to Correct a BOP Deficit

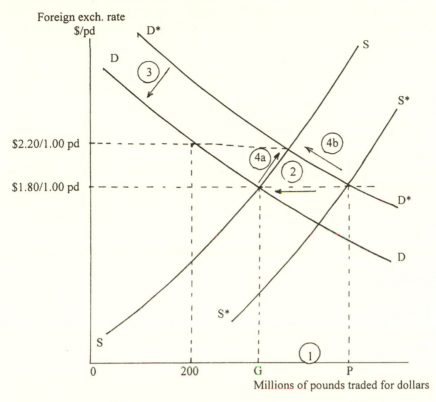

Millions of pounds traded for dollars

The supply of pounds is the flip side of the demand for imports that must be paid for in dollars. If the pound appreciates and the dollar depreciates, the price of imports from the United States will fall in terms of the pound. Thus, the supply of pounds increases. Conversely, a lower quantity of pounds will be supplied when the pound depreciates (the dollar appreciates). The supply curve for the pound, therefore, slopes up to the right as represented by SS in Figure 4.1.

The market establishes a market clearing exchange rate if there is a free market in foreign exchange. This is the rate where the demanded quantity of pounds equals the supplied quantity of pounds, or 1.80 : 1.00 in Figure 4.1. Suppose now that in the United States domestic investment rises, or domestic savings fall, or there is a fall in tax revenue, or an increase in government expenditure; then the national income would increase and there would be a greater demand for British imports. Consequently, the United States would demand a greater quantity of pounds at each and every transaction. This is represented by a shift of the demand curve from DD to D*D*.

With a regime of flexible exchange rates, intervention by central monetary authorities (by selling or purchasing reserves) may still take place in order to defend the existing rate. If the exchange rate is held by central bank intervention, there will be excess demand for the foreign exchange represented by the amount GP in Figure 4.1.

Thus, to hold the rate, the central bank will have to fill the foreign exchange gap of GP with the sale of reserves of pounds. That is, in Figure 4.1 the supply of pounds shifts from SS to S*S*. Holding the rate means that it remains over-valued. If demand and supply were allowed to operate freely in this foreign exchange market, the rate would go to 2.20 : 1.00.

To determine whether a currency is overvalued, one could compare the do-mestic cost relative to foreign cost for a given basket of goods. Such a com-parison is subject to a number of qualifications and criticism (Chapter 1). More directly, one can assume that a country's exchange rate is overvalued if any of the following actions take place:

- the country's central bank continues to lose reserves in an attempt to hold the rate,
- the country has to borrow capital to fill the gap GP,
- the country has to license foreign exchange, and
- the country has to impose tariffs and quantitative restrictions to restrict the demand for foreign exchange.

What remedial policies are available when a foreign exchange gap GP exists? The various possibilities, which are illustrated in Figure 4.1, are:

- the gap can be filled by an outflow of the central bank's foreign reserves, illustrated by (1) in Figure 4.1;
- the gap can be suppressed by imposing direct controls on imports through tariffs or quantitative restrictions that will suppress D*D* back to a level of DD, illustrated by (2) in Figure 4.1;
- the gap can be removed by reducing demand from D*D* back to DD through deflation of national income via a tight monetary policy (a rise in interest rates or a decrease in the money supply) and/or a tight fiscal policy (a decrease in government spending or an increase in taxes), which is illustrated by (3) in Figure 4.1; and
- the exchange rate is allowed to fluctuate freely, resulting into the dollar depreciating and the pound appreciating to a new equilibrium exchange rate of 2.20 dollars for 1.00 pound; the quantity of foreign exchange supplied will then increase (4a), and the quantity of foreign exchange demanded will decrease (4b) as the prices of exports and imports change.

It is noted that the policies involved in (3) and (4) of Figure 4.1 remove the foreign exchange gap by correcting the underlying causes that give rise to GP. Policies involved in (1) and (2) fill and suppress the gap, respectively; they do not correct the underlying causes.

Currency depreciation has a general effect on all prices in the foreign trade sector. It acts as an ad valorem subsidy on all exports and as an ad valorem tax on all imports. A 15 percent depreciation of a country's currency is equivalent to a 15 percent uniform export subsidy and a 15 percent uniform import duty. It may be better for a government to be selective and alter only some prices of selective exports (such as nontraditional new exports) and selective imports (such as luxury products and alcoholic beverages).

The avoidance of BOP deficits is not sought as an end in itself; however, it is important to achieve policy objectives of economic expansion and free trade. Most national governments have as policy target the economic expansion—a satisfactory rate of growth in rich countries and the acceleration of development in poor countries. Internal balance requires this domestic expansion to maintain full employment and stable prices. The reduction of trade barriers is also a frequently avowed policy target for most nations. If a country were content to have a stationary economy, without full employment and growth, or if it were autarkic, it need not worry about its BOP.

The four options of Figure 4.1 to correct a deficit in BOP are not without problems:

- the sale of foreign reserves by the central bank is limited by the amount of reserves it has;
- imposing direct controls on imports is against the policy of free trade resulting in a situation where a country's comparative advantages cannot be exploited;
- deflation of national income leads to unemployment and a slowing down in the rate of economic growth; and
- freely fluctuating exchange rates will lead to a depreciation of these rates.

In assessing the burden of adjustment through depreciation of an exchange rate, one should keep the following possible consequences in mind:

- depreciation requires a shift in resources as the demand for exports increases, the demand for imports decreases and the demand for import-substitutes rises (these re-adjustments in resource allocation are not frictionless or timeless and involve costs of transfer);
- depreciation involves a change in the distribution of income because those consuming imports suffer a rise in their cost of living and a fall in their real incomes while exporters reap a windfall;
- depreciation will have a general effect on all prices in a country's foreign trade sector, acting as an ad valorem tax on all imports and an ad valorem subsidy on all exports;
- unless other countervailing policies (contractionary monetary and fiscal policies, and possibly wage-price controls) are taken, depreciation will generate inflationary forces that exacerbate the resource allocation and distribution of income effects;
- if depreciation is effective in correcting the BOP deficit through price changes, it will ipso facto do so by increasing the volume of exports and decreasing the volume of

Figure 4.2
International Official Liquidity and External and Internal Policy Measures

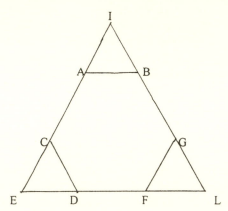

imports, thereby reducing the total amount of resources available for home consumption and investment and, consequently, the rest of the world gains greater command over the depreciating country's resources; and

• from the debtor country's viewpoint, debt-serving payments fixed in terms of the creditor's currency rise in value in proportion to the country's exchange depreciation.

A deficit country should weigh the undesirable side effects against the burden of a more general and deeper deflation in employment and income or the cost of direct controls on trade and capital movements. As we have seen in Chapter 1, the establishment of the IMF enables nations to pursue their domestic economic goals to some extent without suffering the costs of correcting BOP deficits.

The policy options of financing the deficit and internal and external adjustment can also be illustrated with Figures 4.2 and 4.3. The former figure, the so-called "Cooper Triangle," is depicted with the vertices of the triangle indicating the following:

• At L: exclusive use of international liquidity to fill the foreign exchange gap with official reserved assets, which corresponds to policy option (1) of Figure 4.1. As long as the country has enough reserves, or there is a lender of last resort that will provide official liquidity, the country need not reduce its national expenditures to correct the BOP deficit. Conversely, the more the international monetary system dictates that an international imbalance calls for exercising discipline over a country's domestic policies, the less access the country should have to official international liquidity. The less the country's access to liquidity, the more it would then have to resort to either internal measures to remove its BOP problem, or to external measures.

• At E: exclusive use of external measures such as tariffs, quotas and exchange controls, which corresponds to option (2) of Figure 4.1. These measures are "expenditure-switching" since they switch national expenditure away from imports on to import-

Figure 4.3
Feasible Policy Space for Resolving BOP Deficits

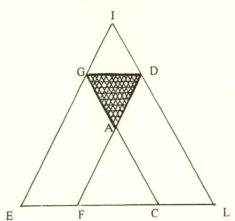

competing goods at home or domestic goods. Depreciation of the country's exchange rate, policy option (4) of Figure 4.1, is also expenditure switching by changing the prices of exportables and importables, so that demand switches on to exports and import-competing goods at home as the exchange rate changes.

- At I: exclusive use of internal measures of adjustment to a country's BOP deficit through reduction of aggregate demand by deflating the domestic economy through an increase in interest rates, a decrease in the money supply, an increase in taxes or a decrease in government spending, which corresponds to option (3) of Figure 4.1. These policies are "expenditure-reducing."

Within the triangle, nations operate in a feasible policy space determined by the degree of international liquidity that is available in the international monetary regime and the national preferences with respect to adjustment policies. In Figure 4.2, for example, the country is only able or willing to deflate to the boundary of AB: any point south of AB can be chosen. With regard to expenditure-switching policies, the country may be constrained to the boundary CD. Any point to the northeast of CD can be realized. Finally, the access to international liquidity is limited to FG: freedom of choice of this expenditure-sustaining policy exists anywhere to the northwest of FG.

In Figure 4.2 each of the vertices represents exclusive use of a sole policy option. In reality, the policy process may well lead to a mix of the policy options. For instance, for political reasons the government may be unwilling to deflate the economy beyond the line represented by DG in Figure 4.3. It may be unable to use official liquidity beyond the boundary DF and it may be unwilling to go in the direction of direct controls or depreciation as represented by the line CG. The line EL of Figure 4.3 represents the *ex ante* deficit and the shaded triangle represents boundaries of the feasible policy space. At point A, EF of the BOP deficit is financed by international liquidity, LC of the deficit is removed by external measures (controls on imports and depreciation of the domestic currency) and FC of the deficit is removed by internal measures that reduce government expenditure (monetary and fiscal policies).

What type of policies a government faced with a BOP deficit will actually undertake depends on:

- what the government wants to do in accordance with the state of its domestic economy (for example, whether there is already domestic inflation or deflation),
- what the country can do in the context of the particular type of international monetary regime that exists (for instance, fixed exchange rates or flexible exchange rates), and
- the expected reaction of foreign governments to any policy that the deficit country undertakes.

In other words, there are limits on what a government is able and willing (for political reasons) to do.

There is a three-way trade-off among L and I and E measures. Thus, the more a government can make use of one type of measure such as internal expenditure-reducing measures, the less it needs the other two of expenditure-switching measures or expenditure-sustaining measures of international liquidity.

The remedial policies taken by a deficit country to adjust its BOP can also affect businesses. For instance, if the deficit country undertakes a tight money policy, the increase in the interest rate will affect the cost of capital of firms, and a decrease in the money supply will reduce demand in the economy. There will be a switch in the composition of demand on to domestic goods that compete with imports, if the government resorts to controls on imports. In addition, the role played by the IMF can affect business because the fund imposes *conditionality* on a country or a set of required policy measures to justify drawing from the fund. Consequently, the IMF affects the country's creditworthiness for lenders and modifies the country risk analysis undertaken by lenders. It behooves managers to pay attention to the BOP policies discussed in this section and to be familiar with the IMF policies affecting countries in which they operate.

CENTRAL BANKS

Central banks (the Federal Reserve System in the United States) in most countries have the following major functions:

- establish and administer monetary policy by controlling the money supply and/or interest rates;
- act as a lender of last resort through the discount window;
- assist in the payments and collections systems (in the United States, the Federal Reserve System plays a major role in the check-clearing process and the electronic wire transfer of funds); and

- regulate commercial banks (in the United States, the Federal Reserve System, the Comptroller of the Currency, the Federal Deposit Insurance Corporation and state bank authorities all have some regulatory authority over commercial banks).

In most industrialized countries, central banks are independent. In the United States, the Federal Reserve System (FRS) is not directly subject to the control of the executive and legislative branches of the government because the FRS's Board of Governors is appointed for 14-year terms and its banks are privately owned. In addition, the FRS earns more money from its operations than it needs to cover operating expenses and consequently does not have to ask Congress for funds. The FRS's earnings are largely interest earned on US Treasury securities held in order to carry out monetary policy. Thus, the FRS has the power to set monetary policy independent of the wishes of the president and both houses of Congress. However, the FRS's actions cannot be too far out of line with congressional preferences, since it was established by an act of Congress and its powers could be changed by further congressional action. The advantage of an independent FRS is that it can consider policy from a long-term perspective as opposed to a shortsighted policy motivated by political expediency. The disadvantage is, however, that there is a danger that the FRS's policies may be in conflict with the rest of government economic policy. The degree of independence of the rest of the government varies among countries. For instance, the central banks of France and the United Kingdom are more subject to politics than the FRS, while those of Germany and Japan are more independent than the FRS. Although there are exceptions, there is some evidence that countries with more independent central banks have lower inflation rates.

Normally, a central bank's objectives of monetary policy are to promote economic growth, full employment and low inflation. By economic growth we mean increases in the wealth of the overall economy by improving the productivity of the average worker. This productivity can be improved by increasing the amount of equipment available to workers and/or by making better use of that equipment. Full employment implies a situation where all people who want to work are able to find work. It does not mean 100 percent employment since some people are always between jobs. Inflation is not desirable since it can result in people's efforts being directed at keeping ahead of inflation and deflected from productive economic activity.

Central banks are sometimes forced to make difficult policy choices, since the aforementioned policy goals can be competing. For instance, it may be difficult to achieve full employment and low inflation. Inflation can be kept low by keeping the money supply growing at a slow rate and pushing up interest rates. From the discussion of the neo-Keynesian model (Chapter 5), we know that a small money supply and high interest rates reduce investment, income and employment. Typically, a central bank adopts some compromise policy which achieves neither low inflation nor full employment. Domestic and international policy goals can also be in conflict when a central bank wishes to control the rate of exchange between its currency and foreign currencies by keeping interest rates high, stimulating inflows of foreign deposits. Such policy is in conflict with an expansionary domestic policy of adequate money growth and low interest rates.

Although money has three characteristics—a medium of exchange, a unit of account and a store of value—it is not always clear what exactly constitutes money. The FRS has adopted M1, M2 and M3 to measure money supply. M1 includes currency and coins in circulation and travelers checks plus private bank deposits upon which checks can be written. M2 includes M1 plus most types of personal savings accounts, including money market funds and money market deposit accounts at banks. M3 includes M2 plus large certificates of deposit and institutional money market funds. The complete definitions of M1, M2 and M3 are as follows:

M1:   Currency and coins held by the public

Checking deposits held by the public

Other checkable deposits

     NOW accounts

     ATS accounts

     Share draft accounts at credit unions

M2:   M1

Savings accounts

Certificates of deposit for less than $100,000

Money market deposit accounts

Money market mutual funds held by individuals

Overnight repurchase agreements

Overnight Eurodollars

M3:   M2

Certificates of deposit over $100,000

Repurchase agreements for longer than overnight

Eurodollars for longer than overnight

Institutional money market mutual funds

M1 includes a category called other checkable deposits consisting of NOW, ATS and share draft accounts. *NOW* (Negotiated Order of Withdrawal) *accounts* are deposits at commercial banks that allow checks to be written and which also pay interest. With *ATS accounts*, funds are automatically transferred from an account that pays interest to a checking account paying no interest when checks come for collection. Share draft accounts at credit unions allow checks to be written. The other checkable deposits category can be used for making immediate payments and are, therefore, transactions balances like currency, coins and checking deposits held by the public; however, they may also be used by some persons as a store of value. They are counted as part of M1 since they are primarily held as transactions accounts.

Money market deposit accounts (MMDAs) are deposits that pay interest and allow checks to be written. In other words, they are similar to NOW accounts. The difference is that MMDAs have large minimum deposits and allow only a limited number of checks to be written. Because of these differences, MMDAs are counted as M2. A money market mutual fund held by individuals is a pooling of funds by many investors and managed on their behalf for a fee; it restricts its investments to short-term money market instruments with maturities of less than one year. Most money market mutual funds allow checks to be written on deposits with some restrictions. They are, therefore, also similar to NOW accounts; however, due to slight differences, they are classified as M2. The institutional money market mutual funds are classified as M3 since they are less likely to be used as transactions balances and more likely to be used as a store of value.

Repurchase agreements (also called repos, or RPs) are generally overnight sales of government securities with an agreement to repurchase on the next business day. Repos, which are counted as part of M2, are extensively used as a means of short-term financing by government security dealers and banks. Consider, for instance, a bond dealer who is closing his/her operations for June 29 with an inventory of $575M of Treasury securities. In his/her role in the market, these securities are held by the dealer hoping to profit by the average bid-ask spread. If the dealer's equity is $75M, an additional $500M is required to pay for these securities since the purchase contract requires same-day payment. The dealer therefore sells the securities to a lender for $500M on the afternoon of June 29, agreeing to repurchase them the following morning of June 30 for $500M plus one day's interest. The sequence of events is as follows:

Points in Time

1:00 P.M.	5:00 P.M.	9:00 A.M.
June 29	June 29	June 30
Dealer buys $575M of bonds	Dealer sells $500M of bonds as repo	Dealer repurchases $500M and pays overnight interest

The price for the overnight repo is the current price plus interest, which is, in the United States, typically slightly below the federal funds rate. Repos involve large dollar amounts per transaction, since otherwise the transaction cost would outweigh the overnight interest. In the aforementioned example, the dealer could also have obtained a bank loan with the securities used as collateral; however, the repo approach is normally a little less expensive. Term repos or repos for longer than overnight are possible but they are not as common as overnight repos. The amount lent in a repo is normally slightly less than the market value of the bonds in order to provide some protection to the lender if the dealer goes bankrupt and the securities are liquidated at the prevailing market price. The difference between the amount lent in a repo and the market value of the bonds is called a *haircut*.

From the viewpoint of the lender of funds, a repo is called a *reverse*. Lenders, including banks, thrift institutions, nonfinancial corporations and municipalities, use reverses in order to invest their temporarily excess funds for short periods of time with minimal risk. For municipalities, which are often restricted in their investments in federal government securities, reverses provide an attractive alternative.

A *Eurocurrency deposit* is a deposit denominated in terms of a foreign currency. Thus, deposits in US dollars terms made in Germany and deposits in Japanese yen terms in Germany are both called Eurodollar deposits, although a deposit of yen in Germany is technically a "Euroyen" deposit. Overnight Eurodollars are counted as part of M2. Eurodollar CDs are dollar-denominated certificates of deposit issued by banks located outside the United States. A US bank may issue Eurodollar CDs through its London branch if the interest rate on a Eurodollar CD compares favorably with the rate on a domestic CD.

The principal task of a central bank is to establish and administer monetary policy guidelines for the money supply and interest rates through:

* open market operations,
* changing reserve requirements, and
* changing the interest rates on loans to banks through the Federal Reserve's discount window.

Open market operations involve the purchase and sale of government securities by a central bank in the open market. If a central bank sells bonds to an individual, the buyer's bank account is reduced and, consequently, the money supply is reduced and interest rates tend to increase. If a central bank buys bonds in the open market from an individual, the seller's bank account is increased by the sale price and, since the money in this account can be spent, the money supply increases. In the United States, the FRS tends to accumulate a large portfolio of US Treasury securities upon which it earns interest. Part of this interest is used by the Federal Reserve to pay its operating expenses and the rest is returned to the Treasury.

Commercial banks in the industrialized world are required to keep a proportion of their deposits as reserves either as vault cash (coins and currency) or/ and deposits with the nation's central bank which has the power to change the reserve requirements within legislatively set bounds. In the United States, federal funds, repos and foreign deposits are exempt from reserve requirements, which makes the cost of these funds a little lower for commercial banks (other things being equal). Reserves serve two purposes: (a) to meet emergency cash needs and, more importantly, (b) to control the money supply by changing reserve requirements. If a central bank reduces reserve requirements, excess reserves become available to commercial banks and these excess reserves are likely to be lent out, thus resulting in an increase in the supply of money. If a central bank increases its reserve requirements, commercial banks tend to reduce their lending (in order to obtain the additional reserve requirements), thereby raising interest rates, reducing the supply of money and decreasing the level of economic activity.

Central banks frequently make loans to commercial banks through a *discount window*, which is a tool for a central bank to be a lender of last resort. A central bank provides funds to individual banks or to the banking system as a whole at times when funds are short. Without this possibility, a relatively small problem might become a large problem. The following types of loans are available form the Federal Reserve in the United States:

- loans to banks which are temporarily short of reserves to meet their reserve requirements;
- seasonal loans to some banks, such as banks serving agricultural communities with a seasonal demand for funds; and
- longer-term loans to banks in serious financial trouble to give these banks some time to work out their problems.

The Federal Reserve is not required to make any of these loans. For instance, if a bank tries too often to borrow under the first type of the aforementioned loans, the Federal Reserve can refuse to make further loans. The discount rate on loans from the Federal Reserve may be lower than the *federal funds rate*, which is the rate at which a bank can lend to other banks. In this case, a bank may be tempted to borrow from the Federal Reserve at the low discount rate and lend these funds at the higher federal funds rate and profiting from the difference. Naturally, the Federal Reserve will refuse making loans to banks engaged in this type of arbitrage.

An example of Federal Reserve action which does not fit into the preceding three types of loans pertains to such action when a major bank has both its main and backup computer systems fail. Consequently, large payments to many other banks to settle their account for the day cannot be settled at the end of the day. Suppose, for example, that the bank with the failed computer systems owed $750M to another bank, which, without this $750M, would have to default on payments to a third bank, which would have to default on payments to a fourth bank, and so on. In other words, default by one bank could bring the entire payments system to a close due to the effect of falling dominoes. To prevent this from happening, the Federal Reserve would immediately step in and make payment on the obligations of the bank with the failed computer systems.

The three methods for making payments are: (a) currency and coins, (b) checks and (c) electronic transfer. In terms of the dollar value of transactions, electronic transfers represent the largest amount, followed by checks and then currency and coins. In terms of number of transactions, this sequence is the reverse. In the United States, electronic transfers can be made for a fee by private wire transfer systems and the Federal Reserve Wire. Without this possibility, it would be difficult to have overnight repos. Central banks have important powers to regulate commercial banks, such as the power to regulate the entry of banks into nonbanking activities. In the United States, many nonbanking activities (e.g., engaging in commerce) are prohibited, while certain types of financial activities are allowed with the permission of the Federal Reserve.

In conclusion, a central bank's primary functions are to set and administer monetary policy, be a lender of last resort and regulate commercial banks. The goal of monetary policy is to promote economic growth, stability, full employment and low inflation. These goals can be competing.

POTENTIAL CONFLICTS BETWEEN AN MNC's OPERATIONS AND GOVERNMENT POLICIES

MNCs' operations sometimes interfere with the smooth functioning of a government's policy instruments to attain a sustainable rate of growth in per capita GNP, full employment, price stability, balance in external accounts and a fair distribution of income. Alternatively, government regulations may hamper the operations of foreign-owned firms. Principal areas where conflict may arise are:

• monetary policy,
• fiscal policy,
• balance of payments (BOP) and exchange rate policy,
• economic development policies, and
• economic protectionism.

An example of a conflict in monetary policy is a situation where a government wishes to control the cost and availability of domestic credit and long-term capital. In this case an MNC's affiliate may turn to its parent or sister affiliates if credit becomes too expensive or unavailable. As a result, the MNC's affiliate is able to implement its spending plans while local competitors are restricted because of lack of access to external capital. MNCs could also move excess working capital to other countries while riding out a foreign exchange crisis. These types of activities may result in an instant change in the supply of local money, which has to be offset by central bank open market operations.

MNCs' operations may have an impact on government revenues and expenditures. For instance, tax concessions used by a government to lure a firm to its country imply that the government will not receive revenue it may need later. An example of the impact on expenditures is an MNC's Greenfield investment creating a need for government spending on new roads, public utilities, and so on. If an MNC provides such infrastructure because the government does not have the required resources, a dependency relationship is established and the foreign firm may be accused of economic imperialism.

BOP and exchange rate problems may lead a government to promulgate regulations that hamper the operations of foreign-owned firms. For instance, exchange control, including inconvertibility of currency, can hurt MNCs, since local currency often diminishes the value of blocked funds. It is therefore important that MNCs understand the causes and likely policy responses to a host country's BOP deficit.

Economic development policies sometimes call for local majority ownership in joint ventures, a majority of local rather than expatriate managers and/or the manufacture of an increasing proportion of components locally rather than the assembling of imported components. While such requirements may have merit in the context of goal-driven government policies, they frequently inhibit an MNC from rationalizing production on a worldwide basis and, consequently, from lowering costs and sales prices to consumers.

During the past three decades, the negotiations under GATT have reduced the general level of tariffs and, therefore, the use of tariffs for economic protectionism. However, nontariff barriers, which often restrict imports by something other than a financial cost, continue to exist in many countries. They are often difficult to identify because they are promulgated as safety, sanitation or health requirements. Examples of nontariff barriers are:

- documentation requirements that are overburdensome,
- quotas limiting the quantity or value allowed for specific imported products for specific time periods,
- proportion restrictions of foreign to domestic goods or content,
- embargoes prohibiting products originating in specific countries,
- application of packaging and labeling standards in unduly stringent ways,
- administrative fees levied, and
- voluntary export restraints by exporting country, often at the request of the importing country.

In the pursuit of national goals, host governments often adopt regulations that hinder MNCs' operations. Regulations with the most potential for conflict for MNCs can be classified as *nondiscriminatory* and *discriminatory* regulations. Nondiscriminatory regulations are usually mild and have an equal impact on foreign subsidiaries, joint ventures and purely domestic firms. Examples of these regulations are laws or administrative rules that:

- require a given percentage of local content in manufactured goods;
- allocate all foreign exchange to purchases deemed in the national interest and, consequently, restricting the availability of foreign exchange for such "nonessential" purposes as dividends or royalty fee payments;

- require that local nationals hold top management positions or seats on boards of directors; and
- require the construction of social overhead facilities such as schools and workers' housing, by the investing firm.

Discriminatory regulations give local firms specific advantages over foreign firms. The intent is often to protect weaker local firms from local-based foreign competition. Examples of discriminatory regulations are laws or administrative rules that:

- require local control in the form of joint ventures with the foreign firms limited to less than 50 percent ownership, in order to have the right to sell to the local government or to have access to credit from local banks,
- require foreign firms to hire labor through a host government agency and to pay wages and social charges set by the government at a higher level than those required for local firms,
- demand special taxes or fees from a foreign firm in order to be allowed to operate locally (for example, very high income taxes on expatriates' salaries or extremely high visa fees for expatriate managers), and
- nationalize an industry dominated by foreigners.

The best approach to avoiding all conceivable areas of potential conflict is to anticipate problems and negotiate understandings. Next, an *investment agreement* spelling out the specific rights and responsibilities of both the foreign firm and the host government has to be prepared. An investment agreement should, as a minimum, include the following:

- the basis on which fund flows (dividends, management fees, loan repayments, royalties and/or patent fees) may be remitted,
- methods of taxation (rate, rate base and type of taxation),
- permission for 100 percent foreign ownership versus required local ownership (joint venture) participation,
- the basis for setting transfer prices (prices for the transfer of goods, services and technology between related affiliates in different countries),
- the right to export to third-country markets,
- obligations to build or fund social and economic overhead projects (retirement systems, schools, hospitals, and so on),
- access to host country capital markets (in particular for long-term borrowing),
- price controls, if any, applicable to sales in the host country markets,
- requirements for local sourcing versus import of raw materials and components,
- permission to use expatriate managerial and technical personnel, and to bring them and their personal possessions into the country without exorbitant visa charges and import duties,

- provision for arbitration of disputes, and
- provisions for planned divestment, should such be required, covering to whom the going concern will be sold and how its value will be established.

MNCs should be aware that, although investment agreements create obligations on the part of both foreign investor and host government, conditions can change and agreements may have to be revised. The changed conditions may be economic and/or the result of political changes within the host government. It behooves an MNC not to stick rigidly to the legal interpretation of its original agreement since the host government could apply pressure in areas not covered by the agreement and/or reinterpret the agreement to conform to the political reality of the country. Most MNCs, in their own self-interest, follow a policy of adapting to changing priorities of the host country whenever possible. Such adaptation calls for anticipating host country priorities and making the MNC's activities of continued value to the host country.

SUGGESTIONS FOR FURTHER READING

De Vries, Margaret Garritsen. *Balance of Payments Adjustment, 1945–1986: The IMF Experience*. Washington, DC: IMF, 1987.

Eichengreen, Barry, and Peter H. Lindert. *The International Debt Crisis in Historical Perspective*. Cambridge, MA: MIT Press, 1990.

Frazer, William. *Central Banking, Crises, and Global Economy*. Westport, CT: Quorum Books, 1999.

Peng, Mike W. *Behind the Success and Failure of US Export Intermediaries*. Westport, CT: Quorum Books, 1998.

Williamson, John, and Donald Lessard, eds. *Capital Flight and the Third World Debt*. Washington, DC: Institute for International Economics, 1987.

Chapter 5

Determinants of Interest Rates

CLASSICAL THEORY

This section as well as the other sections of this chapter deal with a single-period, nontaxed, default-free, noncallable interest rate. In other words, this chapter discusses the economic factors determining the underlying interest rate; determinants unique to individual varieties of debt—taxation, default risk, call features and time preferences for consumption and investment—are discussed elsewhere in this text. In still other words, this chapter deals with the pure time value of money.

According to the classical theory, which prevailed until the 1930s, the money supply does not affect interest rates. Only business investments and savings by individuals are judged to be the determinants of interest rates. Businesses compare the rate of return on their investments with the interest rate. If the return is below the interest rate, a particular investment is not profitable after paying financing costs and is not undertaken. If the return is higher than the interest rate, the firm earns something above the financing costs and a particular investment is undertaken.

For the economy as a whole, one can imagine a list of all possible investments and their rates of return. Figure 5.1 presents a simplified example of six investments of $10 million (M) each; the rate of return versus the cumulative amount invested is shown as the marginal efficiency of investment (MEI) curve. In the classical theory, the cost of funds for business investment is the interest rate. Thus, one assumes that all investments are debt financed and equity financing does not play a role. Of course, in practice, equity financing is important.

The other factor determining interest rates in the classical theory is savings

Figure 5.1
Marginal Efficiency of Investment (MEI) Curve

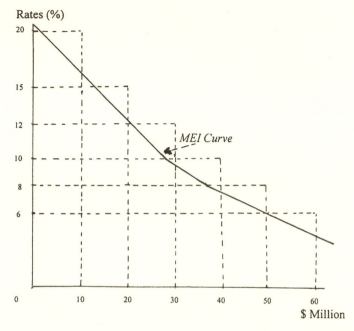

by individuals. Interest payments represent a compensation to savers for postponing consumption. For instance, consumers may be willing to trade $100 of consumption today for $115 of consumption in one year, implying a rate of interest of 15 percent. In the classical model, individuals save more if the interest rate is higher. Figure 5.2 represents savings as a function of the interest rate by the curve labeled *S*; the upward slope indicates greater savings by consumers at higher interest rates. The point where the *MEI* curve and the *S* curve intersect represents *equilibrium*. In equilibrium, the total amount borrowed by investors equals the total amount saved by consumers. In equilibrium, the interest rate equals (a) the return on the marginal (last) investment and (b) the return required by the marginal saver.

If an investment is not equal to saving, a disequilibrium condition exists. In Figure 5.2 the point A represents an investment with a rate of return B. Thus, the rate is above the equilibrium level. Because the amount saved is greater than the amount invested, the surplus savings drive down the interest rate as lenders compete with each other. Point C in Figure 5.2 represents an investment with a rate of return D, which is a rate below the equilibrium level; the amount invested is greater than the amount saved. In this situation borrowers compete with each other for funds, driving up the interest rates and causing savers to save more.

Figure 5.2
MEI and Savings Curves

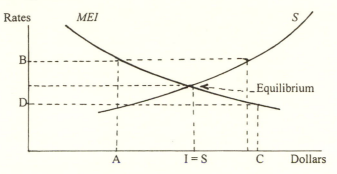

LOANABLE FUNDS APPROACH

The loanable funds approach is similar to the classical approach; however, it includes more entities as demanders and suppliers of funds. The loanable funds approach adds consumers and the government as borrowers to the demand for funds considered in the classical approach (i.e., the demand from business investment only). This approach approximates more realism since consumer and government borrowings are significant. In addition, the loanable funds approach adds savings from businesses and increases in the money supply to the suppliers of savings of the classical approach (the consumers). In other words, the loanable funds approach assumes that the interest rate is determined by the supply and the demand for loanable funds as shown schematically in Figure 5.3. The supply curve shows the relationship between the supply of funds and the interest rate. It has an upward slope, indicating that at higher interest rates more funds are supplied to the market. The demand curve shows the relationship between the demand for funds and the interest rate. This curve is drawn with a downward slope; lower interest rates result in a greater demand for funds. The interest rate and the amount of funds changing hands are determined by the point where the two curves cross.

The total demand for funds consist of consumer borrowing for consumption, business investment in plant and equipment and government budget deficits. The demand for funds by business investors corresponds to the marginal efficiency of capital curve discussed in the section on the classical theory. It is noted that consumer borrowing for "big ticket items" is interest-rate sensitive. For instance, high interest rates cause reductions in consumer purchases of homes and automobiles. However, purchases of relatively low-priced items may not be substantially affected by interest rates. Thus, the demand curve for expensive consumer goods is downward sloping. For other consumer goods, the slope is unclear. For the aggregate of all consumer goods, the demand curve is likely to be downward sloping.

Figure 5.3
Loanable Funds Approach

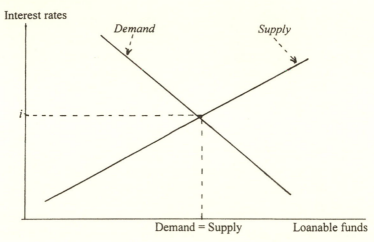

The total amount of funds supplied to the market comprises savings from individual consumers, business savings and an increase in the money supply. The supply curve has been drawn with an upward slope; higher interest rates lead to a larger supply of funds. Consumers save out of current income for future consumption; the amount of savings depends upon current income, wealth, preferences and interest rates. The major determinants of savings are thought to be income, wealth and preferences.

The direction of the effect of interest rates on consumers' savings is not clear. On the one hand, interest rates may attract funds from people who are willing to give up current consumption for a more attractive rate of return and resulting higher consumption in the future, which is called the *substitution effect* and implies an upward sloping supply curve. On the other hand, some savers have a goal for future income derived from savings and are able to reduce the amount saved and maintain the same future income level as interest rates rise. This is called the *income effect* and implies a downward sloping supply curve. The net effect of these two effects on total savings is, therefore, debatable. It is also noted that wealth and interest rates interact. For example, as interest rates decline, the market value of equity and debt instruments is likely to increase.

The impact of the interest rate on business savings may, or may not, be significant. These savings represent depreciation and retained earnings. Depreciation is a function of physical wear and tear on equipment and is not likely to be substantially affected by interest rates. Retained earnings equal earnings minus dividends. The impact of the interest rate on retained earnings can, therefore, be decomposed into the impact of the interest rate on earnings and on dividends. It is not clear how significant these impacts are. For instance, the earnings of some firms, such as banks, may be very sensitive to interest rates,

Figure 5.4
An Increase in the Money Supply

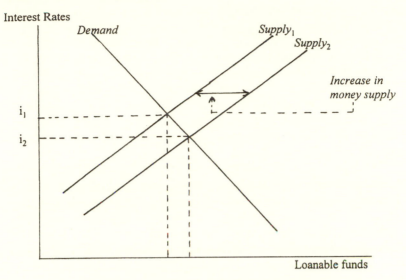

whereas other firms' earnings may be unaffected by interest rates. Interest rates are probably a minor determinant of retained earnings.

Although the level of interest rates affects the total amount of interest paid on the federal debt, it appears unlikely that interest rates significantly affect federal government budget surpluses or deficits. Experience shows, however, that state and local governments tend to postpone capital expenditures when interest rates are high. The money supply is largely determined by a country's central bank as it carries out monetary policy. As shown in Figure 5.4, increases in the supply of money shift the supply curve of funds to the right, resulting in a lower interest rate.

In the United States, the foreign sector has become an increasingly important source of funds in recent years. The supply of these funds is primarily dependent upon interest differentials and expectations of exchange rate changes. Interest rate differentials between countries tend to result into flows of funds from countries with lower interest rates to those with higher interest rates. Expectations of exchange rate changes affect the sources of funds available in the United States, since those who believe that the US dollar will appreciate can shift their funds into dollars in expectation of shifting out of dollars in the future at a more favorable exchange rate. For instance, if US$1 currently equals 10 shillings (Austrian), an investor holding shillings and anticipating an appreciation in the US dollar to $1 equals 12 shillings can exchange 10 shillings for $1. If the forecast is correct, the investor can then exchange the $1 for 12 shillings, resulting in a profit of 2 shillings. Investors expecting the dollar to decline would shift out of dollars and into the foreign currency, expecting to shift back into

Figure 5.5
Increased Government Borrowing

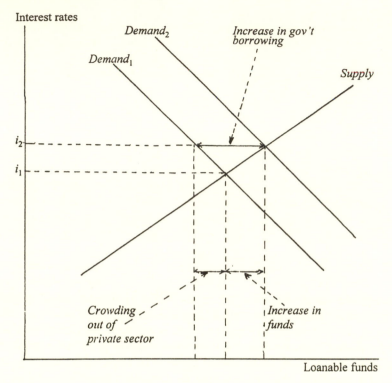

dollars after the dollar has declined. In spite of the aforementioned uncertainties about the individual components of the supply curve, the aggregate supply curve is typically assumed to be upward sloping.

As shown in Figure 5.5, an increase in the government deficit financed by additional borrowing raises the total demand for funds, resulting in a shift to the right of the demand curve for funds and, hence, a rise in the interest rate. This figure also indicates that the total amount of funds supplied to the market does not increase as much as government borrowing since some nongovernment borrowers are crowded out by the government borrowing. Increased government borrowing, therefore, tends to make consumer and business borrowing more expensive, thus reducing consumer expenditures and business capital expenditures in the private economy. In other words, the added government borrowing shifts resources from the private sector to the government. In the crowding-out view, large government deficits reduce business investment in plant and equipment below the level otherwise attainable. Such deficits and the resulting higher interest rates slow the economy's growth rate because business investment is a primary ingredient for increasing productivity and economic growth.

MONETARIST VIEW OF INTEREST RATES

The monetarist view of macroeconomics stresses the importance of money supply as a major factor determining the course of a nation's economy. In simple terms, money supply can be represented as follows:

$$MV = PQ$$

where:

    M = the money supply
    V = the velocity of money (the number of times that an average dollar changes hands during a year)
    P = the price level
    Q = the level of real (physical) output

Thus, the total amount spent in a year is MV, the amount of money times the number of times money turns over. This total amount also equals PQ, the price level times the number of units purchased. The above equation can approximately be stated in terms of rates of change:

$$m + v = p + q$$

where:

    m = the rate of growth in the money supply
    v = the rate of growth of velocity
    p = the rate of growth in prices, or the inflation rate
    q = the rate of growth in real output

Thus, the rates of change in prices and real output are determined by the rates of growth in the money supply and velocity. The classical quantity theory assumes that velocity is constant ($v = 0$) so that:

$$m = p + q$$

Thus, the rate of growth in the money supply must equal the rate of growth in prices plus the rate of growth in real output. Solving for the inflation rate, p:

$$p = m - q$$

In other words, in order to have no inflation, the growth rate of the money supply must equal the growth rate of real output. If the money supply grows faster than real output, inflation occurs.

The classical quantity theory also assumes full employment. Changes in the supply of money are assumed to have no impact upon a nation's GNP since the economy is always producing at maximum capacity and the growth rate of the economy is not affected by changes in the money supply. Changes in the money supply only affect the price level. Thus, if the monetary authorities decide that the expected growth rate of real output is 4 percent, then the money supply should grow at 4 percent in order to ensure a zero inflation rate. If the money supply grows at a faster rate, say 6 percent, inflation occurs at the rate of 2 percent $(0.06 - 0.04 = 0.02)$.

In modern quantity theory, the money supply is the most important determinant of Gross National Product (GNP), which is a measure of production and income. Modern monetarists believe that:

- velocity is a relatively stable and predictable function of economic variables (rather than a never-changing constant as in the classical quantity theory);
- the government should estimate the long-run real growth rate of a nation's economy and that the money supply growth rate should be set equal to this growth rate; however, if the economy is *temporarily* weak, this rule injects money into the system, and if the economy has a temporary, high inflation rate, the money supply rule chokes off the inflation;
- changes in the money supply have wide-ranging effects on the economy; for instance, an increase in the money supply may stimulate purchases of common stocks (and drive up stock prices) and consumer durables such as cars and appliances;
- an increase in the money supply tends to bid the prices of bonds up and interest rates down;
- an increase in the money supply tends to stimulate output and this puts upward pressure on interest rates;
- changes in the money supply affect inflationary expectations; for instance, if bond-holders fear a rapid growth in the money supply with resulting inflation, an inflationary premium is added onto the interest rate;
- the net impact of an increase in the money supply depends upon all of the four preceding factors (i.e., the initial increases in stock and bond prices, the increase in output, and inflationary expectations) with possible offsetting impacts;
- fiscal policy has little impact upon the economy and government policy should, therefore, focus exclusively on monetary policy (controlling the supply of money); and
- contrary to the neo-Keynesian view, an increase in the money supply may result in a net increase in interest rates if inflationary expectations are raised sufficiently.

NEO-KEYNESIAN APPROACH

This approach is perhaps the most general one to explaining the determinants of the interest rate. In the neo-Keynesian model, the following interrelated factors affect the interest rate:

- decisions by investors to save or consume,
- investment decisions by firms,

Figure 5.6
Expenditures = Production = Income

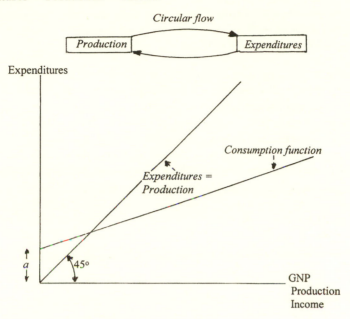

- investors' preferences to hold money balances for speculative purposes,
- demand for money balances for transactions purposes,
- government spending and taxes, and
- total supply of money established by the monetary authorities.

Although consumption by individuals is affected by many factors—income level, wealth, holdings of consumer durables, taxes, attitudes and customs and the population age distribution—the neo-Keynesian approach assumes that consumption is primarily a function of income. The upper part of Figure 5.6 indicates the circular flow between production and expenditures. Production of goods and services results in income to the workers and, as it is spent, this income becomes expenditures, which, in turn determine production. The horizontal axis of this figure measures GNP, production and income, which are three terms with the same meaning. That is, if output is produced in the economy, then someone must be paid for this production; the payment to workers is called income. Thus, total production is total income. The vertical axis of Figure 5.6 measures the following expenditures: consumer expenditures, business investment, and government spending. In other words, the vertical axis measures total expenditures, or

Aggregate Expenditures = C + I + G

where:

C = consumer expenditures
I = total investment
G = total government spending

A nation's economy is in equilibrium if total expenditures equal total production or income. For instance, if total expenditures were greater than total
production, an insufficient quantity of goods would be produced to satisfy demand. Hence, expenditures would have to decrease and/or production increase
until the two were equal. Figure 5.6 shows the equilibrium condition as a straight
line making a 45-degree angle with the origin. The points along this line represent all the possible equilibriums where expenditures equal production.

Aggregate income is defined as follows:

Aggregate Income = C + S + T

where:

S = total savings
T = total taxes
C = as defined above

In equilibrium, aggregate expenditures must equal aggregate income, or

C + I + G = C + S + T

This simplifies to:

I + G = S + T

In other words, the equilibrium condition that expenditures must equal income
is equivalent to the condition that investment plus government spending must
equal total savings plus taxes.

The *consumption function* is a straight line with the following equation:

Expenditures = $a + b$(GNP)

Figure 5.6 also shows a consumption function which represents the desired level
of expenditures under the assumption that this desired level is exclusively dependent upon the level of GNP or income. If GNP is zero, expenditures equal
the intercept a. Since GNP represents income, the consumption function indicates that people still like to consume the amount a if income is zero. In other
words, the intercept a represents consumption in excess of income, or dissavings.

Figure 5.7
Total Expenditures = C + I + G

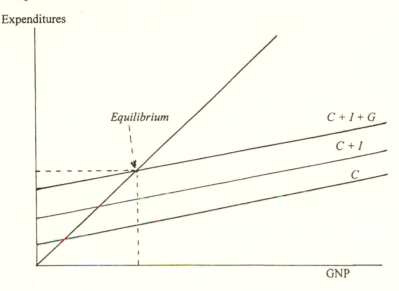

The slope of the consumption function, *b*, which is called the *marginal propensity to consume*, equals the proportion of peoples' incremental income consumed. Note that this slope is less than 1.0 because people consume less than 100 percent of an addition to income. Any drop in income results in a smaller fall in consumption since the slope is less than 1.0. This results in the positive intercept *a* if income is zero. For instance, if C = 70 + (0.8)GNP and if income (GNP) is zero, then consumption is 70. If income is 100, consumption is equal to 70 + (0.8)100 = 150. Out of the $100 increment in income, people spend only $80. The slope, or the marginal propensity to consume, is 0.80, or people consume 80 percent of any increase in income.

The *marginal propensity to save* is 1 minus the slope of the consumption function, or 1 − *b*. In the aforementioned example, the marginal propensity to save is 0.20, or 20 percent. That is, people save 20 percent of any increment to income. If income increases from 0 to 100, people save 20 percent or $20.

The propensities to consume and to save are determined by social customs and attitudes, age distribution of the population, and other factors that change very slowly over time. The consumption function, therefore, assumes that these propensities are stable or constant.

Figure 5.7 adds investment and government spending to consumption since investment and government spending are determined by factors other than income. Investment is determined by the interest rate and the marginal efficiency of investment (MEI), while government spending is assumed to be determined by political factors or exogenous factors (factors determined outside the eco-

Figure 5.8
An Increase in Investment

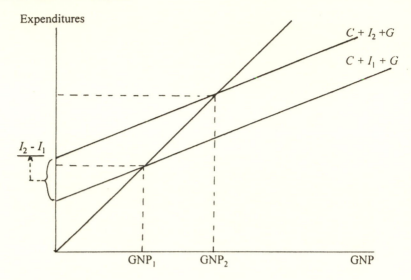

nomic system). Equilibrium is determined by the intersection of the total expenditures function with the 45-degree line with the origin. At this intersection,
consumers have picked their desired level of consumption and production is
equal to expenditures.

Figure 5.8 shows that the expenditures function shifts upward if there is an
outside shock, such as an increase in investment or government spending. The
change in equilibrium GNP is equal to the outside shock times $1/(1 - \text{mpc})$,
where mpc is the marginal propensity to consume or the slope of the consumption function. The ratio $1/(1 - \text{mpc})$ is called the *multiplier*. Since mpc is less
than 1.0, the multiplier must exceed 1.0. The multiplier increases as the mpc
increases or as the consumption function get steeper. The multiplier is bigger if
workers have a tendency to spend a larger proportion of their income. Table 5.1
shows the relationship between mpc, the multiplier and the marginal propensity
to save (mps), which equals $1 - \text{mpc}$. As the mps decreases, the multiplier
increases. Societies which have a smaller savings rate, and a higher propensity
to consume, have a bigger multiplier. In high multiplier societies, a change in
investment and/or government spending has a big impact on GNP. In most
societies, the multiplier is likely to be equal to or smaller than 2.0.

The earlier example had a slope of the consumption function or mpc of 0.80.
According to Table 5.1, the multiplier is 5. Thus, every injection of $1 of in-
vestment or government spending causes a change of $5 in GNP. In order to
enhance our understanding of why an injection of $1 of investment spending
results in a multiple expansion in GNP, it is noted that the $1 of spending is
income to some workers. In the example the mpc is 0.80; consequently, the

Table 5.1
The MPC, the Multiplier and the MPS

mpc	multiplier	mps
0.00	1.00	1.00
0.25	1.33	0.75
0.50	2.00	0.50
0.75	4.00	0.25
0.80	5.00	0.20
0.90	10.00	0.10
1.00	infinity	0.00

Table 5.2
GNP Multiplier

Incremental Income	Incremental Consumption	Cumulative Change in Consumption
$1.00	$0.80	$0.80
0.80	0.64	1.44
0.64	0.512	1.952
0.512	0.4096	2.3616
.	.	.
.	.	.
.	.	.
0.00	0.00	5.00

workers spend $0.80 of this $1 and save $0.20. This $0.80 is income to another set of workers who spend 80 percent of it or $0.64. In turn, this is income, 80 percent of which is spent, and so on. Table 5.2 shows these respendings; it can be shown mathematically that the total change in spending is equal to the original injection of spending times $1/(1 - mpc)$.

As stated earlier, investment is determined by the interest rate and the MEI. Figure 5.9 shows the MEI function, or the amount of business investment for a given interest rate, for two situations, namely a flat and a steep MEI. The figure shows that a decrease in the interest rate results in an increase in business investment or business investments and interest rates are inversely related in the MEI function. If the MEI curve is flat, then changes in interest rates cause large changes in business investment. The change in business investment shifts the consumption function upward (see Figure 5.8) and changes GNP, with the size of the change in the GNP dependent on the GNP multiplier. If the MEI function

Figure 5.9
Flat versus Steep MEI

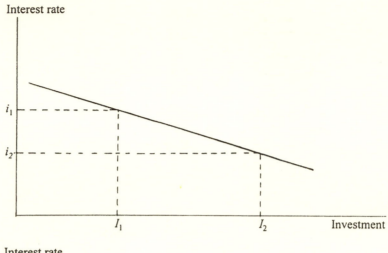

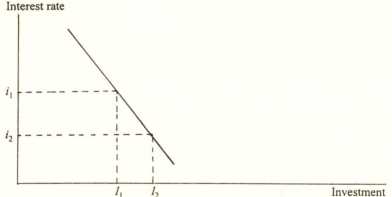

is steep, then changes in the interest rates bring about small changes in business investment and a small shift in the consumption function. For instance, a 1 percent decrease in the interest rate may cause business investment to increase by $20 billion (B) if the MEI is flat; the same decrease in the interest rate may cause only a $10B increase in business investment if the MEI function is steep.

A government decision to reduce the business tax rate (resulting in more profitable business investment) shifts the MEI function upward and to the right since each investment has a higher rate of return. Figure 5.10 shows that if the interest rate is the same, the shift in the MEI function increases the amount of business investment and this, in turn, increases GNP.

The neo-Keynesian approach distinguishes two motives for holding money balances, namely the *transactions motive* and the *speculative motive*. Transac-

Figure 5.10
Shift in MEI

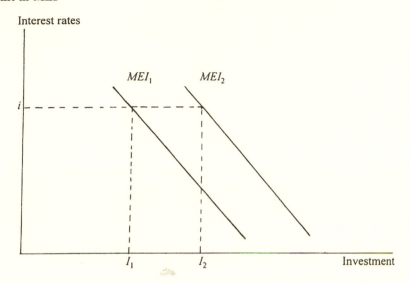

tions balances result from the transactions motive and occur since the exact matching of cash inflows and outflows by businesses is virtually impossible. For instance, a firm may sell part of its output on a Monday but does not need to pay its employees and/or suppliers until the end of the week (it may consider investing the cash until Friday, but search costs and brokerage fees may be higher than the profit from investing the cash for a few days). The amount of transaction balances increases when a firm's production increases since transactions balances are some proportion of production.

Speculative balances are cash balances held to buy securities at lower, more attractive prices in the future. For instance, if people believe that bond prices will be lower in the future, speculative balances are high. Bond prices and interest rates are inversely related: when prices are high, interest rates are low. Figure 5.11 shows that the speculative demand for money is inversely related to the current interest rate. Thus, if investors believe that current bond prices are high (i.e., current interest rates are low), speculative cash balances are increased in anticipation of a decline in future bond prices (that is, higher future interest rates).

It is noted, however, that the Keynesian view of the speculative demand for money contradicts the concept of *efficient markets* or the idea that security markets react rapidly to newly arrived information. The following example elucidates this concept. Company *ABC* anticipates a net cash flow of $10 million (M) per year in perpetuity. There are 10 million shares outstanding; consequently, there is an annual cash flow of $1.00 per share. The company will soon

Figure 5.11
Speculative Balances versus Interest Rates

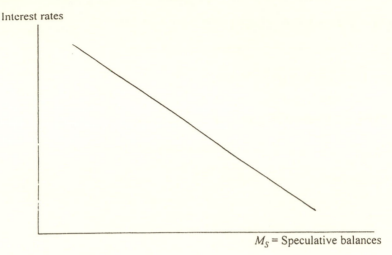

M_S = Speculative balances

build a new plant for $5M; the plant is expected to generate an additional net cash flow of $1M per year in perpetuity. Assuming that Company's *ABC*'s cost of capital is 10 percent, the project's net present value (NPV) is −$5M + $1M/ 0.1 = $5M. Table 5.3 presents market-value balance sheets of Company *ABC* for the following situations:

- prior to the announcement of the equity issue to construct the plant (part A),
- on announcement of the equity issue to construct the plant (part B),
- on issuance of stock but before construction of the plant commences (part C), and
- on completion of the plant (part D).

In part A, the value of the firm is $100M because the annual cash flows of $10M are capitalized at 10 percent. A share of stock sells for $10.00 (or $100M/ 10M) since there are 10 million shares outstanding.

Suppose that Company *ABC* announces it will raise $5M in equity in the near future in order to build a new plant. The stock price will rise to reflect the positive NPV of the plant. According to efficient markets, the increase occurs on the day of the announcement, not on the date of the commencement of construction of the plant or the date of the forthcoming stock offering. An efficient market is one in which stock prices fully reflect available information. Part B of Table 5.3 shows the balance sheet of Company *ABC* after the announcement. Note that the plant's NPV is included in the market-value balance sheet and that the number of outstanding shares remains 10 million because the

Table 5.3
Market-Value Balance Sheets of Company *ABC*

A. Prior to announcement of equity issue to construct plant.

Balance sheet (all equity)

Old assets: $10M/0.1 = $100M	Equity: $100M
	(10 million shares of stock)

B. Upon announcement of equity issue to construct plant.

Balance sheet

Old assets:	$100M	Equity:	$105M
NPV of plant:			(10 million shares of stock)
-$5M + $1M/0.1 =	5M		
Total assets:	$105M		

C. Upon issuance of stock but before construction starts on plant.

Balance sheet

Old assets:	$100M	Equity:	$110M
NPV of plant:	5M		(10,476,190 shares of
Proceeds from new issue			stock)
of stock (currently			
invested in bank):	5M		
Total assets:	$110M		

D.   Upon completion of plant.

Balance sheet

Old assets:	$100M	Equity:	$110M
NPV of plant:			(10,476,190 shares of
$1M/0.1 =	10M		stock)
Total assets:	$110M		

new shares have not yet been issued. The price per share now rises to $10.50 (or $105M/10M) to reflect the news about the plant.

Shortly after the announcement of the equity issue, $5M of stock is floated. Since the stock is selling at $10.50 per share, 476,190 (or $5M/$10.50) shares of stock are issued. The funds are temporarily deposited in a bank before being used to construct the plant. Part C of Table 5.3 presents the market-value balance sheet at this point in time. Note that the number of shares outstanding is now 10,476,190 because 476,190 new shares were issued. Also note that the price per share remains $10.50 (or $110M/10,476,190). The price per share did not change since no new information became available, which is consistent with the operation of efficient markets.

Part D of Table 5.3 reflects a situation in which the $5M is given to a contractor to build the plant and the bank account has been emptied to pay the contractor. To keep the example simple, we assume that the plant is constructed instantaneously (to avoid problems in discounting). The building expenditures of $5M have already been paid and therefore do not represent a future cost. Consequently, they no longer reduce the value of the plant. The NPV of cash flows of $1M a year from the new plant are reflected as an asset worth $10M. Note that total assets do not change, but their composition does. In addition, the price per share remains $10.50, which is consistent with the operation of efficient markets.

Similarly, if investors know that interest rates are going to change in the future, they take action immediately, and the information is immediately reflected in interest rates. In other words, changes in interest rates cannot be predicted and, in an efficient market, they are not too high or too low but are appropriate given current information. Consequently, the Keynesian view of the speculative demand for money should be rejected.

There is, however, another reason for which the interest rate and the money supply are inversely related. That is, when interest rates are high, individuals and business have a strong incentive to move out of cash and into interest-bearing securities. Conversely, when interest rates are low, the incentives for economizing on cash balances are reduced. Consequently, the demand for money is a function of both income and interest rates. In a way, we could consider the aforementioned incentive to move out of the cash a speculative behavior. We therefore continue to refer to the curve of Figure 5.11 as the speculative demand for money.

Figure 5.12 shows that the total demand for money is determined by the transactions demand plus the speculative demand. When income (GNP) increases, the transactions demand increases, and the demand function shifts to the right. The supply of money is established by the monetary authorities and is represented by the vertical line in Figure 5.12. The equilibrium interest rate is given by the point where the demand curve for money crosses the supply curve. At this point, the amount of money demanded by people for transactions and speculative balances is exactly equal to the amount of money supplied by the monetary authorities.

The supply of money curve of Figure 5.12 shifts to the right and interest rates decline, if the monetary authorities increase the supply of money. The extent of the decline in interest rates depends on the slope of the demand for money curve. If this curve is flat, an increase in the money supply has no or little

Figure 5.12
Demand and Supply for Money

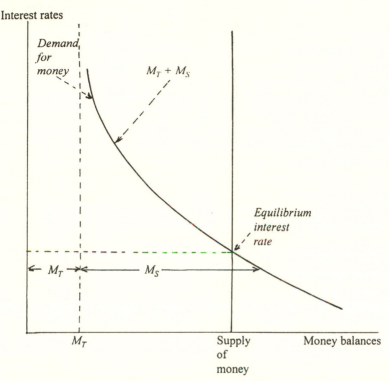

Interest rates

Demand for money

$M_T + M_S$

Equilibrium interest rate

$\leftarrow M_T \rightarrow \leftarrow$ M_S $\longrightarrow$

M_T Supply of money   Money balances

impact on the interest rate; however, if the curve is steep (as shown in Figure 5.12), the interest rate declines sharply. The slope of the demand function affects the impact of changes in the money supply upon the entire economy. A change in the money supply causes a change in the interest rate (because of the speculative demand function), affects business investment, and in turn changes GNP. If the demand for money function is flat, changes in the money supply have little impact on the interest rate and, ultimately, on the GNP. It is noted that the classical quantity theory (see Monetarist View of Interest rates) assumes full employment (which the neo-Keynesian model does not) and does not have speculative balances (existing in the neo-Keynesian model). The absence of speculative balances implies that interest rates do not change when the money supply changes.

In conclusion, based on the money supply, government spending and taxes, the neo-Keynesian approach has four components (Figure 5.13):

• the consumption function,
• the marginal efficiency of investment (MEI) function,

Figure 5.13
Four Components of the Neo-Keynesian Model

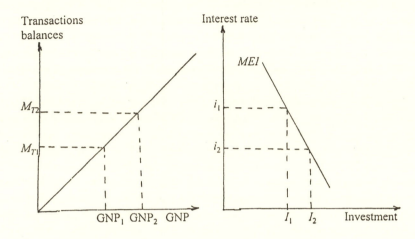

Transactions balances

Transactions balances

M_{T2}

M_{T1}

GNP$_1$ GNP$_2$ GNP

Marginal efficiency of investment

Interest rate

MEI

i_1

i_2

I_1 I_2 Investment

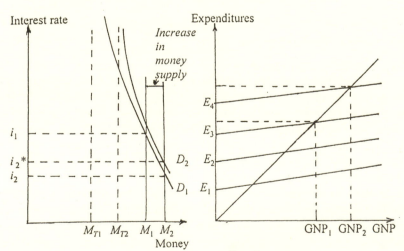

Demand for money

Interest rate

Increase in money supply

i_1

i_2*

i_2

D_2

D_1

M_{T1} M_{T2} M_1 M_2
Money

Consumption function

Expenditures

E_4

E_3

E_2

E_1

GNP$_1$ GNP$_2$ GNP

$E_1 = C$
$E_2 = C + I_1$
$E_3 = C + I_1 + G$
$E_4 = C + I_2 + G$

- the transactions demand for money, and
- the speculative demand for money.

All of the elements are interrelated in the neo-Keynesian approach. Let us, for instance, follow the impact of an increase in the money supply on the entire system. We start with an initial money supply of M_1 established by a nation's central bank as shown in the lower left quadrant of Figure 5.13. The money supply and the total demand function for money imply an interest rate i_1. In the upper right quadrant, i_1 implies an investment of I_1. In the lower right quadrant, the level of investment plus consumption and government spending determine GNP_1. In the upper left quadrant, GNP determines the transactions balances at M_{T1}. In the system all of these elements are simultaneously determined.

Let us now assume that the money supply increases to M_2; the demand function for money in the lower left quadrant of Figure 5.13 shows that as a result of this increase, the interest rate decreases to i_2. In the upper right quadrant, the MEI function indicates that the lower interest rate causes an increase in the investment to I_2. The consumption function in the lower right quadrant shows that the increase in investment is followed by an increase in GNP_2. The transactions demand function tells us in turn that a larger GNP results into an increase in the demand for transactions to M_{T2}. The bigger demand for transactions tends to offset the original drop in the interest rate because the demand function for money in the lower left quadrant shifts to the right. The net impact of an increase in the money supply is still a drop in the interest rate, but to a slightly higher level $(i_2{}^*)$.

The effect of a given change in the money supply on interest rates and the other variables depends on four factors:

- the slope of the MEI function: a change in the money supply has a bigger impact on GNP, if investment is more sensitive to changes in interest rates (a flatter MEI curve);
- the slope of the demand function for money: changes in the money supply cause large changes in interest rates and GNP, if the demand function is steep;
- the size of the multiplier: the impact of a change in the money supply is bigger for a larger marginal propensity to consume (mpc) since the multiplier is directly related to the mpc (a bigger multiplier also implies a steeper consumption function); and
- transactions balances: a change in the money supply has a relatively large impact on GNP, if transactions balances are a small percentage of GNP.

The last point mentioned above may not be evident. Assume, therefore, an increase in the money supply resulting in an initial drop in interest rates, an increase in business investment and an increase in GNP. The increased GNP results, in turn, in more money needed for transactions balances, shifting the demand function for money to the right, boosting interest rates and undoing some of the effect of the original change. The size of the shift in the demand function for money depends on the proportion of GNP held as transactions balances. A small proportion causes a small shift and a small offsetting effect; consequently, an increase in the money supply has a relatively large impact on GNP.

In summary, the interest rate depends on:

- the demand for transactions balances,
- the demand for speculative balances,
- the money supply,
- the marginal efficiency of investment (MEI) curve,
- the marginal propensity to consume and the multiplier, and
- government spending and taxes.

With the above discussion of the neo-Keynesian approach, we can make the following observations:

- Recessions (i.e., low levels of GNP) can be cured by increases in the money supply, resulting in greater production (GNP) and more employment.
- If the demand curve for money is extremely flat, an increase in the money supply has no impact on either interest rates or GNP; increases in the money supply just cannot push interest rates any lower.
- An increase in money supply may increase GNP and have no impact on interest rates, if the MEI function is flat.
- An increase in money supply may reduce interest rates and have no impact on GNP, if the MEI function is almost a vertical line.
- Government spending increases output and employment and gets the economy out of the recession; however, some business investment may be crowded out of the market because interest rates are pushed up.
- Increased government spending may not affect interest rates and not crowd out any business investment, if there is a strong multiplier effect from the increment in government spending and, consequently, a very large impact on GNP.

INFLATION AND INTEREST RATES

Throughout history, inflation—a continual increase in the general price level—has been a frequent occurrence. It often has a significant impact on interest rates and economic activity. In addition, as prices increase, individuals often try to protect their purchasing power by taking actions (e.g., wages tied to the cost of living) which inadvertently perpetuate inflation. In the industrialized world, government statistics provide several price indices to measure inflation: a consumer price index, a producer price index and a GNP deflator. The rate of change in these indices should each measure the inflation rate. The fact that these rates of change can differ significantly indicates that finding the true inflation rate is not an easy task. For instance, finding the consumer inflation rate is difficult since it depends on the price changes of individual consumer goods and the amounts consumed by actual consumers. Since consumer choices change as relative prices change, the basket of goods purchased by the average consumer changes over time.

The *real rate of interest*, which we denote by r, is defined as the rate that would prevail in an inflation-free world. In order to establish the relationship between inflation and interest rates, we first assume complete certainty about the future and a world without taxes. Denote the *completely certain inflation rate* by p and the *observed, nominal* (i.e., money terms) *interest rate* by i. In order to compensate lenders for the declining purchasing power of money, the following relationship must hold:

$$1 + i = (1 + r)(1 + p) = 1 + r + p + rp, \text{ or}$$
$$i = r + p + rp$$

For instance, if the real interest rate is 4 percent and the inflation rate is 5 percent, then the nominal rate, i, equals the real rate, r (0.04), plus the inflation rate, p (0.05), plus the product of rp, (0.04)(0.05). Adding the inflation rate, p, compensates the lender for the declining value of the principal and adding the term rp compensates him for the declining value of the real interest. Since the term rp is rather small, it is often omitted; thus in the example, the nominal rate is frequently approximated by 9 percent.

If the interest income is taxed at the rate t, then the inflation rate must be increased to compensate the lender for taxes paid. That is, 1 plus the after-tax yield to maturity should equal $(1 + r)(1 + p)$, or

$$1 + i(1 - t) = (1 + r)(1 + p), \text{ or}$$
$$i = (r + p + rp)/(1 - t), \text{ or}$$
$$i = r/(1 - t) + (p + rp)/(1 - t), \text{ or}$$
$$\text{before-tax nominal} = \text{before-tax real} + \text{before-tax inflation premium}$$

The before-tax nominal interest rate is represented by i. The term $r/(1 - t)$ is the before-tax real interest rate. The before-tax inflation premium is represented by $(p + rp)/(1 - t)$. If the tax rate is 50 percent, every 1 percent of inflation raises the nominal interest rate by $(p + rp)/(1 - 0.50)$, or by more than 2 percent. For instance, if the real interest rate, r, is 4 percent, the inflation rate is 5 percent, and the tax rate is 50 percent, the before-tax yield to maturity is $(0.04 + 0.05 + 0.002)/(1 - 0.50) = 18.4$ percent. Taxes increase the before-tax interest rate to 18.4 percent, so that the after-tax rate is $i(1 - t) = 0.184(1 - 0.50) = 9.2$ percent.

If the inflation rate is uncertain, a *risk premium* is added to the expected inflation rate:

$$i = [r + E(p) + h]/(1 - t)$$

where:

    $E(p)$ = expected inflation rate
    h   = risk premium
    all other terms are as defined earlier

The risk premium compensates the lender for the possibility of an actual inflation rate which is higher than the expected rate. For example, if the real interest rate is 4 percent, the expected inflation rate is 5 percent, the risk premium is 2 percent, and the tax rate is 50 percent, the nominal interest rate is $(0.04 + 0.05 + 0.02)/(1 - 0.50)$ = 22 percent. Risk premiums may vary over time.

In conclusion, anticipated inflation rates should have an impact on the current interest rate, since investors include anticipation of the future in current security prices. In the case of complete certainty about future inflation, the inflation rate is added to the real interest rate to arrive at the nominal interest rate. If the future is uncertain, the nominal interest rate is equal to the real interest rate plus the anticipated inflation rate plus the risk premium.

As we have seen in the beginning of this chapter, the neo-Keynesians and the monetarists disagree about the proper target of monetary policy. The neo-Keynesians emphasize the importance of the level of interest rates, while the monetarists focus on the growth rate of the money supply. In the United States, the Federal Reserve tended to follow the neo-Keynesian approach by monitoring closely the level of interest rates during the 1950s and 1960s. In the 1970s and 1980s the Federal Reserve's focus was on the growth rate of the money supply, thus following more a monetarist approach, although not completely ignoring the level of interest rates. In the 1990s, more of a focus on interest rates returned. Should a central bank follow a set of predetermined rules in setting the growth rate of the money supply or should it exercise discretion and adapt policy to perceived current needs? Neo-Keynesians tend to favor discretion, while monetarists tend to favor rules (arguing that a central bank has the tendency to make economic problems worse by its discretionary decisions).

SUGGESTIONS FOR FURTHER READING

Landau, Nilly. "Riding Interest Rates: How to Time a New Debt Issue." *Business International Money Report* (May 20, 1991): 193–194.

Maromonte, Kevin R. *Corporate Strategic Business Sourcing*. Westport, CT: Quorum Books, 1998.

Mishkin, F. S. *Money, Banking, and Financial Markets*. New York: HarperCollins, 1992.

Smith, Roy C., and Ingo Walter. *Global Financial Services*. New York: HarperBusiness, 1990.

Wunnicke, Diane B., David R. Wilson, and Brooke Wunnicke. *Corporate Financial Risk Management*. New York: Wiley, 1992.

Chapter 6

Financial Crises:
Insights from East Asia

BACKGROUND OF THE CRISES

The financial crisis in East Asia began in Thailand and was precipitated by a speculative attack on the Thai currency, the baht. Efforts to support the baht through interest rate increases from 12 percent in January to 18 percent by June 1997, and restrictions on foreign speculators, ultimately failed. The reason for this was that by mid-1997 domestic companies added to pressures on the exchange rate as they rushed to protect themselves from foreign exchange risks to their balance sheets by repaying foreign debt and hedging their foreign exchange exposure. On July 2, 1997, the central bank let the exchange rate float after it had lost $8.7 billion in defending the currency. By the end of the year the baht had depreciated by 93 percent (compared to June 1997) and the stock market had fallen to 37 percent of its June level in dollar terms. The devaluation of the baht triggered a collapse of market confidence in Indonesia, Malaysia and the Philippines resulting in a sharp decline in the value of their currencies in July/August 1997 and a fall of 50 to 75 percent in the dollar value of equity prices in the region by the end of the year. In November, turmoil in currency and equity markets extended to South Korea, which became the object of the largest ever international rescue package.

In the wake of the crises, the East Asian economies had been criticized for their mismanaged exchange rate policies, badly regulated financial markets, lack of transparency, wasteful investment, current account deficits and inadequate corporate governance. Although most of this critique was justified, it behooves us to examine in more detail the circumstances which led to the crises. We should also remember that prior to the outbreak of the crises, East Asian economies were widely praised for their rapid growth with equity, which resulted in

Table 6.1
Fiscal Balances and Gross National Savings in East Asia (percent of GDP)

Country	Fiscal Balances 1993-95	1996	Gross National Savings 1993-95	1996
Indonesia	1.2	0.9	31.8	28.7
Malaysia	2.3	1.1	31.8	37.8
Thailand	2.3	2.3	34.7	34.3
Philippines	0.0	-0.4	20.1	19.6
South Korea	0.4	0.3	35.2	34.3

Source: IMF.

large reductions in poverty and extensions in life spans. Between 1966 and 1996, the per capita incomes in Indonesia, Malaysia, South Korea and Thailand grew at an average annual rate of 4.7, 4.4, 7.4 and 5.2 percent, respectively. Over that period the growth rate in these countries was also stable; GDP growth was positive in every year for Indonesia and Thailand and only fell in one year for Malaysia (1985) and South Korea (1980). In other words, it does not make sense to characterize the East Asian economies as vulnerable to crises. Unlike Mexico prior to the 1994–1995 peso crisis, the size of public debt was not a relevant factor in the crises. As indicated in Table 6.1, the East Asian countries had high savings rates prior to the crises; thus, excessive consumption by the private sector also was not an issue. In spite of these high savings rates, foreign capital was still required to finance the substantial investment rates which rose to roughly 40 percent of GDP in Malaysia, South Korea and Thailand and 34 percent in Indonesia between 1993 and 1996. It is also noted that the crises in East Asia occurred against the background of a benign international environment with historically high rates of growth in world trade and low international interest rates, which implied low debt-servicing costs.

Notwithstanding their good macroeconomic track record, the East Asian countries became vulnerable in the mid-1990s due to:

- misallocation of investment,
- large current account deficits,
- maturity/currency mismatches,
- loss of competitiveness,
- policies that worked well in the countries' earlier stage of development and that were ill suited to their current economic conditions, and
- abandonment of some policies that have served well in the past.

Much of the capital inflow and the coincident surge of domestic investment in East Asia was directed into risky and low-productivity investments. A large portion of domestic credit flowed into the nontraded sector, especially real estate.

The surge in the region's real estate investments outpaced demand and made the banking system vulnerable to a downturn in domestic demand. The poor quality of real estate investment in Thailand was reflected in the stock market, where the index for building and furnishing companies collapsed from a peak of just below 8200 in late 1994 to 1100 in late 1997. The misallocation of investment was exacerbated by the change in investor sentiment, both in their perception of risks and their willingness to bear it in the industrialized countries, which had profound effects on East Asia (as well as other developing countries) in the late summer and fall of 1997. The change in investor sentiment was reflected in interest rate spreads not only for emerging market securities, but also for riskier corporate securities in developing countries.

One measure of the productivity of investment is the incremental capital-output ratio (ICOR), which is the ratio of cumulative investment over a period of time to the change in gross domestic output. To reduce cyclical effects, ICORs are often computed as a five-year moving average. In South Korea and Thailand the ICOR rose from 3 in 1991 to over 5 by 1996, which is a significant increase for a five-year period. A rising ICOR is often indicative of poor quality of investment (especially of newer investments) and increased financial vulnerability to a slowdown of the economy if the investment is financed by borrowing that will need to be repaid out of future output. It is noted, however, that other factors such as the business cycle (ICORs rise during a slowdown and fall during a recovery) and structural changes also affect the value of the ICOR. Nevertheless, crises that affected countries in the 1980s also were preceded by a sharp rise in ICORs.

Low productivity of investment can also be observed by the fall of return on assets. The return on equity in Indonesia, Malaysia and Thailand declined to below money market interest rates during 1992–1996. In other words, there was no compensation for the risk of investment in these economies. In 1996, the return on assets of many South Korean companies was 1 percent, which resulted in a number of bankruptcies during 1997 (prior to the spread of the crisis to South Korea).

In general, a large and persistent current account deficit (Chapter 4) is an indication of unsustainable macroeconomic policies. Naturally, the sustainability of large current account deficits depends, in part, on the purposes to which the funds are put. If the funds had been invested in diversified and high-productive investments in East Asia, the borrowing would have been sustainable. The sustainability of a particular level of the current account deficit depends on whether capital inflows are used for productive investment and whether the external liabilities incurred are consistent with the debt servicing capacity of the country.

The vulnerability of many East Asian banks was high since much external borrowing was short term and used to finance local currency denominated assets, particularly in real estate and other nontradables. Although some banks avoided currency mismatches, they were still vulnerable to a fall in the exchange rate since many of their clients had significant foreign exchange exposure. With net

Table 6.2
Mid-1997 Short-Term Debt Ratios (percent)

Country	Short-term debt/total debt	Short-term debt/reserves
Indonesia	24	160
Malaysia	39	55
Philippines	19	66
South Korea	67	300
Thailand	46	107

Source: World Bank.

foreign liabilities rising from 3 percent of total domestic assets in 1990 to 20 percent in 1996 in Thailand, the foreign exchange exposure was particularly severe in that country. The extent of maturity mismatches varied among the East Asian countries. For instance, by mid-1997 the short-term debt levels had risen to 67 percent of total debt in South Korea, 46 percent of total external debt in Thailand and 19 percent in the Philippines. Table 6.2 shows that there was also variation in the ratio of short-term debt to reserves in these countries.

The pegged (or quasi-pegged) exchange rates in East Asian countries resulted in a loss in competitiveness in their economies, which was reflected in a substantial slowdown in exports. Why were the governments of these countries so reluctant to abandon the pegs? First, the governments had successfully kept the quasi-pegged exchange rates for long periods of time. For example, the exchange rate for the Thai baht had largely drifted in a narrow band between 25 and 27 baht to the dollar for 13 years. Second, policymakers wanted to avoid a relatively small increase in inflation, even when this means that the expansion of domestic demand is channeled into a rising current account deficit and a higher probability of a major crisis. Third, policymakers were aware of the fact that, historically, fixed exchange rate systems had frequently been attacked, resulting in large, discrete changes in the exchange rate. Fourth, the option of devaluation had a large potential (and subsequently actual) cost in terms of further weakening the financial system, leading to a collapse of credit and a large fall in aggregate demand (the benefits for exports would not necessarily have been very large).

An example of policies which worked well in the country's earlier stage of development but are ill suited to their current, more advanced situation is South Korea's deliberately pursuing a policy of maintaining high debt-equity ratios to leverage greater investment, in turn leading to rapid growth. However, this high leveraging also left Korean corporations vulnerable to a growth slowdown. In the past, the government had played a complementary role in absorbing such shocks through directed credit and other mechanisms, thereby mitigating much of the risk associated with high debt-equity ratios. When the government of South Korea moved toward a market economy, it limited its role and became reluctant to engage in a massive bail-out.

Abandonment of some policies that served well in the past is clearly seen in the financial market liberalization. Rapid financial liberalization without commensurate strengthening of other/remaining regulation and supervision contributed significantly to the crises in the East Asian countries. Historically, the East Asian financial systems had been highly regulated, with caps on interest rates, directed credit to allocate the scarce supply of credit, restrictions on foreign direct investment and foreign borrowing, limitations on foreign entry into the banking systems and limitations on the asset holding of financial institutions. Over the past decade, many of these restrictions have been eased. For instance, Thailand witnessed the following financial liberalization during the last decade:

- elimination of restrictions on interest rates for many types of lending or borrowing,
- reduction of reserve requirements,
- expansion of the scope of permissible capital market activities by banks (to include activities like financing equity purchases on margin), and
- expansion of the scope in banks' decisions on their loans by relaxing mandates in favor of certain types of lending (e.g., to agriculture) and eliminating rules against other types of lending (e.g., to real estate).

In South Korea, the government adopted a series of progressive policies to loosen the regulations on bank lending:

- sale of government-owned shares in banks,
- increased limits on bank-chaebol links,
- decontrol of interest rates,
- progressive freeing up of the exchange market, and
- relaxation and lifting restrictions on foreign direct investment and borrowing abroad.

Similar financial liberalization took place in Indonesia and Malaysia.

WEAKNESSES IN THE FINANCIAL SECTOR AND CORPORATE GOVERNANCE

The aforementioned liberalization of the financial sectors in East Asia should not be interpreted as meaning that liberalization is bad; perhaps the problem is that the liberalization was too fast. The experience over the last decade of a number of developed as well as developing countries clearly demonstrates the risks posed by rapid financial liberalization unaccompanied by a significant strengthening of supervision and regulation. Liberalization found many banks in a relatively weak position, unable to compete against innovative newcomers. In addition, the erosion of the *franchise value* (the present discounted value of future profits) of banks creates an incentive for more risk taking. If these incentives are not offset by better supervision and regulation, serious problems will emerge. Unfortunately, experience shows that it is much easier to eliminate restrictions than to create new prudential oversight and regulation.

In the previous protected environment, bank managers lacked incentives to invest in risk-monitoring skills and credit assessment. The rapid liberalization placed banks in a position requiring these skills; however, these skills cannot be acquired overnight. As a consequence, banks and financial institutions often had a limited ability to cope with the expanded choices opened up by liberalization.

Prior to the liberalization, many of the financial systems in East Asia were marked by close connections between lenders and borrowers and lending to insiders. Implicit or explicit government guarantees encouraged banks to take excessive risk since the banks would receive high profits if the project were successful, while the government would absorb the losses in the case of failure. This situation further eroded incentives for credit evaluation and contributed to inflated prices of assets. For instance, in South Korea the chaebols were able to obtain loans from banks in part because of their direct shareholdings and the support of associated firms as well as the government's directing a portion of bank lending. Thus, the chaebols obtained sufficient credit to finance continued expansion, despite their high debt-to-equity ratios, which for the 25 largest chaebols averaged 4:1 in 1996. In 1997, as the financial positions of several chaebols deteriorated, the government provided public funds to cover some of the losses.

In view of the lack of transparent and timely balance sheets and other information in most East Asian countries, banks tended to base credit decisions on the availability of collateral rather than on an analysis of cash flows. The over-reliance on collateral skewed the allocation of loans toward real estate and construction where the property or building can serve as collateral. In addition, the use of equities for collateral increased the vulnerability of banking portfolios to a downturn in the stock market. The poor transparency characterizing both banks and corporations impaired the usefulness of equity markets in imposing discipline on corporate behavior. The largest corporations may also have been viewed as "too big to fail," thus encouraging excessive risk taking.

The East Asian countries lacked the institutional capacity to cope with the rapid expansion of domestic credit during the 1990s, which resulted in:

- inadequate reporting and provisioning requirements for nonperforming loans (for example, in Indonesia the permissible length of delinquencies is overly long, allowing a loan to be nonperforming 24 months or more before it is deemed uncollectable),

- lenient capital adequacy requirements [for example, these requirements are more lenient than those suggested by the Bank for International Settlements (BIS) although the East Asian economies face higher risks than the industrial countries that follow BIS standards], and

- a shortage/lack of effective exit mechanisms for failed institutions, meaning that insolvent banks were allowed to continue to lend, although they had little incentive to behave prudently since they had no equity to lose.

Table 6.3
East Asian Loan Growth, 1990–1996 (percent)

Country	Net domestic credit/GDP	
	1990	1996
Indonesia	45	55
Malaysia	80	136
Philippines	26	72
South Korea	68	79
Thailand	84	130

Source: IMF.

As mentioned earlier, these problems were exacerbated by a rapid liberalization of financial markets without a commensurate strengthening of supervision and regulation. In addition, increased access to offshore funding facilitated the taking of excessive foreign exchange risk. The liberalization of financial markets at a time of easy global monetary conditions encouraged a surge in borrowing. Table 6.3 shows that the ratio of domestic credit to GDP increased significantly in the East Asian economies, thus further increasing the vulnerability of the economy to shocks in the banking system. For instance, domestic credit rose to 136 percent of GDP in Malaysia as compared to ratios of 20 to 70 percent in Latin America.

It is noted that the surge in borrowing took place primarily in the private sector. In fact, a shortage of public investment was one of the major bottlenecks to future East Asian growth. Public infrastructure was not up to the demands of the modern economy and education, which had led the East Asian growth and had fallen behind. Reducing public spending would simply have meant agreeing to the diversion of investment from roads and schools to shopping malls and office towers. Thus, it was the short-term maturity structure of private rather than public debt and the pegged exchange rate that were the major sources of financial vulnerability.

Although the supply of adequate levels of credit is critical to an expanding economy and several rapidly growing countries have sustained persistent increases in credit to GDP ratios over considerable time periods, a rapid growth in domestic credit can exceed that warranted by economic fundamentals. In other words, such rapid growth can be a signal of unsustainable macroeconomic policies. Various empirical studies have found:

- a significant correlation between rapid credit expansion and the probability of a devaluation,
- that banking crises were a significant factor in predicting currency crises, as a banking crisis may lead to a loss of confidence in the economy, which then triggers a currency crisis,

- that many of the banking crises were preceded by lending booms, which were typically associated with large capital inflows and financial liberalization, and
- a significant relationship between the level of international reserves and the probability of a currency crisis since reserves may decline prior to a crisis due to (ultimately unsuccessful) efforts to defend the currency.

We may ask ourselves what would have happened if the East Asian governments had maintained the dollar-pegged (or quasi-pegged) foreign exchange policy but had a better-regulated financial sector. Thus, regulators would have limited banks' ability to borrow short in foreign currency and lend long to buy nontradable assets. The expected constancy of the exchange rate would in all likelihood have meant that corporations and nonbank financial institutions rather than banks would have accessed international markets directly. Thus, financial regulation might have succeeded in reducing bank exposure, but the incentives for borrowing would have simply been reflected in the corporate sector. In fact, this is what happened in Indonesia, where about two-thirds of the external debt to BIS-reporting banks was incurred by the nonbank private sector, among the highest fraction of any country in the world. No country can or does regulate individual corporations at the level of detail which would be needed to prevent the maturity and foreign exchange mismatches that resulted.

On the other hand, well-designed bank regulations (e.g., risk-adjusted capital adequacy standards and risk-adjusted deposit premia) may have somewhat reduced the financial market vulnerabilities. For example, banks could have charged higher interest rates to reflect greater risk when lending to borrowers with large uncovered foreign exchange exposures and high debt-equity ratios. The higher interest rate would have provided a disincentive for borrowers to have risky financial positions.

Naturally, restraints on lending, in particular lending for commercial real estate, may have been a more successful way to cope with the surge of capital since it was apparent that there existed a significant nonproductive and speculative real estate lending. Imposing sharp restrictions on this lending would have both dampened investment and strengthened the banking system. Further broad constraints on international capital flows (Chapter 2), especially short-term flows, could have complemented this policy, further lengthening the duration and reducing the risk of the inflows. Such restraints would be justified by the externality imposed by short-term flows.

In Indonesia, Malaysia and Thailand, capital inflows generated considerable upward pressures on domestic demand and the exchange rate. It was thought to be impractical to entirely offset the rise in demand through a fiscal contraction in view of the size of the capital inflows and the relatively strong state of public finances. As current account deficits rose, policymakers therefore turned to monetary policy to restrain the rise in domestic demand. Indonesia and Thailand especially offset a significant proportion of the increase in capital inflows through a contraction in domestic credit. Thus, they relied on *sterilization in-*

tervention. While sterilization reduced domestic demand below the level which otherwise would have occurred, it had disastrous effects on the economy. For instance, in 1996 short-term money market interest rates were 400 basis points above comparable US interest rates, encouraging short-term, unhedged borrowing. Sterilization, by preventing interest rates from falling in response to capital inflows, also encouraged creditors to continue lending. In addition, sterilization resulted in large reserves accumulation. During 1994–1996, international reserves in Indonesia, Malaysia, Philippines and Thailand rose by about $30 billion in total or about a fifth of net capital flows. The holding of large reserves incurs a substantial cost to the economy, since the return on liquid assets is typically well below the cost of attracting capital from abroad.

In all fairness, it should be noted that the financial problems were not exclusively caused by inadequate financial regulation in East Asia or bad choices by the borrowers. The lenders also bear much of the responsibility. For instance, even banks in the supposedly well-regulated advanced economies made loans not just to South Korean banks, but also directly to their chaebols with their high debt-equity ratios. Foreign lenders, including the International Finance Corporation, and investors were not restrained by their awareness of the inadequacies of financial statements, high levels of short-term debt and the unhedged foreign exchange exposure present in the financing structure of banks and firms in East Asia. It appears that sufficient publicly available data existed in Thailand to allow some observers to foresee the problems in Thailand at least one year before the baht devaluation; however, few appreciated the depth of structural weaknesses.

It also appears that the so-called nondebt-creating financial inflows, that is, acquisition of property and securities by nonresidents, have played some role in sustaining speculative bubbles in equity and property markets in East Asia. Indeed, increased access by nonresidents to securities markets (as well as greater access by residents to dollar assets) tends to establish a close link between two inherently unstable markets, namely, currency and equity markets. This generates destabilizing feedbacks: a currency crisis could easily lead to a stock market collapse, while a bearish mood in the equity market could easily translate into a currency crisis. More direct measures to control such destabilizing linkages, including restrictions on foreign acquisition of domestic securities, may be desirable.

International institutions and rating agencies failed to adequately anticipate the vulnerabilities of the East Asian economies. Table 6.4 shows that the foreign currency debt of almost all of the East Asian countries had the same investment grade ratings in June 1997 as a year earlier, and that the rating downgrades only occurred once the crisis was in full swing. The fact that markets and market observers (those whom the market relies on to give and interpret information about the economy) failed to anticipate the scope and severity of the crisis is evidence that a self-fulfilling loss of confidence played an important role. Appendix 4 describes how rating agencies establish bond ratings.

Table 6.4
Credit Ratings for East Asian Countries

| Country | Moody's | | | S&P's | | |
	June 96	June 97	Dec 97|	June 96	June 97	Dec 97
Indonesia	Baa3	Baa3	Ba1	BBB	BBB	BB+
Malaysia	A1	A1	A2	A+	A+	A
Philippines	Ba2	Ba1	Ba1	BB+	BB+	BB+
South Korea	A1	A1	Ba1	AA-	AA-	B+
Thailand	A2	A2	Ba1	A	A	BBB

Source: Moody's and Standard and Poors.

The East Asian crisis was triggered by the events in Thailand during the first half of 1997, when exports remained flat in dollar terms, capital flows slowed down and the stock market fell by 37 percent because the price of companies involved in the burst real estate bubble dropped by almost two-thirds. The rapid spread of the crisis to Indonesia, Malaysia and the Philippines was primarily due to (a) some aspects of their economies being similar to the Thai economy and (b) the four economies being close competitors in world markets so that currency adjustment in one created expectations of a fall in the others. Fears over the sustainability of exchange rates in the region made the market partic-ipants (including domestic corporations) aware (too late) of the riskiness of the currency and maturity mismatches built up during the 1992–1996 surge in cap-ital flows. Foreign investors may also have perceived that loans to banks carried an implicit government guarantee. When this proved not to be the case, a marked reassessment of risks and asset prices ensued.

Although difficult to prove, it is generally believed that the severity of the East Asian crisis was far in excess of the misalignment of exchange rates due to the weaknesses of financial intermediaries and corporations. The high volume of short-term debt falling due in Indonesia, Thailand and South Korea increased pressures on their currencies, as the turmoil in financial markets made creditors reluctant to roll over their credit lines. The resulting currency depreciation in-creased the local currency value of uncovered dollar liabilities of banks, finance companies and corporations, thus impairing balance sheets, lowering stock prices and further increasing the demand for foreign exchange to cover open positions. Increased demand for foreign exchange resulted in further currency depreciation, and so on. The increases in interest rates to defend the currency and the rapid fall in the equity of highly leveraged financial institutions led to a contraction of credit which impaired the position of otherwise healthy com-panies and enhanced foreign lenders' reluctance to roll over short-term debt. Finally, the threat of impending major increases in unemployment raised con-cerns over the potential for social unrest in some countries, in particular Indo-nesia, thus contributing to the downward spiral.

It is of interest to note that Malaysia's central bank adopted much more prudent policies with regard to short-term lending than its neighbors. As a result, its ratio of short-term debt to reserves in end-December 1996 was 0.4 compared to 1.2 for Thailand. Consequently, Malaysia did not suffer as much from the unwillingness of foreign creditors to roll over short-term loans and, as a result, did not face the imminent threat of default that brought Indonesia and South Korea to the brink. Measured by the depreciation of its exchange rate, Malaysia's crisis has, however, been just as severe as that of South Korea or Thailand. It is also of interest to note that Taiwan had strong financial institutions, sound economic policies and an exchange rate that was widely believed to be reasonable. As a consequence, Taiwan's exchange rate gradually depreciated by only 20 percent.

Is the East Asian crisis different from the financial crisis in Chile in 1982 or the one in Mexico in 1994? There were certainly many similarities between the variables leading up to the Mexican and East Asian crises, including rapid growth of credit to the private sector, large capital inflows, a budget surplus, real exchange rate appreciation and, with the exception of Malaysia, a buildup of the short-term debt-to-reserves ratio. However, unlike Mexico and Chile, the East Asian economies' long track record of prudent macroeconomic policies and successful macroeconomic performance were among the most successful in the world. The consequence of the past differences was that East Asian countries had a much smaller stock of government debt than Mexico had. In addition, the East Asian countries did not see the same degree of real appreciation as Mexico had.

SHORT-TERM DEBT-TO-RESERVES RATIO

The ability of this ratio to predict the crises of 1997 appears to be good. Table 6.5 shows that by the end of 1996, 11 developing countries (of the 42 for which data are available) had short-term debt to BIS-reporting banks to reserves ratios above 1.

The only countries with short-term debt-to-reserves ratios above 1 percent at the end of 1996 to economically perform reasonably well in the following two years were Argentina, Mexico and Singapore. As mentioned earlier, Malaysia's prudent policies toward short-term debt were not enough to prevent it from succumbing to the spread of the crisis. Thus, a debt-to-reserves ratio below 1 percent does not mean that a country is immune to a financial crisis. Although the ratio of short-term debt to reserves is not a good measure of solvency (which depends on the level of external debt and the expected future earnings from trade), it is a reasonably good indicator of crises since:

• it does measure liquidity and, therefore, a country's vulnerability to a banking crisis,

• a high short-term debt-to-reserves ratio may be a signal that a country's regulatory or macroeconomic policies are not prudent,

Table 6.5
Short-Term Debt-to-Reserves Ratio (by the end of 1996)

Country	Ratio	Country	Ratio
Indonesia	1.9	Russia	2.3
South Korea	2.0	Bulgaria	2.1
Thailand	1.2	Zimbabwe	1.3
Singapore	2.3	Argentina	1.4
Pakistan	5.1	Mexico	1.4
South Africa	11.6		

Source: World Bank.

- a high short-term debt-to-reserves ratio may indicate that high risk-taking investors are engaged in other high-risk activities (since it is highly risky to use short-term money to finance long-term investments),
- it may draw the attention of investors to the bad equilibrium of the balance of payments, and
- it is indicative of a country's vulnerability to a self-fulfilling withdrawal or flight of capital.

Finally, regardless of whether the ratio of debt to reserves is an accurate indicator of crises, it is clear that if a crisis occurs, it will be significantly more severe if a country does not have reserves to meet short-term obligations.

It behooves policymakers to assess the desirable level of short-term debt. A policy of keeping short-term debt below the level of reserves would certainly be a prudent one. However, if this means that additional short-term borrowing has to be offset by equal increases in reserves because the level of short-term debt has risen too fast, then the aforementioned policy is no longer prudent. This is so since this situation boils down to having a developing country borrowing from industrial-country banks at a high interest rate to relend the money to industrial-country governments at much lower interest rates. Assessment of the desirable level of short-term debt is not an easy task. In principle, we have to weigh the cost of short-term capital flows against the benefits. In particular, the quantification of the cost is not a simple matter since this calls for the determination of the cost of the greater volatility of the economy. The benefits depend on the marginal productivity of the extra investment being financed by the short-term capital. Since the savings rate was high in East Asia, the benefits of the extra capital accumulation that followed liberalization could well have been negative due to standard diminishing returns to capital and costs involved in selecting, implementing and monitoring new investment.

In examining ways of how to restrain capital flows, in particular short-term flows, we may learn from the Chilean experience. In 1991, Chile introduced controls on capital inflows through minimum nonremunerated reserve requirements on external borrowing which were required to be maintained for one year regardless of loan maturity, implying a tax on foreign borrowing that varies inversely with loan maturity. In 1995, these reserve requirements were further extended to all types of foreign financial investments, including issues of American Depository Receipts. Although the overall efficiency of such controls is sometimes questioned, most criticizers of the Chilean system acknowledge that the reserve requirement significantly lengthened the maturity position of capital inflows to Chile without having adverse effects on valuable long-term capital. During 1997–1998, Chile reduced the restrictions on capital inflows since they became less relevant in a period of capital outflows.

In Columbia, capital controls were introduced in 1993 through mandatory, unremunerated reserve requirements on direct external borrowing with a maturity of less than 18 months. The reserve requirements were subsequently tightened by setting a graduated reserve requirement on loans with maturities up to five years. The Chilean and Colombian capital controls may be thought of as an implicit tax that significantly increased the interest differential between domestic and foreign short-term interest rates. A number of econometric studies using this approach to quantify the impact on short-term flows suggest that this implicit tax resulted in a substantial change in the term structure of external borrowing (i.e., discouraging short-term inflows) in Chile and Columbia. An alternative to the Chilean system could be limiting the extent of tax deductibility for interest in debt denominated in, or linked to, foreign currencies. Naturally, the employment of other tax policies may be explored.

Most Latin American economies were not greatly affected by spillover effects from the devaluation of East Asian currencies in July/August, although the Brazilian stock market declined by 20 percent in July. The ability of Latin American countries to weather the storm can be explained by the following factors:

- Their previous experience of high inflation and large exchange rate changes have made lenders and borrowers of that part of the world familiar with and adverse to the risks of currency and maturity mismatches;

- Although considerable further progress is required to address financial weaknesses in many of the Latin American economies, countries in the region have been making progress in strengthening their financial systems (closure of some weak institutions, privatization of public banks, improvement of prudential regulation and bank supervision, and the easing of restrictions on foreign participation in the financial sector), particularly since the Mexican peso crisis of 1994–1995;

- In recent years, Latin American countries have not experienced lending booms comparable to those of the East Asian countries and domestic credit was a smaller share of GDP than in East Asia (in 1996, the ratio of net domestic credit to GDP varied from 20 to 70 percent in the major Latin American countries, compared to 55 to 136 percent in East Asia); and

• In recent years, a few of the Latin American countries have come to depend more heavily than most East Asian countries on direct foreign investment to finance current account deficits, which tends to be more stable in response to capital market shocks than debt flows and portfolio equity.

The rapid response by the policymakers, particularly in Brazil, contained contagion in the Latin American region. Brazil was perceived as vulnerable due to its high fiscal deficit (rather than high private capital inflows as in East Asia), relatively inflexible exchange rate regime and growing external account deficit. The government more than doubled nominal interest rate levels overnight and introduced an emergency package of fiscal measures projected to yield about 2.5 percent of GDP. In mid-December 1997, Congress approved the package with some amendments but the same aggregate impact.

In contrast, the severity of the East Asian crisis was probably increased by a hesitant policy response and political uncertainties. In Indonesia, uncertainty over the depth of commitment to restructuring the financial sector and concerns over the political transitions process are believed to have impeded recovery. In Thailand, the government did not move sufficiently quickly to deal with insolvent financial institutions and market confidence was further reduced by revelations that losses on forward foreign exchange transactions to defend the baht were substantially higher than believed. In Malaysia, government statements raised concerns over the possible imposition of capital controls, which encouraged further capital outflows.

Latin American countries with more flexible exchange rate systems, such as Chile, Columbia, Mexico and Peru, absorbed the external shocks by some depreciation of their currencies and some increase in interest rates. As discussed earlier, Chile and Columbia also may have avoided many of the difficulties affecting the East Asian economies due to policies discouraging short-term external borrowing.

The many investors who did not see the East Asian crisis coming often complain that the countries "lied" to them by not disclosing all the relevant information to them; the countries were not transparent. These investors should raise the question whether there was a lack of *relevant* information. The East Asian countries have statistical services that are significantly better than the average within the developing world. Our previous discussion identified several factors that appear to be related to crises:

• debt-to-reserves ratio,
• ratio of net domestic credit to GDP,
• incremental capital-output ratio,

- large current account deficits,
- lack of transparent and timely balance sheets and other information,
- the speculative real estate boom,
- level of international reserves, and
- the unhedged foreign exchange exposure of the financing structure of banks and firms.

Information about most of these factors was and is available with the statistical services and international organizations like the IMF and World Bank. In addition, there is no evidence that there was any significant misreporting on these critical variables. It therefore appears that investors who complain that the East Asian countries were not transparent had not done their homework. It is also noted that the major financial-cum-currency crises in Scandinavia roughly 15 years ago cast doubt on whether lack of transparency is a significant factor that leads to a financial crisis, since these countries were (and are) the paragons of transparency. What these countries did share with East Asia were rapid financial liberalization, fixed exchange rates and, in some cases a real estate boom and in others adverse external shocks.

The above discussion should not be interpreted as meaning that there is no room for improvement of transparency in the East Asian countries. For instance, in the East Asian crisis the market observed that some firms were weak but it could not easily identify which were and which were not. Consequently, the market shut off the supply of capital to all firms or charged all of them a high risk premium, thus exacerbating the downturn.

THE ROLE OF INTEREST RATES

The typical policymaker claims that a period of temporarily higher interest rates suffices to permanently strengthen the exchange rate. In addition, the fact that higher interest rates are only temporary is publicly announced. Some policymakers also claim that temporary higher interest rates are not very costly to the economy. One could argue that if a government makes a credible commitment to reform, interest rates do not necessarily have to rise at the time of the announcement of the "reform bailout." One could also argue that raising the interest rate only makes sense if the government and/or the market do not believe that the policy package is credible. In general, we conclude that the more credible the promised reforms, the less interest rates have to rise to defend the currency.

Unfortunately, our knowledge about how reforms affect future exchange rates is very limited since there are many market participants with different expectations, portfolios and preferences. In addition, policies may have one effect on outside investors and a different effect on those inside the country. Extreme care must be exercised with increasing interest rates if a country has low inflation and many firms with high debt-equity ratios because in this case the increased interest rate could result in banks reluctant to roll over the loans and/or to lend. Consequently, the number of bankruptcies will increase, which in turn could lead to a weaker rather than a stronger exchange rate. Thus, the exchange rate could be persistently weakened if the period of high interest rates leads to a long-lasting increase in the probability of bankruptcy.

It is of interest to compare the situation in East Asia with the one in Latin America towards the end of 1997. In East Asia, banks were very fragile, firms were highly leveraged, capital markets were not highly segmented and much of the debt was short-term. In addition, the economy was initially in a situation were aggregate demand and supply were roughly in balance. As a result, there were significant adverse macroeconomic effects from raising interest rates. These adverse effects, combined with the high indebtedness, led to a large increase in bankruptcy probabilities, lowering expected returns and thus making investments less, not more attractive, in the country. In Latin America, firms were (and are) not highly indebted and, in most cases, capital markets are highly segmented so that, for instance, an increase in the interbank lending rate does not get translated into higher lending rates for most borrowers. Most debt was long term. Consequently, increases in interest rates may have worked in stabilizing the economy in Latin America. That is not to say that in some countries substantial macroeconomic sacrifices were made.

When speculative pressures on the Brazilian real increased in October 1997, the authorities responded by raising the overnight interest rate from 30 percent to 70 percent. After having stayed at high levels for almost two months, the Brazilian authorities brought the interest rates down to pre-attack levels. The exchange rate maintained its trajectory even after the rates were lowered. The Indonesian experience was quite different from the one in Brazil. In the aftermath of Thailand's devaluation, the rupiah fell by about 6 percent. In mid-August speculative pressures intensified and the rupiah fell by another 10 percent. The Indonesian authorities responded by raising interest rates from 20 percent to almost 100 percent. After one and a half months, the authorities tried to lower the rates only to see the exchange rate slip, leading them to quickly raise rates again. When rates eventually came down to 40 percent (20 percent higher than their pre-crisis level), the exchange rate began to drop. In both the Brazilian and Indonesian situations, the high interest rates prevented the currency from depreciating. Why did the exchange rate maintain its value after interest rates were reduced in Brazil but not in Indonesia? Although many factors may have played a role, the following two observations perhaps best explain the reason:

- Due to its greater financial fragility, Indonesia's economy was more sensitive to high interest rates than Brazil's. As a result, the increase in the probability of bankruptcy was significantly higher in Indonesia than in Brazil. Consequently, the direct economic effect on the interest rate hikes in Indonesia was probably to weaken rather than strengthen the equilibrium exchange rate.

- Brazil was subject to a temporary shock which could have been a period of irrational contagion. The high interest rates provided a defense of the currency that was required only until the market regained its senses. Indonesia, on the other hand, was subject to a much larger permanent shock and the attack on the rupiah was more rationally grounded and could not be defended. Thus, when interest rates were reduced, the exchange rate quickly depreciated to its equilibrium value.

Unfortunately, existing macroeconomic models do not predict crises and the consequences of higher interest rates, since they simply summarize financial markets in money demand equations rather than explaining how the growth of modern finance has changed the dynamics of market economics.

It is noted that a large depreciation of a currency may also result in a substantially higher probability that firms will default on their foreign currency denominated debts. This, together with weaker economic conditions, reduces capital inflows and decreases the demand for the local currency. Normally, exchange rate depreciation leads to increased exports and, hence, greater demand for local currency. The aforementioned decrease in demand for the local currency due to the large depreciation of a currency may more than offset the increased demand for local currency to export.

In the above discussion we emphasized the role of the probability of bankruptcy and increased uncertainty about the future. As a result, increased interest rates can lead to stronger or weaker exchange rates. The effect of higher interest rates could outweigh the higher default probability in the short run and thus increase the expected return. Consequently, the exchange rate would strengthen, at least in the short run. To enhance our understanding of the macroeconomic and financial effects of high interest rates, we list the following channels through which interest rates affect the economy:

- *Debtors' Net Worth.* Higher interest rates significantly erode debtors' net worth, leading them to reduce investment, employment, inventories and production (Chapter 5). In addition, increases in interest rates result in a decrease in asset values, which further undermines the value of banks, which unavoidably have long-term assets and short-term liabilities. It may take some time before the depletion of net worth resulting from temporary higher interest rates is restored and, consequently, these higher rates may do more harm than good.

- *Portfolio Effects.* Although the higher interest rate is likely to make holding the country's interest-bearing securities more attractive, this will be offset by a markedly lower value of net worth due to the higher probability of default and the generally perceived higher riskiness. A decrease in the value of domestic assets will lead to a portfolio shift away from domestic assets. In fact, domestic residents often move their money out first since they are better informed about the problems in the country. Future taxes that may need to be imposed to repay debt (particularly when the government assumes responsibility for it) may exacerbate this tendency, as happened in Latin America in the 1980s. Gross capital outflows by residents is often referred to as *capital flight*.

- *Financial Distress Effects*. The decline in net worth may lead some firms to follow selfish strategies or engage in looting behavior. Examples of such strategies are (a) firms near bankruptcy may take great chances because they think they are using some-one else's (i.e., bondholders') money and (b) firms near bankruptcy may pay out extra dividends, leaving less in the firm for bondholders in case of bankruptcy. In the finan-cial sector such behavior has been credited with exacerbating the problems of that sector and increasing the losses, as in the case of the S&L debacle in the United States. It is also noted that sometimes the taint of impending bankruptcy suffices to drive away customers. For example, when the Chrysler automobile company skirted insolvency in the 1970s, a number of its loyal customers switched to other car manufacturers because of fear that parts and service would not be available were Chrysler to fail.

- *Bankruptcy Effect*. Even with a well-functioning bankruptcy law with a smoothly work-ing Chapter 11, as in the United States, bankruptcy can have severely disruptive effects. First, the organizational capital that is the firm's core asset dissipates quickly after its bankruptcy and rebuilding that capital may be a costly and lengthy process. Second, the bankruptcy of some firms has adverse effects on the net worth of that firm's cred-itors, especially of banks. To offset the effects of bankruptcy, old firms have to be expanded and/or new ones have to be created. Neither of these events is likely to happen in the midst of a recession.

- *Credit Availability*. As financial institutions go bankrupt and banks reduce their lending, credit may become highly constrained. Consequently, a credit crunch may occur and the economic downturn will be exacerbated. In fact, the higher interest rates offered on government securities may induce banks to hold their assets in these securities rather than lending (especially if the level of government indebtedness is low so that the probability of default is low). Severe liquidity constraints imposed by a weakening financial system make it difficult for firms to find outside financing while the low level of profits associated with an economic downturn makes it difficult to finance investment expansion through retained earnings. Consequently, even short-lived interest rate in-creases could have persistent negative effects.

- *Information Effects*. Large interest rate hikes lead to increased imperfections of infor-mation about, for instance, net worth values of firms, since these hikes change asset values and there is almost always imperfect information about asset structures of firms. These adverse information effects make decisions regarding lending and increased risk premia more difficult. As a result, the chances of misallocation of resources are in-creased and contribute further to the contraction of the economy.

As firms reduce their employment, aggregate demand is reduced further. As the uncertainty of the reduction in credit availability and the anxiety caused by increased bankruptcies are felt, even firms that do not face credit constraints may reduce their demand for investment. The reduced demand pushes more firms into bankruptcy. In other words, the probability of bankruptcy and the increase in uncertainty are increasing functions of the interest rate.

Interest rate increases and exchange rate depreciations create winners and losers. It is important to raise the following questions while analyzing the potential effects of the increases and depreciations:

- Who are the winners and losers?
- What is the net magnitude of the gains and losses?
- How long will it take for the winners to feel the gains and for the losers to feel the losses?
- What is the role of compensatory policies (if any) in minimizing losses?

In the case of a weaker exchange rate, exporters and net holders of foreign assets will benefit, while those relying on imports and net debtors in foreign currency will lose. It takes on average 16 to 18 months for exports to rise after an exchange rate depreciation. The rise in exports is expected to increase overall output, although this need not be the case for very large devaluations, which may increase bankruptcies just as high interest rates do. Unexpected increases in interest rates hurt fixed-rate creditors and variable rate debtors. They typically weaken financial institutions and result in a lower level of investment and thus, lower output.

The examination of the trade-offs of interest rate increases and exchange rate depreciations depends on the domestic circumstances. If the primary concern is the likelihood of a financial crisis, exchange rate decreases should get a higher priority than interest rate increases since:

- well-managed firms normally can easily find cover for their exchange rate risk; however, even these well-managed firms will have some indebtedness which leaves them exposed to large increases in interest rates, especially when these increases coincide with an economic downturn;
- from the equity point of view, we may ask ourselves "why should borrowers in general (i.e., workers and firms), all of whom will be adversely affected by interest rate increases, be made to pay the price to benefit speculators?" (the increase in interest rates would only be desirable if everybody in the economy would benefit, which is highly unlikely);
- high interest rates have adverse effects on all firms with short-term debt and/or loans with variable interest rates, including small firms that never gambled by taking on liabilities denominated in foreign exchange; very high interest rates can bring bankruptcy even to firms with moderate indebtedness; and
- if a government is serious with stabilizing the exchange rate it should commit itself not to intervene to stabilize the exchange rate, either directly or through interest rate policies, since every intervention will reinforce the belief that the government will be there to help stabilize the exchange rate.

A useful lesson on what needs not to be done and what needs to be done under conditions of high indebtedness can be drawn from recent US history. During the 1980s, recovery in the Unites States was driven by spending financed by increased indebtedness relative to income. The government, business firms and consumers all raised their indebtedness to unprecedented levels, while financial institutions increased their lending against risky assets. This meant that corporate as well as household incomes and spending became increasingly sensitive to interest rates. After the 1987 crash, the Fed started tightening by introducing tax increases and a less expansionary fiscal policy in order to check asset-price inflation. The result was one of the deepest post-war recessions. However, in reaction to the weakness in the financial system and the economy, the Fed started to reduce short-term interest rates in the early 1990s, almost to negative levels in real terms, thus providing relief not only for banks, but also for firms and households, which were able to refinance debt at substantially lower interest servicing costs. This eventually produced a boom in the securities market, thereby lowering long-term interest rates, helping to restore balance-sheet positions and producing a strong recovery at the end of 1993.

Appendix 5 discusses the establishment of cash flows of a direct foreign investment and how to deal with issues of changing exchange rates, inflation and taxation. It also introduces the concepts of *net present value* and *modified internal rate of return*.

MATCHING LIABILITIES WITH ASSETS

Banks sometimes invest large portions of their assets in mortgages with long durations and fixed interest rates. An asset's *duration* is the weighted average time of its cash flows. If much of the funds available for mortgages are financed by short-term credit such as savings accounts, a bank is faced with a large interest rate risk because any increase in interest rates would significantly reduce the value of the mortgages. The bank's equity would be reduced since an interest rate rise would only reduce the value of liabilities slightly.

The matching of liabilities with assets is also important in other areas of finance. For instance, the manager of a pension fund with obligations to retirees analogous to interest payments on debt, and with assets of the fund invested in fixed-income securities, should choose pension assets so that their duration is matched with the duration of the liabilities. In this way, changing interest rates will not affect the value of a pension fund. Another example pertains to insurance firms, which frequently invest in bonds whereby the duration is matched with the duration of future death benefits. Similarly, leasing companies often structure debt financing so that the duration of the debt matches the duration of the leases.

The concept of matching liabilities with assets is based on the market-value balance sheet, which is a useful tool in financial analysis (Chapter 5). It has the same form as the balance sheet used by accountants. Thus, assets are placed on the left side and liabilities and owners' equity on the right. In addition, the left and right sides must be equal. However, the difference in this balance sheet is in the numbers. Financiers value items in terms of the market value, whereas

Table 6.6
Market-Value Balance Sheet of Bank XYZ

Assets	Market Value	Duration
Overnight money	$ 40M	0
Accounts receivable-backed loans	750M	3 months
Inventory loans	375M	6 months
Industrial loans	85M	24 months
Mortgages	250M	180 months
	$1,500M	
Liabilities and Owners' Equity		
Checking and savings accounts	$ 550M	0
Certificates of deposit	450M	12 months
Long-term financing	300M	120 months
Equity	200M	
	$1,500M	

accountants value items in terms of historical cost (original purchase price less depreciation).

Let us consider the following example in order to enhance our understanding of the concept of matching liabilities with assets. Consider the market-value balance sheet of Bank XYZ, as shown in Table 6.6. The bank has $1,500 million in assets and $1,300 million in liabilities. Thus, its equity is the difference between the two (or $200 million). Table 6.6 shows both the market value and the duration of each individual item of Bank XYZ's balance sheet. Note that overnight money and checking and savings accounts have a duration of zero, since interest paid on these instruments adjusts immediately to changing interest rates in the market.

The managers of Bank XYZ believe that interest rates are likely to move quickly in the coming month but do not know in which direction. Hence, they are concerned about the bank's vulnerability to changing interest rates. To make the bank immune to the risk of changing interest rates, the following relationship must hold:

(duration of assets)(market value of assets) =
(duration of liabilities)(market value of liabilities)

Thus, we first establish the duration of assets and the duration of liabilities:

Duration of assets = 0($40M)/($1,500M) + ¼($750M)/($1,500M) +
½($375M)/($1,500M) + 2($85M)/($1,500M) +
15($250M)/($1,500M) = 2.86 years,

Duration of liabilities = 0($550M)/($1,300M) + 1($450M)/($1,300M) +
10($300M)/($1,300M) = 2.65 years.

In these calculations we assumed that the duration of a group of items is a weighted average of the duration of the individual items (weighted by the market value of each item). This simplification significantly increases the concept's practicality.

In order not to violate the aforementioned relationship, we must now either decrease the duration of the assets without changing the duration of the liabilities or increase the duration of the liabilities without changing the duration of the assets, as follows. Decrease the duration of the assets to:

(duration of liabilities)(market value of liabilities/market value of assets) =
2.65($1,300M/$1,500M) = 2.30 years,

or increase the duration of liabilities to:

(duration of assets)(market value of assets/market value of liabilities) =
2.86($1,500M/$1,300M) = 3.30 years.

In other words, to make the bank immune to the risk of changing interest rates, we can either decrease the duration of the assets from 2.86 years to 2.30 years and keep the duration of the liabilities at 2.65 years or increase the duration of liabilities from 2.65 years to 3.30 years and keep the duration of the assets at 2.86 years. In the former case, we get (2.30)($1,500M) = (2.65)($1,300)— the equality is approximate rather than exact due to rounding—and in the latter case, we have (2.86)($1,500M) = (3.30)($1,300M). Thus, in either case the aforementioned relationship holds. A decrease in the duration of the assets may be achieved by replacing some of the mortgages of the balance sheet by inventory loans; an increase in the duration of the liabilities may be realized by replacing certificates of deposits by long-term financing. If replacements cannot be obtained, the management of Bank XYZ could add short-term loans to assets or long-term financing to liabilities.

Finally, in this example it would be incorrect to simply match the duration of the assets (2.86 years) with that of the liabilities (2.65 years) because the assets total $1,500M while the liabilities total only $1,300M. That is, if, in another problem, the durations of the assets and the liabilities are approximately the same, we cannot conclude that the bank is immune to risk of changing interest rates because the aforementioned relationship is not likely to hold.

FINANCIAL DISTRESS

Although debt may provide tax benefits to a firm, it also exerts pressure because interest and principal payments are obligations. The firm may risk some

Table 6.7
Cash Flows of Companies *ABC* and *XYZ*

	Company *ABC*		Company *XYZ*	
	Boom times[1]	Recession[2]	Boom times[1]	Recession[2]
Cash flow	$100	$50	$100	$50
Payment of interest and principal on debt	45	45	60	30
Distribution to stockholders	$ 55	$ 5	$ 40	$ 0

[1]Probability of boom times is 50 percent.
[2]Probability of a recession is 50 percent.

sort of financial distress if these obligations are not met. In most cases it is difficult to arrive at a precise estimation of the cost of financial distress. Sometimes, the taint of impending bankruptcy suffices to drive away customers. As mentioned earlier, when the Chrysler automobile company skirted insolvency in the 1970s, a number of loyal customers switched to other car manufacturers because of fear that parts and service would not be available were Chrysler to fail.

The ultimate distress is *bankruptcy*, whereby ownership of the company's assets is legally transferred from the stockholders to the bondholders. Let us consider the following simple example to examine the effect of the possibility of bankruptcy on the value of a firm. The example ignores taxes since we want to concentrate on costs related to a possible bankruptcy.

Suppose two companies, *ABC* and *XYZ*, have the cash flows shown in Table 6.7. Company *ABC* plans to be in business for one more year and expects a cash flow of either $100 or $50 in the coming year, depending on whether boom times or a recession will take place. Each of these possibilities has a probability of occurrence of 50 percent. Previously issued debt requires *ABC* to make payments of $45 on interest and principal. Company *XYZ* has identical cash flow prospects but has $60 of interest and principal obligations. Table 6.7 indicates that company *XYZ* will be bankrupt in a recession. Under American law, corporations have limited liability. That is, *XYZ*'s bondholders will receive only $30 in a recession (*XYZ* has $20 in bankruptcy costs) and cannot get the additional $30 from the stockholders.

Although one normally assumes that investors are risk averse, we assume, for simplicity, that both bondholders and stockholders are risk neutral, and therefore, the cost of debt capital equals the cost of equity capital. Consequently, cash flows to both stockholders and bondholders are to be discounted at the interest rate, which we assume to be 10 percent. We evaluate the debt, D; the equity, S; and the value, V, of the entire firm for both *ABC* and *XYZ* as follows:

Company ABC	Company XYZ

$S = [0.5(\$55) + 0.5(\$5)]/1.10$

$= \$27.27$

$D = [0.5(\$45) + 0.5(\$45)]/1.10$

$= \$40.91$

$V = S + D = \$68.18$

$S = [0.5(\$40) + 0.5(\$0)]/1.10$

$= \$18.18$

$D = [0.5(\$60) + 0.5(\$30)]/1.10$

$= \$40.91$

$V = S + D = \$59.09$

The bondholders of company *XYZ* only receive $30 because the cash flow is only $50. Since they are likely to hire lawyers to negotiate or sue the company, the management of *XYZ* is also likely to hire lawyers to defend itself. Additional costs will be incurred by company *XYZ* if the case goes to a bankruptcy court. In this simple example we assume that bankruptcy costs amount to $50 − $30 = $20. It is clear that in the real world these costs will be much higher since lawyers' fees are high. The fees related to bankruptcy costs are always paid before the bondholders get paid. If, in the example, the costs of bankruptcy were zero, the bondholders of company *XYZ* would receive $50. Determining the value of the company in the same manner gives, for this case, *V* = $68.18. In other words, companies *ABC* and *XYZ* have the same value, even though *XYZ* runs the risk of bankruptcy. By comparing *XYZ*'s value in a world with no bankruptcy costs (*V* = $68.18) to *XYZ*'s value with such costs (*V* = $59.09), we conclude that the possibility of bankruptcy has a negative effect on the value of the company. It is, however, impossible to quantify this negative effect, since this depends on the number of lawyers' hours to be hired and the *selfish strategies* described earlier.

COVERAGE RATIOS

Management can control the probability of financial distress by limiting the amount of interest to which the firm commits. It does so by determining the probability of a firm's operating income smaller than or equal to a specified amount. Assuming that the probability distribution of the firm's possible operating incomes is approximately normal, we are able to determine this probability by using the table in Appendix 6, which presents probabilities of a value of Z being smaller than (or equal to) the values tabulated in the margins.

The Z value is defined as follows:

$$Z = [P - E(P)]/\sigma$$

where:

P = the net present value considered for the use of Appendix 6
$E(P)$ = expected net present value
σ = the standard deviation of possible net present values

To illustrate the use of the above expression and Appendix 6, let us assume that the net present value (NPV) and standard deviation of a project are $2,592,000 and $1,718,000, respectively, and that we wish to determine the probability that this net present value will be equal to or less than zero. Thus, in the above equation we enter $P = 0$, $E(P) = 42,592,000$, and $\sigma = 1,718,000$, and find:

$$Z = [0 - 2,592,00]/1,718,000 = -1.509$$

Looking in Appendix 6, we find that there is a 0.0559 probability that the NPV of our project will be zero or less. Notice that the numerals 1.5 and 09 of $Z = -1.509$ are read from the left and upper margins of Appendix 6, respectively. It is noted that Appendix 6 can also be used to find the probability that the NPV is greater than a specific value; in this case the expression for the Z value would be positive rather than negative.

Suppose a firm's operating income before interest and taxes (EBIT) over the past years has a normal distribution with a mean of $1,500,000 and a standard deviation of $450,000, and suppose the firm wishes to limit interest payments to $500,000. In this case we can determine the Z value as follows:

$$Z = [500,000 - 1,5000,000]/450,000 = -2.22$$

Next, we find, with the help of Appendix 6, that there is about a 1 percent chance that the firm will experience a shortfall in EBIT so severe that it cannot cover its interest.

Since management is often reluctant to work with probabilities and Z tables because the concepts are difficult to understand, there is another way to view this by considering the *expected coverage*, namely:

interest coverage $= 1,500,000/500,000 = 3$

Thus, maintaining an interest coverage ratio of 3 is equivalent to restricting the probability of distress to about 1 percent for this firm.

Alternatively, if the firm limits interest to $750,000, the Z value is:

$$Z = [750,000 - 1,500,000]/450,000 = -1.67$$

Now there is about a 5 percent chance that the firm's income will not cover its interest expense. In this case the expected coverage is:

interest coverage $= 1,500,000/750,000 = 2$

Thus, a coverage of 2 corresponds to a probability of distress of 5 percent for this firm.

In general, higher coverage means a lower chance of getting into financial difficulty. The various possibilities for the above-mentioned example are as follows:

Expected Coverage	Chance of a Shortfall
3.0	0.01
2.0	0.05
1.5	0.13
1.0	0.50

In other words, by targeting a minimum interest coverage ratio, management can control the risk of a shortfall. An expected coverage ratio of 1.0 means there is a 50:50 chance that income from operations will not cover interest payments. In general, the higher the coverage, the lower the likelihood of a firm being unable to cover its interest payments.

In the example, we used the *interest-rate coverage ratio*, or *the times interest earned ratio* defined as EBIT/(interest expense). Thus, we ignored principal repayments since most companies can reschedule their loans if they cannot make the principal repayments. However, we could use the *times burden covered ratio* and develop a similar argument if we do not wish to ignore principal repayments. The times burden covered ratio is defined as follows:

$$\text{times burden covered} = \text{EBIT}/[\text{interest} + \text{principal repayment}/(1 - \text{tax rate})]$$

When we include the principal repayment as part of a company's financial burden, we must express the figure on a before-tax basis comparable to interest and EBIT. Unlike interest payments, principal repayments are not a tax-deductible expense. In the definition of the times burden covered ratio, the before-tax burden of the principal repayment is found by dividing the repayment by 1 minus the company's tax rate. For instance, if a company is in, say, the 50 percent tax bracket, it must earn $2 before taxes to have $1 after taxes to pay creditors. (The other dollar goes to the tax collector.)

How much coverage is enough? The answer to this question depends on (1) variability and (2) vulnerability. The variability relates to how likely the firm is to experience dramatic declines in operating income (EBIT), while the vulnerability is an indication of bankruptcy cost or how much of the firm's value could be lost in the event of financial distress. In general, the higher the variability and vulnerability, the greater the target coverage ratio required.

If vulnerability increases, how can the firm maintain the same probability of distress as before? It can do so by increasing its coverage, namely, by lowering interest payments through using less debt and more equity to finance investments. For instance, in the example of the firm with an expected operating income of $1,500,000 and a standard deviation of $450,000, we observed that it could limit the chance of financial distress to 5 percent with an interest rate coverage of 2. When the variability increases so that the standard deviation becomes $600,000, the firm must increase coverage to 3 to maintain the 5 percent chance of distress.

We can only use the Z table of Appendix 6 if we are willing to assume that the probability distribution of possible NPVs or operating incomes is approximately normal. In view of the Central Limit Theorem of mathematical statistics, there is a good chance that this approximation is reasonable. This theorem informs us that when summing random variables having distributions other than normal, the distribution of the sum still approaches a normal distribution under certain conditions. The required conditions are not very stringent. Although the most common version of the Central Limit Theory requires that the random variables be independent and identically distributed, various other versions also exist in which one or both assumptions can be replaced by much weaker conditions.

Chebyshev's Inequality Theorem rather than Appendix 6 may be used to make reasonable strong probability statements if the normal distribution assumption cannot be made. A discussion of this theorem requires an advanced knowledge of mathematical statistics and is, therefore, not presented here. Readers with such knowledge will most likely be able to use Chebyshev's Inequality Theorem, since the approach is similar to the one used in Appendix 6.

SUGGESTIONS FOR FURTHER READING

Arogyaswamy, Bernard. *The Asian Miracle, Myth, and Mirage.* Westport, CT: Quorum Books, 1998.

Mourdoukoutas, Panos. *Collective Entrepreneurship in a Globalizing Economy.* Westport, CT: Quorum Books, 1999.

Organization for Economic Co-operation and Development (OECD). *Regulatory Reform in the Global Economy: Asian and Latin American Perspectives.* Paris: OECD, 1998.

Rao, C. P. *Globalization, Privatization and Free Market Economy.* Westport, CT: Quorum Books, 1999.

Richter, Frank-Jürgen. *Business Networks in Asia.* Westport, CT: Quorum Books, 1999.

Chapter 7

Managing Foreign Exchange Exposure

TYPES OF FOREIGN EXCHANGE EXPOSURE

Foreign exchange exposure can be classified as *transaction exposure, operating exposure* and *accounting exposure*. Transaction exposure measures changes in the value of outstanding financial obligations incurred prior to a change in exchange rates but not due to be settled until after the exchange rates change. In other words, transaction exposure deals with changes in cash flows that result from existing contractual obligations. Operating exposure measures the change in the present value of a firm as a result from any change in the future operating cash flows of the firm caused by an unexpected change in exchange rates. The change in value depends on the impact of the exchange rate change on future costs, prices and/or sales volume. It is noted that both transaction exposure and operating exposure are the result of unexpected changes in future cash flows. The difference lies in the fact that transaction exposure deals with pre-existing cash flows which will occur in the near future, whereas operating exposure is concerned with expected future cash flows that are potentially affected by changing international competitiveness. Accounting exposure is the potential for accounting-derived changes in owners' equity that occur because of the need to "translate" foreign currency financial statements of foreign affiliates into a single reporting currency to prepare worldwide consolidated statements. It is noted that operating exposure is sometimes referred to as *competitive exposure, economic exposure* or *strategic exposure*. Accounting exposure is also called *translation exposure*.

Many MNCs manage their currency exposure through *hedging*. An MNC hedges by taking a position, such as acquiring a cash flow, an asset or a contract that will rise (fall) in value and offset a drop (rise) in value of an existing

Figure 7.1
Impact of Hedging on a Company's Expected Cash Flows

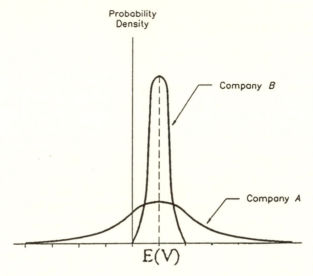

position. In other words, hedging protects the owner of an existing asset from loss. Financial theory defines the value of a firm as the net present value of all expected future cash flows. If the currency value of these cash flows changes due to changes in exchange rates, an MNC that hedges its currency exposures reduces some of the variance in the value of its expected cash flows. Thus, currency risk can be defined as variance in expected cash flows arising from exchange rate changes. Figure 7.1 presents the probability distributions of expected net cash flows (NCFs) of two identical companies A and B; the only difference between the two companies is that company A does not hedge, while B does. The figure demonstrates that hedging NCFs narrows the distribution about the mean of the distribution or it reduces currency risk. It is important to realize that hedging does not shift the mean [the expected value of the firm or E(V) in Figure 7.1] of the distribution to the right; consequently, it does not increase the value of Company B.

If hedging only reduces the variability of cash flows, we may ask ourselves whether it is worth the effort. Hedging is likely to be worthwhile since it results in:

- a reduction of risk in future cash flows, which improves the MNC's planning capability and reduces the likelihood that its cash flows fall below necessary minimum or the point of *financial distress*; and

- management's comparative advantage over the individual stockholder in knowing the actual currency risk of the MNC.

Naturally, a disadvantage of hedging is that precious resources of the MNC are used.

TRANSACTION EXPOSURE

Transaction exposure arises from:

- borrowing or lending funds when repayment is to be made in a foreign currency,
- purchasing or selling on credit goods or services whose prices are stated in foreign currencies,
- being a party to an unperformed foreign exchange forward contract, and
- otherwise acquiring assets or incurring liabilities denominated in foreign currencies.

For example, suppose a US firm borrowed SF100,000 in 1971 at a time when that amount of Swiss francs was worth US$25,000. If the loan came due six years later, the cost of repayment of principal would have been US$55,000, or more than double the amount borrowed. Another example pertains to selling on credit. Suppose a US company sells merchandise on open account to an Austrian buyer for ASh600,000, payment to be made in 60 days. The current exchange rate is ASh11/$ and the US seller expects to exchange the ASh600,000 for $54,545 when payment is received. Transaction exposure arises since the US seller may receive something other than $54,545. For instance, if the exchange rate is ASh12/$ when payment is received, the seller will get only $50,000; however, if the exchange rate is ASh10/$, the seller will get $60,000. Naturally, the seller may insist that he/she be paid in US dollars (although he/she may not obtain the sale by doing so). This does not eliminate the currency risk but transfers it to the Austrian buyer.

Another example involves the hedging of an existing transaction exposure by buying a *forward* exchange contract. For instance, a US firm may want to offset an existing obligation to purchase DM1 million to pay for an import from Germany in 60 days. One way to offset this payable is to purchase DM1 million in the forward market for delivery in 60 days. In this manner any change in the value of the mark relative to the dollar will be neutralized. The account payable will cost more if the mark increases in value; however, the forward contract has already fixed the number of dollars needed to buy the DM1 million. In other words, the potential loss, or gain, on the account payable is offset by the transaction gain or loss in the forward market.

To illustrate how *contractual hedging techniques* may be used to protect against transaction exposure, we consider the following example. A US manufacturing firm *XYZ* sells a data processing system (DPS) to *ABC*, a Swiss firm, in March for SF1,000,000. Payment is due three months later, in June. *XYZ*'s cost of capital is 12 percent. The following quotes are available:

- Spot exchange rate: $0.5210/SF
- Three-month forward rate: $0.5170/SF
- Swiss three-month borrowing interest rate: 10.0% (or 2.5%/quarter)
- Swiss three-month investment interest rate: 8.0% (or 2.0%/quarter)
- US three-month borrowing interest rate: 8.0% (or 2.0%/quarter)
- US three-month investment interest rate: 6.0% (or 1.5%/quarter)
- June put option in the over-the-counter (bank) market for SF1,000,000; strike price $0.5130 (nearly at-the-money); 1.5% premium
- June put option in the over-the-counter (bank) market for SF1,000,000; strike price $0.4800 (out-of-the-money); 1.0% premium
- *XYZ*'s foreign exchange advisory service forecasts that the spot rate in three months will be $0.5200/SF

XYZ is concerned about the possibility that the Swiss franc will fall since it operates on relatively narrow margins. When *XYZ* budgeted this contract, it determined that its minimum acceptable margin was at a sales price of $490,000. The *budget rate*, the lowest acceptable dollar per Swiss franc exchange rate, was, therefore, established at $0.4900/SF. Any exchange rate below this budget rate would result in a loss on the transaction for *XYZ*. Four alternatives are available to *XYZ*: remain unhedged; hedge in the forward market; hedge in the money market; and hedge in the options market.

XYZ may decide to accept the transaction risk if it believes its foreign exchange advisor, since it would receive SF1,000,000 × $0.5200/SF = $520,000 in three months. However, that amount is at risk. If the Swiss franc would fall to, say, $0.4850/SF, *XYZ* would only receive $485,000. On the other hand, if the Swiss franc would strengthen even more than forecast by the advisor, *XYZ* could receive considerably more than $520,000. The essence of the unhedged approach is as follows:

Today   **Three months hence**

Do nothing   Receive and sell SF1,000,000
                                                   and receive dollars at spot
                                                   rate existing then

XYZ could also have entered into a *forward contract* at the time when the sale was booked to *ABC* as an account receivable (March). A forward contract is a private contract or agreement to buy or sell an asset at a fixed price (called the *delivery price*) at a specific date in the future. Funds to fulfill the contract will be available in June, when *ABC* pays SF1,000,000 to *XYZ*. Thus, if *XYZ* wishes to hedge its transaction exposure in the forward market, it will sell

SF1,000,000 today at the three-month forward quotation of $0.5170/SF. This is a *covered* (also called *perfect* or *square*) transaction in which the firm no longer has any exchange risk. In three months it will receive SF1,000,000 from *ABC*, deliver that sum to the bank against its forward sale, and receive $517,000. This certain sum is $3,000 less than the uncertain $520,000 from the unhedged position since the forward quotation differs from the firm's three-month forecast. Naturally, under the unhedged position *XYZ* could also receive considerably less than $520,000. The essence of the forward hedge is as follows:

Today   Three months hence

Sell SF1,000,000   Receive and deliver
forward @ $0.5170/SF   SF1,000,000 against
                                                        forward sale; receive
                                                        $517,000

Like the aforementioned forward hedge (also called a forward market hedge), a *money market hedge* also involves a contract and a source of funds to fulfill that contract. In this instance the contract is a loan agreement. The firm seeking the money market hedge borrows in one currency and exchanges the proceeds for another currency. To hedge in the money market, *XYZ* will borrow Swiss francs in Switzerland at once, immediately convert the borrowed Swiss francs into dollars, and repay the Swiss franc loan in three months with the proceeds from the sale of the DPS. *XYZ* needs to borrow just enough to repay both the principal and interest with the sale proceeds. Assuming that x is the amount of Swiss francs to borrow at 10 percent per annum, or 2.5 percent for three months, we have:

$$1.025x = \text{SF1,000,000 or}$$
$$x = \text{SF975,610}$$

XYZ should borrow SF975,610 and in three months repay that amount plus SF24,390 of interest from the sale proceeds. In addition, it should exchange the SF975,610 loan proceeds for dollars at the current spot exchange rate of $0.5210/SF, receiving $508,293 at once. The essence of the money market hedge is as follows:

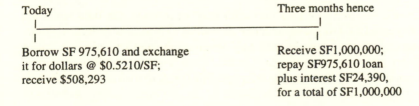

Today   Three months hence

Borrow SF 975,610 and exchange   Receive SF1,000,000;
it for dollars @ $0.5210/SF;   repay SF975,610 loan
receive $508,293   plus interest SF24,390,
                                                        for a total of SF1,000,000

In order to compare the forward hedge with the money market hedge, we have to examine how *XYZ* will use the loan proceeds in the next three months. If *XYZ* is cash rich, the loan proceeds may be invested in US dollar market instruments, yielding 6 percent per annum. It may also use the Swiss franc loan proceeds to substitute for an equivalent dollar loan that it would otherwise have taken at an assumed rate of 8 percent per annum. Finally, *XYZ* may invest the loan proceeds in the general operations of the firm, in which case the cost of capital of 12 percent per annum would be the appropriate rate. The future value at the end of three months under each of these investment alternatives is as follows:

Received Today	*Invested at*	*Future Value in Three Months*
$508,293	1.5%/quarter	$515,917
$508,293	2.0%/quarter	$518,459
$508,293	3.0%/quarter	$523,542

Since the proceeds in three months from the forward hedge would be $517,000, the money market hedge would be superior to the forward hedge if *XYZ* used the loan proceeds to replace a dollar loan (8%) or to conduct general business operations (12%). A break-even investment rate can be established that would make *XYZ* indifferent between the forward hedge and the money market hedge. Assuming that r is the unknown three-month investment rate, expressed as a decimal, that would equalize the proceeds from the forward hedge and the money market hedge, we have:

$$(\text{loan proceeds})(1 + r) = (\text{forward proceeds})$$
$$508,293(1 + r) = \$517,000$$
$$r = 0.0171$$

Assuming a 360-day financial year, we can convert the three-month investment rate to an annual percentage equivalent:

$$0.0171(360/90)(100\%) = 6.84\%$$

Thus, if *XYZ* can invest the loan proceeds at a rate higher than 6.84 percent per annum, it would prefer the money market hedge. If it is unable to do so, it would prefer the forward hedge. A money market hedge can cover a single transaction like *XYZ*'s SF1,000,000 receivable, or repeated transactions. Hedging repeated transactions is called *matching*, which requires an MNC to match the expected foreign currency cash inflows and outflows by currency and maturity.

It is noted that the cost of the forward hedge depends on the forward rate quotation, whereas the cost of the money market hedge is determined by differential interest rates. In efficient markets, interest rate parity (Chapter 1) would ensure that these costs are nearly the same; however, not all markets are efficient at all times. In addition, the difference in interest rates faced by a private MNC which is borrowing in two separate national markets may be different than the difference in risk-free government rates in these markets. It is the latter differential that is relevant for interest rate parity.

XYZ could also cover its SF1,000,000 exposure by purchasing a put option (Chapter 1). In this instance *XYZ* can speculate on the upside potential for appreciation of the Swiss franc while limiting downside risk to a known amount. It can purchase from its bank a three-month put option on SF1,000,000 at either (a) a nearly at-the-money (ATM) strike price of $0.5130/SF and a premium cost of 1.50 percent, or (b) an out-of-the-money (OTM) strike price of $0.4800/SF and a premium cost of 1.00 percent. It is noted that an option with a strike price which is (nearly) the same as the forward rate is called *forward at-the-money* and an option with a strike price which is below the forward rate is called *forward out-of-the-money*. The cost of the option with a strike price of $0.5130/SF is:

(size of the option)(premium)(spot rate) = (cost of option)
SF1,000,000 × 0.015 × $0.5210/SF = $7,815.

The premium cost of the option has to be projected three months forward since we are using future value to compare the hedging alternatives. We could again justify several investment rates (6%, 8% and 12% per annum); for the sake of brevity, we will use the cost of capital or 12 percent per annum (3% per quarter). Consequently, the premium cost of the put option as of June would be $7,815 × (1.03) = $8,049 or $0.0080 per Swiss franc ($8,049/SF1,000,000).

The value in dollars of SF1,000,000 in June depends on the spot rate at that time. As in the unhedged alternative, the upside potential is unlimited. At any exchange rate above $0.5130/SF, *XYZ* would allow its option to expire unexercised and would exchange the Swiss francs for dollars at the spot rate. For instance, if the expected rate of $0.5200/SF materialized, *XYZ* would exchange the SF1,000,000 in the spot market for $520,000 and the net proceeds would be $520,000 − $8,049 = $511,951. In contrast to the unhedged alternative, downside risk is limited with an option. *XYZ* would exercise its option to sell (put) SF1,000,000 at $0.5130/SF if the Swiss franc depreciated below $0.5130/SF. It would receive $513,000 gross or $504,951 net ($513,000 − $8,049). Although this downside result is worse than the downside of the forward or money market hedges, the upside potential is not limited the way it is with those hedges. In other words, whether the option strategy is or is not superior to a forward or money market hedge depends on the degree to which management is risk averse. The essence of the option hedge is:

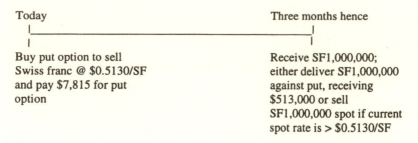

Today   Three months hence

Buy put option to sell   Receive SF1,000,000;
Swiss franc @ $0.5130/SF   either deliver SF1,000,000
and pay $7,815 for put   against put, receiving
option $513,000 or sell
                                SF1,000,000 spot if current
                                spot rate is > $0.5130/SF

A trading range for the Swiss franc which defines the break-even points for the option compared with the other strategies can be established. The upper bound of the range is determined by comparison with the forward rate. The Swiss franc must appreciate sufficiently above the forward rate of $0.5170/SF to cover the $0.0080/SF cost of the option. Thus the break-even upside spot price of the Swiss franc must be $0.5170 + $0.0080 = $0.5250. In other words, the proceeds under the option strategy will be greater than those under the forward strategy, if the spot Swiss franc appreciates above $0.5250. If the spot Swiss franc ends up below $0.5250, the forward hedge would be superior in retrospect. The lower bound of the range is established by a comparison with the unhedged alternative. *XYZ* will exercise its put option and sell the proceeds at $0.5130/SF if the spot price falls below $0.5130/SF. The net proceeds per Swiss franc will be $0.5130 minus the cost of the option or $0.5130 − $0.0080 = $0.5050. If the spot rate falls below $0.5050, the net proceeds from exercising the option will be greater than the net proceeds from selling the unhedged Swiss francs in the spot market. At any spot rate above $0.5050, the spot proceeds from the unhedged alternative will be greater.

We can carry out the same calculations for the second option or the one with the strike price of $0.4800/SF and the premium cost of 1.0 percent. It has a smaller premium cost since it is out-of-the-money. The cost of this option is:

SF1,000,000 × 0.010 × $0.5210/SF
= $5,210, or in future value terms $5,210 × 1.03 = $5,366 or $0.0054/SF

The break-even rate versus the forward contract rate is $0.5170/SF + $0.0054/SF = $0.5224. A comparison of the two alternative over-the-counter options is as follows:

Put Option Strike Price	ATM Option $0.5130/SF	OTM Option $0.4800/SF
Option cost (future value)	$8,049	$5,366
Proceeds if exercised	$513,000	$480,000
Minimum net proceeds	$504,951	$474,634
Maximum net proceeds	unlimited	unlimited
Break-even spot rate	$0.5250	$0.5224

XYZ's alternative hedging strategies may be summarized as follows:

Unhedged alternative	*Result*
Wait 3 months then sell SF1,000,000 for dollars in the spot market.	Receive in 3 months: 1. An unlimited maximum; 2. An expected $520,000; 3. A zero minimum.

Forward market hedge	*Result*
Sell SF1,000,000 forward for dollars at once.	Certain receipt of $517,000 in 3 months.

Money market hedge	*Result*
1. Borrow SF975,610 in Switzerland@ 10%; 2. Exchange for $508,293 at spot rate; 3. Invest in US for 3 months.	Receive $508,293 at once. Value in 3 months depends on US investment assumption: 1. At break-even rate of 6.84%, receive $517,000; 2. At cost of capital of 12%, receive an expected $523,542.

Options market hedge	*Result*
Purchase a 3-month put of SF1,000,000 with strike price of $0.5130/SF and premium cost of $8,049 (after 3 months).	Receive in 3 months: 1. An unlimited maximum less $8,049; 2. An expected $502,000 less $8,049 or $493,951; 3. A minimum of $513,000 less $8,049 or $504,951.

The forward hedge yields a certain $517,000 in three months, which is equivalent to a money market hedge if the loan proceeds are invested at 6.84 percent per annum. At any higher rate (e.g., the 12% cost of capital), the money market hedge is preferred. If *XYZ* does not hedge, its exchange advisory service forecasts $520,000 in three months. However, this forecast is at risk and might be greater or smaller. The expected results from an unhedged position are identical to the certain results from the forward hedge if the forward rate is accepted as the most likely future spot rate. Under such conditions, the advantage of hedging over remaining unhedged is the reduction of risk. Except for their up-front costs, the two put options have the same upside potential as the unhedged alternative. However, if the exchange rate moves against *XYZ*, the put options limit the downside risk. A put option can be used to hedge the foreign exchange risk when construction firms or exporters must submit a price in a foreign currency without knowing until some later date whether their bid was successful. If the bid is rejected, the loss is limited to the cost of the option. In contrast, if the risk is hedged by a forward contract and the bid is rejected, the forward contract must be reversed or eventually fulfilled at an unknown potential loss or gain. The bidder has an uncovered forward contract.

Heretofore, we have assumed a foreign currency denominated receivable. The management of an account payable (i.e., the firm is required to make a foreign currency payment at a future date) is similar but not identical in form. If *XYZ* had a SF1,000,000 account payable in 90 days, the hedging choices are as follows:

- *Remain unhedged.* XYZ could wait 90 days, exchange dollars for Swiss francs at that time and make the payment. If *XYZ*'s foreign exchange advisory service expects the spot rate in 90 days to be $0.5200/SF, the payment would be expected to cost $520,000. However, this amount is uncertain since the spot rate could be different from that expected.

- *Forward market hedge.* XYZ could buy SF1,000,000, locking in a rate of $0.5170/SF and a total dollar cost of $517,000. This is $3,000 less than the expected cost of remaining unhedged and, therefore, the preferred alternative.

- *Money market hedge.* This hedge is distinctly different for a payable as opposed to a receivable: in this case XYZ exchanges US dollars spot and invests them for 90 days in a Swiss franc denominated interest-bearing account. The principal and interest in Swiss francs at the end of the 90 days is used to pay the SF1,000,000 account payable. XYZ discounts the SF1,000,000 by the Swiss franc investment interest rate of 8 percent for 90 days in order to determine the Swiss francs needed today:

    SF1,000,000/[1 + (.08 × 90/360)] = SF980,392
    or SF980,392 × $0.5210/SF = $510,784 at the current spot rate of $0.5210/SF

    or in future value terms (using 12% cost of capital)

    $510,784 × [1 + (.12 × 90/360)] = $526,108

    which is higher than the forward hedge and therefore unattractive.

- *Option hedge.* XYZ could cover its SF1,000,000 account payable by purchasing a call option on SF1,000,000. A June call option on Swiss francs with a near ATM strike price of $0.5130/SF would cost 1.5 percent or SF1,000,000 × 0.015 × $0.5210/SF = $7,815. This premium, regardless of whether the call option is exercised or not, has to be paid up-front. Its value carried forward 90 days at the 12 percent cost of capital raises its end of the period cost to $8,049. If the spot rate in 90 days is less than $0.5130/SF, the option would be allowed to expire and the SF1,000,000 purchased on the spot market. If the spot rate in 90 days is greater than $0.5130/SF, the call option would be exercised. The total cost of the call option if exercised is (SF1,000,000 × $0.5130/SF) + $8,049 = $521,049.

As with *XYZ*'s account receivable, the final hedging choice depends on its confidence in the foreign exchange rate forecast of $0.5200/SF and its willingness to bear risk. The forward hedge gives the lowest cost of making the account payable payment, which is certain. However, if the dollar were to strengthen against the Swiss franc and end up at a spot rate less than $0.5130/SF, the call option could be potentially the lowest-cost hedge. On the other hand, the forward hedge appears the preferred alternative in view of the expected spot rate of $0.5200/SF. The four methods of managing a SF1,000,000 account payable for XYZ may be summarized as follows:

Hedging Alternative	Cost to XYZ	Degree of Risk
1. Remain unhedged	$521,000	Uncertain
2. Forward hedge	$517,000	Certain
3. Money market hedge	$526,108	Certain
4. Call option hedge	$521,049	Limited

Today, a few MNCs with appreciable quantities of transaction exposure do no hedging at all. An increasing number of MNCs are actively hedging not only backlog exposures, but also anticipated exposures or transactions for which there are at present no contracts or agreements but are anticipated on the basis of historical trends and/or continuing business relationships. The choice of which contractual hedge to use depends on the individual MNC's currency risk tolerance and its expectation of the probable movement of exchange rates over the transaction exposure period. In general, if an exchange rate is expected to move:

• against the MNC, the preferred contractual hedges are the ones that lock in an exchange rate, such as the forward contract hedge and the money market hedge; and

• in an MNC's favor, the preferred alternatives are probably those that allow it to participate in some upside potential (remaining unhedged or using a currency option), but protect it against significant adverse exchange rate movements.

OPERATING EXPOSURE

Operating exposure measures any change in the present value of a firm resulting from changes in future operating cash flows caused by any unexpected change in exchange rates. The analysis of operating exposure examines the impact of changing exchange rates over coming months and years on a firm's own operations, and on its competitive position vis-à-vis other firms, in order to identify strategic moves or operating techniques the firm may wish to adopt to improve its value in the face of unexpected exchange rate changes. For the long-run health of a firm, operating exposure is more important than transaction or accounting exposure. It depends on estimates of future cash flow changes over an arbitrary time horizon. Planning for operating exposure calls for the interaction of strategies in finance, marketing, purchasing and production. An *expected* change in foreign exchange rates is not included in the definition of operating exposure, since both management and investors should have factored this information into their evaluation of the anticipated operating results and market value. Thus, budgeted financial statements already reflect information about the effect of an expected change in exchange rates. For instance, management may use the forward rate when preparing the operating budgets if it does not believe that the spot rate would remain unchanged.

MNCs' cash flows can be categorized as *operating cash flows* and *financing cash flows*. Operating cash flows arise from interfirm (between unrelated firms) and intrafirm (between units of the same firm) receivables and payables, rent and lease payments for the use of facilities and equipment, royalty and license fees and assorted management fees for services provided. Financial cash flows are payments for the use of interfirm and intrafirm loans (principal and interest) and stockholders' equity (dividends and new equity investments). Naturally, each of these cash flows can occur at different time periods, in different amounts and in different currencies of denomination.

Depending on the time horizon, an unexpected change in exchange rates can affect a firm's expected cash flows at the following levels:

- *Short run*. This impact is on expected cash flows in the one-year operating budget. The currency of denomination cannot be changed for existing obligations (such as those defined by transaction exposure) or even for implied obligations such as sales or purchase commitments. In the short run it is difficult to change sales prices or renegotiate factor costs. Consequently, realized cash flows will be different from those expected in the budget.

- *Medium run: equilibrium case*. This impact is on expected cash flows of two- to five-year budgets assuming that parity conditions hold among the foreign exchange rates, national inflation rates and national interest rates (Chapter 1). Under equilibrium conditions a firm should be able to adjust prices and factor costs over time to maintain the expected level of cash flows, provided it is allowed to adjust prices and costs. Whether equilibrium conditions exist or not depends on national monetary, fiscal and balance-of-payments policies.

- *Medium run: disequilibrium case*. This impact is on cash flows of two- to five-year budgets assuming disequilibrium conditions, in which case the firm may not be able to adjust prices and costs to reflect the new competitive environment caused by a change in exchange rates. Consequently, the firm's realized cash flows may differ from its expected cash flows and its market value may change due to the unanticipated results.

- *Long run*. This impact is on long-run cash flows or those beyond five years. At this level a firm's cash flows are affected by the reactions of existing and potential competitors to exchange rate changes under disequilibrium conditions. In the long run, all firms (both domestic and multinational) that are subject to international competition are exposed to foreign exchange operating exposure whenever foreign exchange markets are not continuously in equilibrium.

One way of measuring an MNC's operating exposure is to classify the cash flows into different income statement items and subjectively predict each income statement item based on a forecast of exchange rates. Next, an alternative exchange rate scenario can be considered and the forecasts for the income statements revised. By examining how the earnings forecast in the income statement changes in response to alternative exchange rate scenarios, the firm can assess the impact of currency movements on earnings and cash flows. Consider, for example, a US-based company, Alpha Inc., which conducts a portion of its business in Canada. Its US sales are denominated in US dollars and its Canadian sales in Canadian dollars. Its pro forma income statement (in millions of US and Canadian dollars) for next year is as follows:

	US Business	Canadian Business
Sales	$456.0	C$ 6.0
Cost of goods sold	75.0	300.0
Gross profit	$381.0	−C$294.0
Operating expenses:		
Fixed	$ 45.0	—
Variable	46.1	—
Total	$ 91.1	—
Earnings before interest and taxes (EBIT)	$289.9	−C$294.0
Interest expense	4.5	15.0
Earnings before taxes (EBT)	$285.4	−C$309.0

Let us assume that Alpha Inc. wishes to assess the effect of the following three possible exchange rate scenarios on the income statement items.

Possible Exchange Rate of C$	Forecast US Sales (millions)
$.75	$450.0
.80	456.0
.85	460.5

Note that the above US sales data indicate that Alpha's sales in the United States are higher when the Canadian dollar is stronger since Canadian competitors will be priced out in the US market.

Table 7.1 shows how Alpha Inc. can determine the impact of different exchange rate scenarios on its pro forma income statements. The assumed impact of exchange rates on US sales is shown in row 1. Row 2 shows the amount in US dollars to be received as a result of the Canadian sales (after converting the C$6 million of Canadian sales into US dollars). Row 3 represents the estimated US dollars to be received from total sales, which is established by combining rows 1 and 2. Row 4 shows the cost of goods sold in the United States. Row

Table 7.1
Impact of Exchange Rate Changes on Pro Forma Income Statement (US and Canadian millions of dollars)

		Exchange rate scenario				
		C$ = $.75		C$ = $.80		C$ = $.85
Sales:						
(1) US		$450.0		$456.0		$460.5
(2) Canadian	C$6 =	4.5	C$6 =	4.8	C$6 =	5.1
(3) Total		$454.5		$460.8		$465.6
Cost of goods sold:						
(4) US		$ 75.0		$ 75.0		$ 75.0
(5) Canadian	C$300 =	225.0	C$300 =	240.0	C$300 =	255.0
(6) Total		$300.0		$315.0		$330.0
(7) Gross profit		$154.5		$145.8		$135.6
Operating expenses:						
(8) US fixed		$ 45.0		$ 45.0		$ 45.0
(9) US variable (10% of sales)		45.5		46.1		46.6
(10) Total		$ 90.5		$ 91.1		$ 91.6
(11) EBIT		$ 64.0		$ 54.7		$ 44.0
Interest expense:						
(12) US		$ 4.5		$ 4.5		$ 4.5
(13) Canadian	C$15 =	11.3	C$15 =	12.0	C$15 =	12.8
(14) Total		$ 15.8		$16.5		$ 17.3
(15) EBT		$48.2		$38.2		$ 26.7

5 converts the estimated C$300 million cost of goods sold into US dollars for each exchange rate scenario. Row 6 presents the estimated US dollars needed to cover the total cost of goods sold, which is determined by combining rows 4 and 5. Row 7 estimates the gross profit in US dollars by subtracting row 6 from row 3. Rows 8 through 10 show estimated operating expenses. Row 11 subtracts total operating expenses from gross profit to determine earnings before interest and taxes (BIT). Row 12 estimates the interest expenses paid in the United States, while row 13 estimates the US dollars needed to make interest payments in Canada. Row 14 combines rows 12 and 13 to estimate total US

dollars needed to make all interest payments. Finally, row 15 presents earnings before taxes (BET), estimated by subtracting row 14 from 11.

Table 7.1 illustrates that a stronger Canadian dollar would:

- increase both US sales and the US dollar value of Canadian sales,
- result in a negative impact on gross profit because Alpha's cost of goods sold exposure (C$300 million) is much greater than its Canadian sales exposure (C$6 million),
- increase the total amount in US dollars needed to make interest payments, and
- in general adversely affect Alpha Inc.

Alpha Inc. would be favorably affected by a weaker Canadian dollar since the reduced value of total revenues would be more than offset by the reduced cost of goods sold and interest expenses. Our example is based on a one-period time horizon. Naturally, the example can be easily expanded to cover several periods ahead once forecasts of sales, expenses and future exchange rate scenarios have been established. A general conclusion from our example is that firms with more (less) in foreign costs than in foreign revenues will be unfavorably (favorably) affected by a stronger foreign currency. The precise impact, however, can only be established by using the procedure described here.

Some MNCs assess the effect of changes in the exchange rate on particular corporate characteristics, such as earnings, exports or sales. For example, Toyota Motor Corporation measures the sensitivity of exports to the yen exchange rate relative to the US dollar and, therefore, is able to forecast the expected impact of a forecast yen value on future exports.

If the Canadian dollar strengthens consistently over the long run, Alpha's cost of goods sold and interest expense are likely to increase at a higher rate than US dollar revenues. Hence, it behooves Alpha to introduce some policies to create a more balanced impact of Canadian dollar movements on its revenues and expenses. At the moment, its high exposure to exchange rate changes is due to its expenses being more susceptible than its revenues to the changing value of the Canadian dollar. Consequently, a policy to either reduce orders of Canadian materials or increase Canadian sales would provide more balance.

Alpha believes that it can:

- achieve Canadian sales of C$30 million if it spends $3 million more on advertising (which is part of its fixed operating expenses) and an additional $15 million on materials from US suppliers;
- reduce its reliance on Canadian suppliers and increase its reliance on US suppliers, which is expected to reduce the cost of goods sold attributable to Canadian suppliers by C$150 million and increase the cost of goods sold attributable to US suppliers by $120 million (not including the $15 million increase resulting from increased sales to the Canadian market); and

• borrow additional funds in the United States and retire some existing loans from Canadian banks resulting in an additional interest expense of $6 million to US banks and a reduction of C$7.5 million owed to Canadian banks.

Table 7.2 shows the anticipated impact of the aforementioned strategies on the pro forma income statement for the three exchange rate scenarios.
    Table 7.2 illustrates that:

• the projected total sales increase in response to intentions to penetrate the Canadian market,

• the US cost of goods sold is now $135 million higher than before, resulting from a $15 million increase to accommodate increased Canadian sales and a $120 million increase due to the shift from Canadian suppliers to US suppliers,

• the Canadian cost of goods sold decreases from C$300 to C$150 million,

• the revised fixed operating expenses of $48 million include the increase in advertising expenses necessary to penetrate the Canadian market,

• the variable operating expenses are revised because of revised estimates of total sales,

• the interest expenses are revised due to the increased loans from US banks and reduced loans from Canadian banks, and

• the variation in EBT due to movements in the exchange rate is much smaller than the variation in the EBT of Table 7.1.

The way an MNC restructures its operations to reduce operating exposure to exchange rate risk depends on the form of exposure. In the case of Alpha Inc., future expenses are more sensitive than future revenues to the possible values of a foreign currency. Consequently, operating exposure could be reduced by increasing the sensitivity of revenues and reducing the sensitivity of expenses to exchange rate movements. MNCs that have a greater quantity of exchange-rate-sensitive revenues than expenses, however, would reduce operating exposure by reducing the quantity of exchange-rate-sensitive revenues or by increasing the quantity of exchange-rate-sensitive expenses. It is also noted that some revenues or expenses may be more exchange-rate-sensitive than others. Thus, a simple matching of the quantity of exchange-rate-sensitive revenues to the quantity of exchange-rate-sensitive expenses may not completely insulate an MNC from exchange rate movements. An MNC can best evaluate a proposed restructuring of operations by forecasting various income statement items for various possible exchange rate scenarios, as done in Table 7.2, and then assessing the sensitivity of earnings to these different scenarios.
    The management of operating exposure serves as a long-term solution; once the restructuring is complete it should decrease operating exposure over the long run. This is different from the hedging of transaction exposure, which deals with each upcoming foreign currency transaction separately. Any restructuring which is used to reduce operating exposure can only be reversed or eliminated at high

Table 7.2
Restructuring to Reduce Operating Exposure (US and Canadian millions of dollars)

		Exchange rate scenario		
		C$ = $.75	C$ = $.80	C$ = $.85
Sales:				
US		$450.0	$456.0	$460.5
Canadian	C$30 =	22.5 C$30 =	24.0 C$30 =	25.5
Total		$472.5	$480.0	$486.0
Cost of goods sold:				
US		$210.0	$210.0	$210.0
Canadian	C$150 =	112.5 C$150 =	120.0 C$150 =	127.5
Total		$322.5	$330.0	$337.5
Gross profit		$150.0	$150.0	$148.5
Operating expenses:				
US fixed		$ 48.0	$ 48.0	$ 48.0
US variable (10% of sales)		47.3	48.0	48.6
Total		$ 95.3	$ 96.0	$ 96.6
EBIT		$ 54.7	$ 54.0	$ 51.9
Interest expense:				
US		$ 10.5	$ 10.5	$ 10.5
Canadian	C$7.5 =	5.6 C$7.5 =	6.0 C$7.5 =	6.4
Total		$ 16.1	$ 16.5	$ 16.9
EBT		$ 38.6	$ 37.5	$ 35.0

cost. It therefore behooves MNCs to be very confident about potential benefits before they decide to restructure their operations. They should address the following questions when deciding how to restructure operations to reduce operating exposure:

• Should the MNC try to increase or decrease sales in new or existing foreign markets?
• Should the MNC increase or decrease its dependency on foreign suppliers?
• Should the MNC establish or eliminate production facilities in foreign markets?
• Should the MNC increase or decrease its level of debt denominated in foreign currencies?

The possibilities of restructuring operations in order to reduce the risk of exchange rate movements may be summarized as follows:

	Recommended action when a foreign currency has a greater impact on:	
Type of operation	*cash inflows*	*cash outflows*
Sales in foreign currency units	Reduce foreign sales	Increase foreign sales
Reliance on foreign supplies	Increase foreign supply orders	Reduce foreign orders
Proportion of debt structure representing foreign debt	Restructure debt to increase debt payments in foreign currency	Restructure debt to reduce debt payments in foreign currency

ACCOUNTING EXPOSURE

Accounting exposure arises when an MNC translates each subsidiary's financial data to its home currency for consolidated financial statements. Some people argue that it is not necessary to hedge or reduce accounting exposure, since cash flow is not affected. For instance, Phillips Petroleum has stated in its annual report that accounting exposure is not hedged since accounting effects do not influence cash flows. However, some MNCs are concerned with accounting exposure because of its potential impact on reported consolidated earnings. Other MNCs attempt to avoid accounting exposure by matching foreign liabilities with foreign assets.

Accounting exposure depends on:

• the degree of foreign involvement by foreign subsidiaries,
• the locations of foreign subsidiaries, and
• the accounting methods used.

The greater the proportion of an MNC's business that is conducted by its subsidiaries, the greater the proportion of a given financial statement item that is susceptible to accounting exposure will be. For instance, if the foreign involvement of an MNC is primarily in the form of exporting, it does not have much of its business conducted by foreign subsidiaries and the consolidated financial statement will not be substantially affected by exchange rate movements. This does not mean, however, that such an MNC could not have a high degree of transaction and operating exposure. The location of subsidiaries plays a role in the degree of accounting exposure since the financial statement items of each subsidiary are typically measured by that country's home currency. For instance, a US MNC with an Indonesian subsidiary must develop consolidated financial statements that require translation of the Indonesian subsidiary figures for assets, liabilities, earnings, and so on, which are measured in Indonesian rupiahs, into US dollar terms. If the subsidiary had been located in Morocco instead of Indonesia, the risk of accounting exposure would be lower, since the Moroccan dirham is more stable against the US dollar.

An MNC's degree of accounting exposure can also be affected by the accounting procedures it uses. The December 1981 Financial Accounting Standards Board No. 52 (FASB-52) significantly changed the consolidated accounting rules for US-based MNCs. The important points of FASB-52 are:

- The functional currency of an entity is the currency of the economic environment in which the entity operates.
- The current exchange rate as of the reporting date is used to translate the assets and liabilities of a foreign entity from its functional currency into the reporting currency.
- The weighted average exchange rate is used to translate revenue, expenses, gains and losses of a foreign entity from its functional currency into the reporting currency.
- Translated income gains and losses due to changes in foreign currency values are not recognized in current net income but are reported as a second component of stockholders' equity; an exception to this rule is a foreign entity located in a country with high inflation.
- Realized income gains and losses due to foreign currency transactions are recorded in current net income, although there are some exceptions.

Thus, consolidated earnings under FASB-52 are sensitive to the functional currency's weighted average exchange rate. Consider a Swiss subsidiary of a US-based MNC that earned SF10,000,000 in Year 1 and SF10,000,000 in Year 2. These earnings are translated at the weighted average exchange rate when they are consolidated along with other subsidiary earnings. Let us assume that the weighted average exchange rate is $0.52/SF in Year 1 and $0.48/SF in Year 2. The translated earnings for each reporting period in US dollars are determined as follows.

Reporting period	Assumed local earnings of Swiss subsidiary	Weighted average exchange rate of Swiss franc over the reporting period	Translated US dollar earnings of Swiss subsidiary
Year 1	SF10,000,000	$0.52/SF	$520,000
Year 2	SF10,000,000	$0.48/SF	$480,000

The above figures show that even though the earnings in Swiss francs were the same in each year, consolidated MNC dollar earnings translated from the Swiss subsidiary were reduced by $40,000 in Year 2. The drop in earnings (when measured in US dollars) is not the fault of the Swiss subsidiary, but rather of a weakened Swiss franc.

The following example demonstrates that MNCs can use forward contracts to hedge accounting exposure. Consider a US-based MNC with a subsidiary in Switzerland. As of the beginning of its fiscal year the subsidiary forecasts earnings at SF30,000,000 and it plans to reinvest the entire amount in earnings in Switzerland. In other words, no earnings will be remitted to the parent in the United States. While there is no foreseeable transaction exposure from the future earnings since the Swiss francs will remain in Switzerland, accounting exposure does exist for the MNC. The Swiss earnings would be translated at the weighted average value of the Swiss franc over the course of the year. Assuming that the Swiss franc is currently worth $0.52/SF and that its value is constant during the year, the forecast translation of Swiss earnings into US dollars would be $15,600,000. The MNC may be concerned that the translated value of the Swiss earnings will be reduced if the Swiss franc's average value decreases during the year. It could, therefore, implement a forward hedge on the expected earnings by selling SF30,000,000 one year forward. Let us assume that the forward rate is the same as the spot rate or $0.52/SF. At the end of the year, the MNC could buy SF30,000,000 at the spot rate and fulfill its forward contract obligation to sell SF30,000,000. If the Swiss franc depreciates during the fiscal year, then the MNC will be able to purchase Swiss francs at the end of the fiscal year at a cheaper rate than it could sell them for ($0.52/SF) to fulfill the forward contract. Consequently, it will have generated income that could offset the translation loss.

It is noted, however, that the forward-rate gain or loss reflects the difference between the forward rate and future spot rate, whereas the translation gain or loss reflects the average exchange rate over the period of concern. In addition, translation losses are not tax deductible, whereas gains on forward contracts used to hedge translation exposure are taxed. Another limitation with a hedging strategy (forward or money market hedge) on accounting exposure is that a subsidiary's forecast earnings for the end of the year are not guaranteed. The most critical limitation with such a strategy is, however, that the MNC may be increasing its transaction exposure. For instance, assume a situation in which the subsidiary's currency appreciates during the fiscal year, resulting in a translation gain. If the MNC enacts a hedging strategy at the beginning of the fiscal year, this strategy will generate a transaction loss that will somewhat offset the translation gain. The problem is that the translation gain is simply a paper gain while the loss resulting from the hedging strategy is a real one. The reason for the gain being a paper gain is that the MNC's parent net cash flow is not affected if the subsidiary reinvests the earnings; the reported dollar value of earnings is higher due to the subsidiary currency's appreciation. Perhaps the best way to deal with accounting exposure is for MNCs to clarify how their consolidated earnings have been affected by exchange rate movements.

THE CURRENCY HEDGE RATIO

The discussion of transaction exposure at the beginning of this chapter as-sumed—without discussion—a *hedge ratio* of 1.0. The hedge ratio is defined as the percentage of an individual exposure's nominal amount covered by a financial instrument such as a forward or futures contract or a currency option. Thus, the ratio, frequently termed *beta* (β), is:

$$\beta = \text{(value of currency hedge)/(value of currency exposure)}$$

The value of an individual currency position can be expressed as a portfolio of two assets, namely a spot asset (the exposure) and a hedge asset. We are interested in constructing a hedge so that whatever spot value is lost as a result of adverse exchange rate movements (ΔS) is replaced by an equal but opposite change in the value of the hedge asset as, for instance, the futures position (ΔF):

$$\Delta \text{ Position value} = \Delta \text{ Spot} - \Delta \text{ Futures} = \text{(about) } 0.$$

Thus, our goal is to establish the effective hedge that will indeed result in $\Delta V = 0$.

The determination of the *optimal hedge ratio* can best be explained by way of an example. For instance, an MNC is expecting a foreign currency–denom-inated payment, an account receivable at a future date, time t_1, which we call the spot or *cash position*. However, the amount of the hedge must be determined now, at time t_0. The expected value of this future receivable is:

$$E(X_{s,1}) = X_1 \times E(S_1)$$

where:

$E(X_{s,1})$ = the expected dollar value of the foreign currency receivable at time t_1

X_1 = the amount of the foreign currency to be received (in foreign currency)

$E(S_1)$ = the expected spot ratio to occur at time t_1 (dollars per unit of foreign currency)

It is noted that the *present* spot rate is not part of the expected value at time t_1.

The MNC wishes to hedge its foreign currency exposure since it does not know what the exchange rate will actually be on the future date. It can sign a forward contract for a specific exchange rate for US dollars per unit of foreign currency at time t_1, for whatever amount of foreign currency it wishes. Next, the MNC forms a portfolio of the aforementioned $X_1 \times E(S_1)$ and a forward contract as a hedge asset. The expected dollar value of the portfolio at time t_1, $E(P_{\$,1})$, is:

$$E(P_{\$,1}) = X_1 E(S_1) + X_f [E(F_1) - F_0]$$

where:

X_f = the amount of foreign currency sold forward at time t_0
F_0 = the current price of the futures contract
$E(F_1)$ = the expected futures price at time t_1

This is the expectation now of the portfolio's total value when the receivable is paid at time t_1.

The expected spot rate at time t_1 is the only unknown. The decision variable is the amount of the foreign currency the MNC chooses to sell forward. In order to minimize the risk that the aforementioned ΔV will not be equal to zero, the MNC should choose the amount of the hedge such that the variance of the expected return of the portfolio is minimized. In other words, the value of X_f should be selected so that the variance of the portfolio's final value is minimized.

The variance of the expected portfolio value is:

$$\text{var}[E(P_{\$,1})] = X_1^2 \text{var}(S_1) + 2X_1 X_f \text{cov}(S_1, F_1) + X_f^2 \text{var}(F_1)$$

The minimum value of the variance of the portfolio's expected return can be obtained by differentiating this expression with respect to X_f and setting the result equal to zero, which gives the following:

$$2X_f \text{var}(F_1) = 2X_1 \text{cov}(S_1, F_1)$$

Thus, the amount of foreign currency to be sold forward (X_f) to minimize the portfolio's terminal variance is:

$$X_f = X_1 \text{cov}(S_1, F_1)/\text{var}(F_1)$$

Finally, if this equation is rearranged to determine the relative size or the optimal hedge amount to the amount of the original exposure, the optimal hedge ratio or beta is found:

$$X_f/X_1 = \beta = \text{cov}(S_1, F_1)/\text{var}(F_1)$$

As an example of the application of the optimal hedge ratio, we consider a US-based MNC that expects the receipt of DM1,000,000 in 90 days. The only values necessary for this application are the variance of the 90-day forward, 0.005572, and the covariance between the spot rate (\$/DM) and the forward rate (\$/DM) of 0.0054997. The optimal hedge ratio is:

β = 0.0054997/0.005572 = 0.987024
or about 98.70%

This optimal hedge ratio means that if the MNC wishes to minimize the variance of the expected value of the two-asset portfolio (spot position and forward position) at the end of the 90 days it should sell 98.70 percent of the DM exposure forward, or 0.987024 × DM1,000,000 = DM987,024. A beta of 1.0 would imply that 100 percent of the amount of the exposure should be sold forward, yet the theoretical model implies a value slightly less than 100 percent. The reason for the discrepancy is that the spot rate and the futures rate are not perfectly correlated. This less than perfect correlation is called *basis risk*. In general, hedgers do not bother to evaluate and hedge less than the beta of 1.0 when selling currency forward to eliminate exchange risk, since the spot and forward rates for most major currencies typically indicate similar high hedge ratios (0.97 and up).

Sometimes there are no available futures or forward markets for currencies. In these cases, the risk manager may wish to use a substitute, or *proxy*, for the underlying currency that is available. The above described methodology for establishing the optimal hedge ratio is also helpful in the analysis of *proxy-hedging* or *cross-hedging*. The cross-hedger is likely going through a simple two-step process to determine the *optimal cross-hedge*: first, find the currency futures that is most highly correlated with the actual currency of exposure; second, find the optimal hedge ratio using the covariance between the proxy futures and the actual currency, as in the preceding model. This would then tell the risk manager the amount of the proxy futures that should be purchased to hedge the currency exposure.

The Deutschmark (DM) has long been used as a proxy for the hedging of all European Monetary System (EMS) currencies. A US-resident MNC with long currency positions in many EMS currencies could effectively hedge all positions at once using the DM as a proxy futures. Naturally, the validity of the proxy hedge depends on the covariance and the variance of the recent past applying to the future, and in periods in which the fundamental relations between EMS currencies change (as in September 1992 and July 1993), the proxy hedge may prove sub-optimal.

It is noted that the optimal hedge ratio may be rewritten as follows:

β = cov(S_1,F_1)/var(F_1) = [cov(S_1,F_1)/$\sigma(S_1)\sigma(F_1)$][$\sigma(S_1)\sigma(F_1)$/var(F_1)] = $\rho(S_1,F_1)\sigma(S_1)/\sigma(F_1)$

where:

$\sigma(S_1)$ = the standard deviation of S_1

$\sigma(F_1)$ = the standard deviation of F_1

$\rho(S_1,F_1)$ = the correlation coefficient between S_1 and F_1

all other terms are as defined before

As illustrated in the following example, the use of the hedge ratio is not limited to proxies for currencies.

Suppose an airline wishes to hedge a future payment for 1 million gallons of jet fuel in three months using heating oil futures as a proxy. One heating oil futures contract is on 45,000 gallons. The standard deviation of jet fuel is 0.034 over a 3-month period, that of heating oil futures is 0.042 over a 3-month period, and the correlation coefficient is 0.8. The hedge ratio is $\beta = (0.8)(0.034)/(0.042) = 0.65$. Since one futures bears on 45,000 gallons, the company should buy $0.65(1,000,000)/45,000 = 14.4$ contracts, or (rounding to the nearest whole number) 14 contracts.

DESIGN OF THE FINANCIAL STRUCTURE

The financial structure of each affiliate of an MNC is relevant only to the extent that it affects an MNC's goal of minimizing the cost of capital for a given level of business risk and capital budget. Thus, an individual affiliate does not have an independent cost of capital and its finance structure should not be based on an objective of minimizing its own independent cost of capital. On the other hand, we could argue that an MNC should take differing country debt ratio norms into consideration when determining its desired debt ratio for foreign affiliates, since a finance structure for foreign affiliates that conforms to local debt norms has the following advantages:

• it helps management evaluate the return on equity relative to local competitors in the same industry,

• it reminds management that unless return on assets is greater than the local price of capital, they are likely to misallocate scarce domestic resources (this is particularly important in economies with relatively high interest rates),

• it reduces criticism of foreign affiliates that they have been operating with too high debt ratios and, therefore, do not contribute a fair share of risk capital to the country, and

• it may result in a better match of foreign liabilities with foreign assets and, therefore, reduce accounting exposure.

The *debt ratio* is defined as the ratio of total debt to total assets. The debt considered here should be only what is borrowed from sources outside the MNC (local and foreign currency loans). Both investment firms and host countries consider parent loans to affiliates as equity investment. A parent debt is generally subordinated to other debt and does not have the same threat of insolvency as an external loan. Is there a conflict between minimizing an MNC's consolidated worldwide cost of capital and the use of localized financial structures? If debt is available to a foreign affiliate at equal cost to what could be raised elsewhere, after adjusting for foreign exchange risk, then localizing the foreign affiliate's financial structure should incur no cost penalty and yet would also enjoy the advantages just listed. Naturally, if a particular foreign affiliate has access to local debt at a lower cost, after adjusting for the foreign exchange risk, than other sources of debt available to the MNC, the MNC should borrow all it can through that affiliate. The reverse would be true if the foreign affiliate only had access to higher cost debt than available elsewhere. The fact that a lower cost of debt exists elsewhere is indicative of market imperfections or segmentation.

Capital market segmentation is a major imperfection. A national capital market is segmented if the required rate of return on securities (debt and equity) in that market differs from the required rate of return on securities of comparable expected return and risk that are traded on other national securities markets (for example, New York or London). Securities of comparable expected return and risk should have the same required rate of return in each national market if these capital markets are fully integrated. Market segmentation is caused by government constraints and investor perceptions. The important imperfections are:

- *Information barriers*. The main information barriers are language, accounting principles and quality of disclosure.
- *Transaction costs*. Taxes imposed on securities transactions, high quotation spreads or fixed brokerage commissions are a quick way to segment a market (business will flee to other capital markets).
- *Foreign exchange risk*. An exceptionally volatile exchange rate is not conducive to attracting long-term foreign investors.
- *Regulatory barriers*. Taxation of capital gains varies significantly from country to country and some countries have restrictions on the amount of shares foreigners can own.
- *Small country bias*. Small country capital markets lack economies of scale and scope and are usually too illiquid to handle block purchases by international institutional investors.
- *Political risk*. Fear of government intervention and lack of capital market laws and judicial systems to enforce these laws are not conducive to attracting long-term foreign investors.

If a firm is located in a segmented market it can still escape from this market by sourcing its debt and equity abroad. The result should be a lower marginal cost of capital, improved liquidity for its shares and a larger capital budget.

As a US-based MNC tries to attract more new dollars, the cost of each dollar will at some point rise. In other words, the weighted average cost of capital (WACOC) depends on the amount of new capital raised; the WACOC, which is a weighted average of the component costs of debt, preferred stock and common equity, will, at some point, rise if more and more capital is raised during a given period. This is so since (a) flotation costs cause the cost of new equity to be higher than the cost of retained earnings, and (b) higher rates of return on debt, preferred stock and common stock may be required to induce investors to supply additional capital to the MNC, which increases the risk. The *marginal cost of capital* (MCC) is defined as the cost of the last dollar of new capital that the MNC raises; the marginal cost rises as more and more capital is raised during a given period.

In the domestic case, the total availability of capital to a firm is determined by supply and demand in the domestic capital markets. A firm should always expand its capital budget by raising funds in the same proportion as its optimal financial structure, but as its budget expands, its marginal cost of capital will eventually increase. In the multinational case an MNC is able to increase its market liquidity by raising funds in the Euromarkets, by directed security issues in individual national capital markets and by tapping local capital markets through foreign affiliates. Increased market liquidity results in the MNC being able to raise more capital at about the same low cost of capital available in the domestic market.

A graph which shows how the WACOC changes as more and more new capital is raised during a given period is called the *marginal cost of capital schedule*. Figure 7.2 shows how the WACOC changes for the following example. From $0 to $150 million (M) of new capital the WACOC is 10 percent, whereas just beyond $150M, the WACOC rises to 11 percent since the cost of debt rises. This may be due to the fact that a bank is willing to lend to a firm at a given interest rate up to a given limit; beyond this limit, the interest rate will be higher due to the additional risk exposure the bank is taking. At $200M, the WACOC rises again to 12 percent, since at this point, external equity is required and the cost of external equity is higher than the cost of retained earnings. There could, of course, be still more break points, or points at which the WACOC would increase: they would occur if the interest rate continued to rise or if there was a rise in the cost of preferred and/or common stock.

Since the cost of capital depends on how much capital a firm raises, the question of which WACOC it should use arises. Specifically, in the example of Figure 7.2, should we use 10, 11 or 12 percent? The answer is based on the concept of *marginal analysis*, which tells us that firms should expand output to the point where marginal revenue equals marginal cost. At this point, the last unit of output exactly covers its cost—further expansion would reduce profits and the firm would forego profits at any lower production rate.

To apply the concept of marginal analysis, we introduce a schedule that is analogous to the MCC schedule. This is the *investment opportunity schedule* (IOS), which shows the rate of return on each potential investment opportunity, including, for instance, the establishment of a foreign affiliate. Figure 7.2 shows an IOS for projects *A, B, C* and *D*. The first three projects all have expected rates of return that exceed the cost of capital that will be used to finance them, but the expected return on project *D* is less than its cost of capital. Consequently, projects *A, B* and *C* should be accepted and project *D* should be rejected. As indicated at the bottom of Figure 7.2, the required capital to implement projects *A, B* and *C* is $170 million; this is the *optimal capital budget*. The WACOC at the point where the IOS intersects the MCC curve is defined as the *corporate cost of capital*—this point reflects the marginal cost of capital to the MNC.

Figure 7.2
Combining the MCC Schedule and the IOS to Determine the Optimal Capital Budget

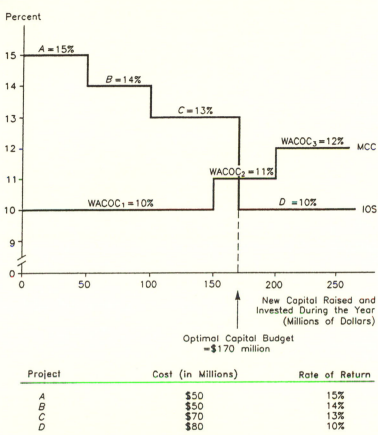

Project	Cost (in Millions)	Rate of Return
A	$50	15%
B	$50	14%
C	$70	13%
D	$80	10%

Naturally, most MNCs would have more than four potential investments to analyze; however, the application of the concept of marginal analysis remains the same if there are many potential investments.

Up to this point we have not yet considered the determination of the optimal capital budget when among the identified set of investment opportunities there are some mutually exclusive projects. Consider, for example, that we have identified projects *A, B, C, D* and *E* and that projects *B* and *C* are mutually exclusive and each has a return larger than the MCC. In this case we develop two graphs as in Figure 7.2, one for projects *A, B, D* and *E* and one for projects *A, C, D* and *E*. Next, we determine the MCC related to each graph and the corresponding sum of net present values of projects with a return larger than the MCC. Project *B* is selected if the sum of net present values of the projects including *B* is larger than the sum of net present values of the projects including C. Naturally, if the former sum is smaller than the latter, we select project C.

Although the procedures set forth in the preceding paragraphs are conceptually correct and an understanding of their underlying logic is important, management often uses a more judgmental, less quantitative process for establishing the final capital budget. Typically, the financial vice president of a company acquires reasonably good estimates of the MCC schedule and the IOS from the treasurer and the director of capital budgeting, respectively. These two schedules are then combined, as in Figure 7.2, to get a reasonably good approximation of the company's MCC. The corporate MCC is then scaled up or down for each division and each foreign affiliate (where applicable) to reflect the division's and foreign affiliate's risk characteristics and capital structure, which is included if a company finances different assets in different ways. For instance, one division may have most of its capital tied up in special-purpose machinery, which is not very well suited as collateral for loans, while another division may have a lot of real estate, which is normally good collateral. As a result, the division with the real estate has a higher debt capacity than the division with the machinery, and consequently, an optimal capital structure that contains a higher percentage of debt.

Suppose, for instance, that the corporate MCC is 11.0 percent. The financial vice president may then decide to assign a factor 0.9 to a stable and low-risk division, but a factor of 1.1 to a more risky division or foreign affiliate. Therefore, the cost of capital of the low-risk division is 0.9(11.0%) = 9.9 percent, while that of the more risky division is 1.1(11.0%) = 12.1 percent. Next, each project within each division is classified into one of three groups—high risk, average risk and low risk—and the same factors, 0.9 and 1.1, are used to adjust the divisional MCCs. For example, a low-risk project in the low-risk division would have a cost of capital of 0.9(9.9%) = 8.9 percent, and a low-risk project in the more risky division would have a cost of capital of 0.9(12.1%) = 10.9 percent. A high-risk project in the low-risk division would have a cost of capital of 1.1(9.9%) = 10.9 percent, and a high-risk project in the more risky division would have a cost of capital of 1.1(12.1%) = 13.3 percent. Naturally, the corporate MCC of 11.0 percent is not adjusted for an average-risk project in an average-risk division.

After having established the adjusted cost of capital for each project in each division, we determine the net present value (NPV) for each project by using its risk-adjusted cost of capital. The optimal budget consists of all independent projects with risk-adjusted, positive NPVs plus those projects from mutually exclusive projects which result in the risk-adjusted, highest positive NPVs among that group.

This approach to establishing the final capital budget has the advantage that it forces a company to think carefully about each division's and foreign affiliate's risk, the risk of each project in each division/affiliate and the relationship between the total amount of capital raised and its cost. In addition, the MNC's capital budget is adjusted to reflect capital market conditions—the cost of capital to evaluate projects will increase if the cost of debt and equity rises, and projects that are marginally acceptable when capital costs are low will be ruled unacceptable when capital costs are high.

To deal with projects with different risks (for instance, political risks), we can also determine the corporate cost of capital for groups of projects with about equal risk. Thus, the first group of projects may consist of high-risk projects; the second group, of average-risk projects; and the third group, of low-risk projects. Next, we determine the IOS and MCC schedules for each group to arrive at the corporate costs of capital.

Figure 7.2 shows three WACOCs (10%, 11% and 12%). Each of these WACOCs should be based on an analysis of debt-assets ratios (D/A ratios) in order to minimize its value. In other words, we are interested in finding the optimal capital structure or the one which minimizes the WACOC, where *capital structure* is defined as the combination of debt and equity. The concept of optimal capital structure is based on a capital structure policy which involves a trade-off between risk and return. That is, using more debt raises the riskiness of a firm's earnings; however, a higher debt ratio generally leads to a higher expected rate of return. In other words, higher risk associated with greater debt tends to decrease the stock's price, but the higher expected rate of return increases it. The optimal capital structure is the one that strikes the optimal balance between risk and return, and by doing so, maximizes the stock's price and minimizes the WACOC.

Appendix 7 shows a capital budgeting analysis which starts with simplifying assumptions. Next, the simplifying assumptions are relaxed to demonstrate the potential complexity of such analysis.

Financial leverage, which is the extent to which fixed-income securities (debt and preferred stock) are used in a firm's capital structure, affects the firm's expected earnings per share (EPS), their riskiness, and, consequently, its stock price. As a result of using financial leverage, an additional risk is placed on common stockholders. This additional risk, called the *financial risk*, is the portion of stockholders' risk over and above the basic business risk.

The following example illustrates how financial leverage affects a company's EPS and stock price and how we determine the optimal capital structure. Suppose a company's annual sales are $400,000; its fixed costs are $80,000; its variable costs are 60 percent of sales, or $240,000; and its marginal tax rate, T, is 40 percent. The company's total assets are worth $400,000. We first consider two cases:

- D/A ratio = 0, or there is zero debt and 20,000 shares outstanding, and
- D/A ratio = 50 percent; the interest rate, i, is equal to 12 percent; and there are 10,000 shares outstanding.

Thus, in the first case the company is capitalized with 0 debt and 100 percent equity, while in the second case, the company is capitalized with 50 percent debt and 50 percent equity. The EPS is defined as:

$$EPS = [(\text{sales} - \text{fixed costs} - \text{variable costs} - \text{interest})$$
$$(1 - T)]/\text{shares outstanding}$$

Thus, for D/A = 0 we have:

$$EPS = [(\$400{,}000 - \$80{,}000 - \$240{,}000 - 0)(0.6)]/20{,}000 = \$2.40$$

For D/A = 50 percent, we have:

$$EPS = [(\$400{,}000 - \$80{,}000 - \$240{,}000 - \$24{,}000)(0.6)]/10{,}000 = \$3.36$$

In order to determine the required rate of return on common stock, k, we use the *capital asset–pricing* model (CAPM):

$$k = k_{rf} + (k_m - k_{rf})\beta$$

where:

k_{rf} = the risk-free rate, generally taken to be either the US Treasury
       bond rate or the short-term US Treasury bill rate
k_m = the expected rate of return on the market (or on an average stock)
β = the stock's beta coefficient

The expected rate of return on the market may be obtained by taking, for instance, the average return of the stocks included in the New York Stock Exchange Composite Index, the Standard & Poor's 500 Index or the Nikkei 225 Stock Average.

A stock's beta coefficient, β, is defined as follows:

$$\beta = \text{cov}(k, k_m)/\sigma^2(k_m)$$

where:

$\sigma^2(k_m)$ = the variance of the market
and all other terms are as defined previously

Note that the above β is a special case of the β introduced in the previous section (the Currency Hedge Ratio).

Based on statistics kept by the University of Chicago since 1926, financial analysts in the United States often assume that $(k_m - k_{rf}) = 8.5$ percent. Others have taken a value for $(k_m - k_{rf})$ based on the most recent 15, 25 or 40 years. For instance, if you do not believe that another world war will take place during the next 20 years, there is no reason to include the effect of World War II on $(k_m - k_{rf})$ by going back to 1926. Values for $(k_m - k_{rf})$ may also vary from country to country.

A stock has, by definition, a *beta coefficient* equal to 1.0 if its price moves up, or down, by percentage, in accordance with the market's movement. A portfolio of such ($\beta = 1.0$) stocks will go up or down exactly with the broad market averages, and its riskiness is the same as that of the averages. A $\beta = 0.5$ value means that a stock moves up or down by half as much as the average stock moves up or down, or the stock is half as volatile as the market average. A portfolio of $\beta = 0.5$ stocks is half as risky as a portfolio of $\beta = 1.0$ stocks. On the other hand, if $\beta = 2.0$, the stock is twice as volatile as an average stock and a portfolio of such stocks will be twice as risky as an average portfolio. The beta coefficients of thousands of companies are calculated and published by organizations like Value Line and Merrill Lynch.

It can be shown mathematically that if dividends are expected to grow at a constant rate, g, the present value of a stock, V, is as follows:

$V = D/(k - g)$

where:

D = the stock's estimated dividend one year hence
all other symbols as defined above

Let us assume that the company pays all its earnings out as dividends, so that EPS = DPS or dividend per share. Thus, no retained earnings are plowed back into the business and, consequently, growth in EPS and DPS will be zero. Suppose the risk-free rate of return is 6 percent; the required return on the average stock is 10 percent; the β pertaining to the D/A = 0 case is 1.50; and the β pertaining to the D/A = 50 percent case is 2.35. The application of the above expressions for k and V gives for D/A = 0:

$k = 6\% + (10\% - 6\%)1.50 = 12.0\%$
$V = DPS/k = \$2.40/0.120 = \$20.00$

For D/A = 50 percent:

$k = 6\% + (10\% - 6\%)2.35 = 15.4\%$
$V = DPS/k = \$3.36/0.154 = \$21.82$

Next, we determine the price earnings (P/E) ratio and WACOC for each of the cases considered. For D/A = 0:

P/E = V/EPS = $20.00/$2.40 = 8.33
WACOC = (D/A)i(1 − T) + (1 − D/A)k = 0 + k = 12.0%

For D/A = 50 percent:

P/E = V/EPS = $21.82/$3.36 = 6.49
WACOC = (D/A)i(1 − T) + (1 − D/A)k = 0.5(12.0%)(0.6) + 0.5(15.4%)
        = 11.3%

This example illustrates that changing a company's capitalization from 0 debt and 100 percent equity to 50 percent debt and 50 percent equity decreases the WACOC from 12.0 percent to 11.3 percent, increases the EPS from $2.40 to $3.36 and increases the company's estimated stock price from $20.00 to $21.82. In other words, using financial leverage is to the advantage of the company, since it increases the company's stock price. How far should the company go with substituting debt for equity? The answer is that the company should choose the capital structure that will maximize the price of its stock. To elucidate this concept, we consider the same example as the one discussed above, and increase the number of cases pertaining to different D/A ratios as given in Table 7.3.

The values of columns 2 and 4 of Table 7.3 are given, while the values of the other columns are calculated in the same manner as we computed them for D/A = 0 and D/A = 50 percent. For instance, for D/A = 20 percent, we have:

EPS = [($400,000 − $80,000 − $240,000 − $6,800)(0.6)]/16,000 = $2.75
k = 6% + (10% − 6%)1.65 = 12.6%
V = $2.75/0.126 = $21.83
P/E = $21.83/$2.75 = 7.94
WACOC = 0.2(8.5%)(0.6) + 0.8(12.6%) = 11.10%

Table 7.3 shows that at a 40 percent debt ratio, the expected stock price is maximized and the WACOC is minimized. Thus, the optimal capital structure calls for 40 percent debt and 60 percent equity. The company should set its target capital structure at these ratios; it should move toward this target when new security offerings are made if the existing ratio is off target.

The following observations are made about the figures of Table 7.3:

• Column 2 shows that the company's cost of debt varies if different percentages of debt are used in its capital structure; the higher the percentage of debt, the riskier the debt, and, consequently, the higher the interest rate lenders will charge.
• Column 3 demonstrates that the expected EPS is maximized at a D/A ratio of 50 percent; however, this does not mean that the company's optimal capital structure calls

Table 7.3
Estimates of Stock Price and Cost of Capital for a Company According to Different D/A Ratios

D/A	i	Exp.	β	k	V	P/E	WACOC
(%)	(%)	EPS		(%)		(%)	
(1)	(2)	(3)	(4)	(5)	(6)	(7)	(8)
0	-	$2.40	1.50	12.0	$20.00	8.33	12.00
10	8.0	2.56	1.55	12.2	20.98	8.20	11.46
20	8.5	2.75	1.65	12.6	21.83	7.94	11.10
30	9.0	2.97	1.80	13.2	22.50	7.58	10.86
40	10.0	3.20	2.00	14.0	22.86	7.14	10.80
50	12.0	3.36	2.35	15.4	21.82	6.49	11.30
60	15.0	3.30	2.75	17.8	18.54	5.62	12.52

for a 50 percent debt, since the optimal capital structure is the one that maximizes the price of the company's stock, which always calls for a D/A ratio smaller than the one that maximizes expected EPS.

- The beta coefficients of Column 4 measure the relative volatility of the company's stock as compared with that of an average stock; it has been demonstrated both empirically and theoretically that a company's beta increases with its degree of financial leverage.

- Column 5 shows that the values of k increase when the estimated beta coefficients increase (by definition of k); note that $(k_m - k_{rf})$ is not equal to 8.5 percent, as is often the case in the United States, since the example pertains to a European country.

- As mentioned above, the values of Column 6 are computed to establish the optimal capital structure—the one that results in the highest estimated stock price.

- The P/E ratios of Column 7 demonstrate that, other things held constant, they will decline as the riskiness of a company increases; the P/E ratios are computed as a check on the reasonableness of the other data of Table 7.3 and they can be compared for consistency with those of zero-growth competitive companies with varying amounts of financial leverage.

- Column 8 shows that as the D/A ratio increases, the costs of both debt and equity rise and the increasing costs of the two components begin to offset the fact that larger amounts of the lower-cost component are being used; at 40 percent debt, WACOC hits a minimum; it rises after that as the D/A ratio is increased.

SUGGESTIONS FOR FURTHER READING

Beenhakker, H. L. *Risk Management in Project Finance and Implementation*. Westport, CT: Quorum Books, 1997.
Hack, G. D. *Site Selection for Growing Companies*. Westport, CT: Quorum Books, 1999.
Lewent, J. C., and A. J. Kearney. "Identifying, Measuring, and Hedging Currency Risk at Merck." *Journal of Applied Corporate Finance* 2, no. 4 (Winter 1990): 19–28.

Moffett, M. H., and J. K. Karlsen. "Managing Foreign Exchange Rate Economic Exposure." *Journal of International Financial Management and Accounting* 5, no. 2 (June 1994): 157–175.
Schniederjans, M. J. *Operations Management in a Global Context*. Westport, CT: Quorum Books, 1998.

Chapter 8

Financing from a Global Perspective

SOURCING EQUITY INTERNATIONALLY

We define sourcing equity internationally as cross-listing shares abroad as well as the selling of new shares to foreign investors. A firm hopes to achieve one or more of the following objectives by cross-listing its shares on foreign exchanges:

- provision of a liquid secondary market to support a new equity issue in the foreign market,
- improvement of the liquidity of its existing shares by making it easier for foreign shareholders to trade in their home markets and currencies,
- establishment of a secondary market for shares used to acquire local firms,
- increase of its share price by overcoming mispricing in a segmented, illiquid home capital market,
- increase of the firm's visibility and political acceptance to its customers, suppliers, creditors and host government, and
- creation of a secondary market for shares that will be used to compensate local management and employees in foreign affiliates.

Cross-listing is usually accomplished by *depository receipts*. In the United States, foreign shares are usually traded through American depository receipts or ADRs. These are negotiable certificates issued by a US bank in the United States and which represent the underlying shares of stock, which are held in trust at a custodian bank. ADRs are sold, registered and transferred in the United States in the same manner as any share of stock. Each ADR represents some multiple of the underlying foreign share, which enables ADRs to be traded in an appropriate price range for the US market even if the price of the foreign share is inappropriate when converted to US dollars. Dividends paid by a foreign firm are passed to its custodian bank and then to the bank that issued the ADR. The issuing bank exchanges the foreign currency dividends for US dollars and sends the dollar dividend to the ADR holders.

ADRs can be *sponsored* or *unsponsored*. Sponsored ADRs come into being at the request of a foreign firm interested in having its shares traded in the United States. The firm applies to the SEC and a US bank for registration and issuance of ADRs. All costs of creating sponsored ADRs are paid by the foreign firm. If a foreign firm does not seek to have its shares traded in the United States but US investors are interested, a US securities firm may initiate the creation of ADRs, in which case we call these unsponsored ADRs.

It has not been conclusively demonstrated that cross-listing on a foreign stock exchange has a favorable effect on share prices. What we can say is that this depends on the degree to which markets are segmented. For instance, if a firm's home capital market is segmented it could benefit by cross-listing in a foreign market if that market values the firm or its industry more than does the home market. MNCs often list in markets where they have substantial physical operations in order to advertise trademarks and products, get improved local press coverage, enhance their corporate image and become familiar with the local financial community in order to raise working capital locally.

Disadvantages of cross-listing are an increased commitment to full disclosure and a continuing investor relations program. For firms resident in the Anglo-American markets, listing abroad is not likely to be much of a barrier. For instance, the SEC's disclosure rules for listing in the United States are so stringent and costly that any other market's rules are rather simple. Non-US firms, however, must think twice before listing in the United States. In addition to stringent disclosure requirements, there is a continuous demand for timely quarterly information. This means that the foreign firm must supply a costly continuous investor relations program for its US shareholders. Since the US level of required disclosure is an onerous, costly burden, it chases away potential listers, thus narrowing the choice of securities available to US investors at reasonable transaction costs. For instance, the number of foreign firms listed on the Frankfurt Stock Exchange is more than twice the number of foreign firms listed on the New York Stock Exchange.

In addition to cross-listing on multiple stock exchanges, firms can lower their cost of capital and increase their liquidity by selling their shares to foreign investors through a new share issue or resale of existing shares. This can be accomplished in three alternate ways:

- sale of a *directed* share issue to investors in one particular foreign equity market,
- sale of a *Euro-equity* share issue to foreign investors simultaneously in more than one market, including both foreign and domestic markets, and
- sale of shares to a foreign firm as part of a strategic alliance.

A directed share issue is defined as one targeted at investors in a single country and underwritten in whole or in part by investment institutions from that country. The issue can be denominated in the currency of the target market, but it does not have to be. In addition, the shares may or may not be listed on a stock exchange in the target market. The motivation of a directed share issue might be the need to fund acquisitions or major capital investments in a target foreign market. This is an important source of equity for firms resident in smaller capital markets which have outgrown that market.

The same financial institutions that had created an infrastructure for the Euronote and Eurobond markets are responsible for the introduction of the Euro-equity market. Accordingly, a firm can issue equity which is underwritten and distributed in multiple foreign equity markets, sometimes simultaneously with distribution in the domestic market. The term *Euro* does not imply that the issuers are located in Europe; it is a generic term for international equity issues originating and sold anywhere in the world. Large Euro-equity share issues have been in conjunction with privatizations of government-owned enterprises such as the sale of shares for $3.04 billion by Argentina's state-owned oil company (YPF Sociedad Anonima) in 1993, and the sale of shares for $2 billion by the Mexican telephone company (Telefonos de Mexico) in 1991. In 1984 the Thatcher government in the United Kingdom created the model when it privatized British Telecom. That issue was so large that it was necessary to sell *tranches* to foreign investors in addition to the sale to domestic investors. A tranche means an allocation of shares to underwriters that are expected to sell to investors in their designated geographic markets. The objective is to raise funds and to ensure post-issue worldwide liquidity. In retrospect, in the case of British Telecom the issue was underpriced. Most of the foreign shares, especially those placed in the United States, flowed back to London, leaving a handsome profit behind for the US underwriters and investors. However, other large British privatization issues that followed British Telecom have been successful.

Strategic alliances are generally formed by firms that expect to gain synergy such as sharing the cost of developing technology or pursuing complementary marketing activities. An industrial purchaser might be willing to pay a higher price for a firm that will provide it some synergy than would a portfolio investor that does not receive this synergy. Normally, portfolio investors cannot anticipate the value of synergy that might accrue to a firm from an unexpected strategic alliance partner. They are only pricing a firm's shares based on the risk versus return trade-off.

SOURCING DEBT INTERNATIONALLY

Chapter 6 stressed the importance of maturity matching when a firm acquires debt, while chapter 7 emphasized the importance of currency matching. Naturally, these forms of matching are important when sourcing debt internationally.

Let us now examine other issues related to MNCs raising debt capital on the international markets.

When an MNC issues foreign currency–denominated debt, its effective cost equals the after-tax cost of repaying the principal and interest in terms of the MNC's own currency. Principal and interest must be adjusted for any foreign exchange gains or losses, since they are in foreign currency terms. Let us calculate the dollar cost of a one-year debt for SF1,500,000 at 5.00 percent interest, assumed by a US-based firm. During the year the Swiss franc appreciated from an initial rate of SF1.5000/$ to SF1.4500/$.

The dollar proceeds of the initial borrowing are calculated at the current spot rate of SF1.5000/$:

$$(SF1,500,00)/(SF1.5000/\$) = \$1,000,000$$

At the end of the year the US-based firm is responsible for repaying the SF1,500,000 principal plus 5 percent interest, or a total of SF1,575,000. This repayment is to be made at an ending spot rate of SF1.4500/$:

$$(SF1,500,000 \times 1.05)/(SF1.4500/\$) = \$1,086,207$$

Thus, the actual dollar cost of the loan's repayment is not simply 5.00 percent, which was paid in Swiss franc interest, but 8.62 percent:

$$\$1,086,207/\$1,000,000 = 1.086207$$

The dollar cost is higher than expected due to appreciation of the Swiss franc against the US dollar. Assuming a corporate income tax rate of 34 percent, the after-tax cost of this Swiss franc denominated debt is 8.62 percent $\times$ 0.66 = 5.689 percent. The percentage change in the value of the Swiss franc versus the US dollar, when the home currency is the US dollar is:

$$(SF1.5000/\$ - SF1.4500/\$)/(SF1.4500/\$) \times 100\% = 3.4483\%$$

The added 3.4483 percent cost of this debt in terms of US dollars can be reported as a foreign exchange transaction loss and is deductible for US tax purposes.

Similarly, when investing internationally, "what you see is not always what you get". For instance, a 10 percent interest rate on a dollar-denominated bond is not comparable to a 6 percent rate on a yen bond or a 14 percent rate on a British sterling bond. To see why, let us calculate the rate of return on $1,000 invested today in a one-year British sterling bond yielding 14 percent interest when today's exchange rate is 1 pound = $1.50 and the rate in one year is 1 pound = 1.35.

$1,000 will buy 666.67 pounds today (1,000/1.50 = 666.67), and in one year interest and principal on the sterling bond will total 760 pounds (666.67[1 +

.14] = 760). Converting this amount back into dollars yields $1,026 in one year (760 × 1.35 = 1,026). So the investment's rate of return, measured in dollars, is only 2.6 percent ([1,026 − 1,000]/1,000 = 2.6%). Why is the dollar return so low? Because investing in a foreign asset is really two investments: a purchase of a foreign-currency asset and speculation on future changes in the dollar value of the foreign currency. Here the foreign asset yields a healthy 14 percent, but the sterling depreciates 10 percent against the dollar ([1.50 − 1.35]/1.50); thus, the combined return is roughly the difference between the two. The exact relationship is:

(1 + return) = (1 + interest rate)(1 + change in exchange rate), or
(1 + return) = (1 + 14%)(1 − 10%), or
return = 2.6%

The international debt markets offer the borrower a variety of different maturities, repayment structures and currencies of denomination. The three principal sources of debt funding on the international markets are as follows:

Markets and Instruments	Maturities	Rate
International Bank Loans		
Short- to Medium-Term Bank Loans	1 yr.–5 yrs.	floating
Syndicated Credits	2 yrs.–10 yrs.	floating
Euronote Market		
Euronotes	3 yrs.–7 yrs.	floating
Euro-Commercial Paper (ECP)	30 days–365 days/ 1–5 yrs.	fixed
Euro-Medium Term Notes (EMTN)	2 yrs.–6 yrs.	fixed
International Bond Market		
Straight Fixed Rate Issues	2 yrs.–20 yrs.	fixed
Floating Rate Notes (FRNs)	2 yrs.–20 yrs.	floating
Equity-Related Issues	2 yrs.–10 yrs.	fixed (equity dependent)

An MNC normally needs debt in a variety of maturities, currencies and payment structure; it will, therefore, often use all three markets—international bank loans, the Euronote market and the internatioanl bond market—in addition to its traditional domestic funding base.

International bank loans have traditionally been made in the Eurocurrency markets. Eurodollar bank loans are also referred to as *Eurodollar credits* or *Eurocredits*. The latter title is perhaps more correct because it encompasses nondollar loans in the Eurocurrency market. Eurodollars are lent for both short- and medium-term maturities. Most Eurodollar loans are for a fixed term with no provision for early repayment. The narrow interest rate spread (difference between loan and deposit rates) within the Eurocurrency loan market is a key factor attracting both borrowers and depositors to that market. The interest rate spread is small (often less than 1%) since:

- the Eurodollar market is a "wholesale" market with deposits and loans made in amounts of $500,000 or more on an unsecured basis,
- borrowers are usually large corporations or government agencies that qualify for low rates because of their credit standing and because the transaction size is large, and
- overhead assigned to the Eurodollar operation by participating banks is small.

Syndicated credits are bank loans to business firms, international institutions, sovereign governments and other banks, denominated in Eurocurrencies and extended by banks in countries other than the country in whose currency the loan is denominated. In view of the large size of these loans, the banks form a syndicate (group) in order to diversify the risks. The basic borrowing interest rate for Eurodollar loans has long been tied to the LIBOR, which is the deposit rate applicable to interbank loans within London. Today, the use of LIBOR is supplemented by the use of a US money market rate base. Borrowers usually pay a premium over the base rate determined by their creditworthiness and the terms of the credit. A syndicated bank credit is arranged by a *lead bank* on behalf of its client; the lead bank works with the borrower to establish the amount of the total credit, the floating-rate base and spread over the base rate, maturity and fee structure for managing the participating banks. Before finalizing the loan agreement, the lead bank seeks the participation of a group of banks. A syndicated loan can be a *revolving credit* or a *term credit*. If a revolving credit, a commitment fee on any unused portions of the credit must be paid. If a term credit, the borrower has a specified drawdown time schedule for the loan, and there is usually no commitment fee. Spreads in the syndicated loan market vary from as little as .16 percent to over 2.5 percent.

The Euronote market refers to short- to medium-term debt instruments sourced in the Eurocurrency markets. In principle, they can be divided into *underwritten facilities*, which are used for the sale of Euronotes in a number of different forms, and *nonunderwritten facilities*, which are used for the sale and distribution of Euro-Commercial Paper (ECP) and Euro-Medium-Term Notes (EMTNs). Euronotes are short-term, negotiable, promissory notes, which were established in the early 1980s. The Euronote market essentially died in the late 1980s due to competition from ECPs and EMTNs and the development of newly established, nonunderwritten, domestic commercial paper markets in many countries. The ECP, like the commercial paper issued in domestic markets, is a short-term debt obligation of a corporation or bank. Maturities are typically one, three and six months. In general, the ECP is sold at a discount. The market price of the ECP issued by corporate borrowers at a discount is calculated as follows:

$$\text{Market Price} = \text{Face Value}/\{1 + [(N/360) \times (Y/100)]\}$$

where:

    Y = yield in annual percent
    N = days remaining until maturity

For instance, the market price (proceeds) of the sale of a $1,000 face-value 90-day ECP priced to yield 8.0% annually is:

Market Price = $1,000/{1 + [(90/360) $\times$ (8.0/100)]} = $980.39

It is noted that Germany, Japan and the United States use a 360-day financial year; however, the British pound sterling–denominated ECP market uses a 365-day financial year.

The EMTN's basic characteristics are similar to a bond, with principal, maturity and coupon structures and rates being comparable. Its typical maturities range from two to six years. Coupons are typically paid semiannually and coupon rates are comparable to similar bond issues. However, the EMTN has three unique features:

- it is a facility allowing continuous issuance over a period of time (unlike a bond issue that is sold at once);
- coupons are paid on set calendar dates regardless of the date of issuance (in order to make coupon redemption manageable, since EMNTs are sold continuously); and
- it is issued in relatively small denominations, from $2 million to $5 million, making medium debt acquisition more flexible than the large minimums customarily needed in the international bond markets.

International bonds can be classified as *Eurobonds* and *foreign bonds*. The distinction between these two categories is based on whether the issue is denominated in the local currency or a foreign currency. A Eurobond is underwritten by an international syndicate of banks and other security firms, and is sold exclusively in countries other than the country in whose currency the issue is denominated. For instance, a bond issued by a firm resident in Switzerland, denominated in Swiss francs but sold to investors in the United States and Japan (not to investors in Switzerland), would be a Eurobond. Eurobonds are usually issued in bearer form, meaning the name and country of residence of the owner is not on the certificate. To receive interest, the bearer cuts an interest coupon from the bond and turns it in at a banking institution listed on the issue as a paying agent. A foreign bond is underwritten by a syndicate composed of members from a single country, sold primarily within that country and denominated in the currency of that country. The issuer, however, is from another country. For instance, a bond issued by a firm resident in Germany, denominated in dollars and sold in the United States to US investors by US investment bankers, would be a foreign bond. Foreign bonds have nicknames: those sold in the

United States are *Yankee bonds*, those sold in the United Kingdom are *Bulldogs* and those sold in Japan are *Samurai bonds*.

The *straight fixed-rate* issue is structured like most domestic bonds, with a fixed coupon, set maturity date and full principal repayment upon final maturity. Since the bonds are bearer bonds and annual coupon redemption is more convenient, coupons are normally paid annually. The *floating-rate note* (FRN) normally pays a semiannual coupon that is determined using a variable-rate base. A typical coupon would be set at some fixed spread over LIBOR. Like most variable-rate interest-bearing instruments, the FRN was designed to allow investors to shift more of the interest rate risk of an investment to the borrower. Although many FRNs have fixed maturities, a number of major issues since 1985 are perpetuities; the principal will never be paid back.

The *equity-related international bond* resembles the straight fixed-rate issue in practically all price and payment characteristics, with the added feature that it is convertible to stock prior to maturity at a specified price per share (or number of shares per bond). The added value of the equity conversion feature enables the borrower to issue debt with lower coupon payments.

The Eurobond market has the following attractive features:

- *Absence of regulatory interference*. National governments frequently impose tight controls on foreign issuers of securities denominated in the local currency and sold within their national boundaries. However, generally governments have less stringent limitations for securities denominated in foreign currencies and sold within their markets to holders of those foreign currencies.

- *Less stringent disclosure*. Disclosure requirements in the Eurobond market are much less stringent than those of the SEC for sales within the United States. US firms often find that the registration costs of a Eurobond offering are less than those of a domestic issue and that less time is needed to bring a new issue to market.

- *Favorable tax status*. In 1984 the US tax laws were revised to exempt foreign holders of bonds issued by US corporations from withholding tax. Repeal of the US withholding tax caused other countries (e.g., France, Germany and UK) to liberalize their tax rules as a defensive measure to avoid an outflow of capital from their markets.

Rating agencies, such as Standard & Poor's (S&P's) and Moody's provide ratings for selected international bonds for a fee. Credit ratings are critical to borrowers and investors alike. An MNC's credit rating determines its cost of capital. The higher the credit rating, the lower the cost of capital. A higher cost of obtaining debt capital does not only add significantly to the annual financial expenses of the firm, but over the long term could form the basis for a continuing source of international competitive weakness. Purchasers of Eurobonds do not only rely on bond-rating services or on detailed analyses of financial statements. General reputation of the issuing corporation and its underwriters is a major factor in obtaining favorable terms. Large and better-known MNCs, well-run state enterprises and sovereign governments are able to obtain the lowest interest rates.

INTEREST RATE RISK MANAGEMENT

We distinguish two basic types of interest rate risk: *basis risk* and *gap risk*. Basis risk is the risk related to mismatching of interest rate bases for associated assets and liabilities (discussed in Chapter 7). It is particularly important for financial institutions to pay attention to basis risk since their primary revenues and costs consist of interest rate payment flows. Gap risk, which is more typical of a nonfinancial firm, arises from mismatched timing in repricing interest-rate-sensitive assets and liabilities. The typical nonfinancial firm possesses a relatively small amount of interest-sensitive assets, while funding may consist of a relatively large amount on interest-bearing debt.

The instruments or techniques available for reducing gap risk are:

* mismatched maturities,
* foreign exchange forward mismatching,
* forward rate agreement,
* interest rate and currency swaps,
* interest rate futures,
* interest rate caps and floors,
* interest rate collars, and
* interest rate options.

MISMATCHED MATURITIES

The *mismatching of maturities*, lending long and borrowing short, is probably the oldest interest rate management technique. It is based on the assumption that the *yield curve* is a forecast of future spot interest rates. A yield curve is a graph of equivalent annual percentage interest rates versus maturities in days. Figure 8.1 gives an example of a yield curve. If the yield curve is upward sloping, a firm wishing to lock in a future rate of interest on investments that are more attractive than current rates should borrow short and invest long. In other words, the short-term borrowing provides the funds for the long-term investment, and the repayment of the short-term borrowing is covered by the inflow of cash to the firm in the medium term. It is this inflow that the firm wishes to invest at higher rates. With an upward sloping yield curve, a firm wishing to reduce borrowing costs over the long run would be forced to borrow short and continually roll over the debt at market rates of interest. A negatively sloped yield curve provides a firm with a set of conditions for relatively low-cost long-term

Figure 8.1
Example of a Yield Curve

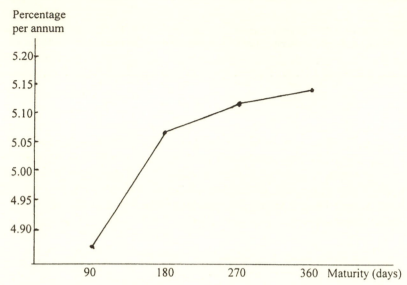

borrowing. If the funds are not needed immediately, short-term loans/invest-ments allow a firm to cover its cheap long-term debt service expenses.

FOREIGN EXCHANGE FORWARD MISMATCHING

A *foreign exchange forward mismatching* consists of a combined position of selling one currency forward at one maturity while buying the same currency forward at a different maturity to lock in a future interest rate on the foreign currency. The following example elucidates this technique. Assume a firm in Germany knows that it will need $10,000,000 beginning in six months for a six-month period. The firm wishes to reduce the uncertainty of exchange rates related to borrowing the US dollar funds six months later. In addition, the firm wishes to take advantage of the fact that US dollar interest rates are currently relatively low compared to German mark interest rates, but may not remain so. This future borrowing of a foreign currency is achieved by signing two forward contracts:

• buy $10,000,000 180 days forward at DM1.5380/$, and
• sell $10,000,000 360 days forward at DM1.5740/$.

With these two contracts, the German firm has assured itself of (a) obtaining $10,000,000 in six months at a certain exchange rate and (b) selling the same $10,000,000 for German marks at a second exchange rate six months later. Since the exchange rate is specified on both ends of the agreement, the cost of the US dollar funds has been locked in. The actual cost of the Eurodollar funds to the German firm is obtained by determining the internal interest rate that equates the amount of German mark funds put up at the beginning of the six-month period with the funds returned at the end of the total period:

[($10,000,000 × DM1.5740/$)/($10,000,000 × DM1.5380/$)] − 1 =
[DM15,740,000/DM15,380,000] −1 = 0.02341
or 2.341% for six months or 4.682% per annum.

Although the cost of Eurodollar funds could actually be cheaper at maturity of the first forward contract, the cost could also be higher. This enables the German firm to eliminate the interest rate uncertainty now, and assure itself of the cost of acquiring the US dollar funds without formally taking out a Eurodollar loan.

FORWARD RATE AGREEMENT

A *forward rate agreement* (FRA) is an agreement to exchange a fixed-rate payment at a rate k for a LIBOR on an underlying loan with a principal P for a period T to $T + m$. At time T, the FRA's settlement is made in discounted form. The use of LIBOR is based on a discount factor (DF), which is defined as the value at t of $1 paid at T, or:

$$DF = 1/[1 + i(N/M)] \tag{1}$$

where:

N = number of days between interest reset days
M = the money market day convention (360 for LIBOR)
i = LIBOR

The difference between paying fixed and receiving floating interest payments at time $T + m$ on a loan of P from time T to time $T + m$ is:

$$P(i_{m,T} - k)(N/M) \tag{2}$$

where:

$i_{m,T}$ = an m month LIBOR at time T
N = the number of days between T and $T + m$ (number of days between interest reset days)
all other symbols are as previously defined

The settlement amount for an FRA at time T is:

$$\text{FRA}_T = P(i_{m,T} - k)(N/M)/[1 + i_{m,T}(N/M)] \tag{3}$$

Note that equation (3) is based on equations (1) and (2).

The payoff on an FRA involves the exchange of LIBOR payments and a fixed-rate payment. A long FRA involves receiving LIBOR and paying a fixed-rate interest, while a short FRA involves paying LIBOR and receiving a fixed-rate interest. No loan principal changes hands with an FRA; however, the interest payments are determined by the size of the notional underlying loan principal P.

Let us consider the following example to enhance our understanding of FRAs. Suppose on April 2 (the "dealing" date), a firm buys a 12-month FRA on a 3-month LIBOR. The principal is $6 million, and the rate is fixed at 7 percent. The contract takes effect two days later, on April 4 (the "spot" date). The contract position is long, indicating that the firm buys the FRA; it will receive LIBOR and pay a fixed rate. Thus, in the example, the notional underlying loan principal is $6 million, and the underlying interest rate index on which payments will be based is the 3-month $LIBOR where $LIBOR indicates the LIBOR applicable to the dollar. The contract has a maturity of 12 months, meaning that the settlement date, T, is 12 months after the spot date. The loan maturity date is 3 months (91 days) after T. The payoff on this FRA is positive if $LIBOR in 12 months after the spot date exceeds 7 percent. Suppose, for example, that the 3-month LIBOR will be 8 percent. With equation (3) we determine the payoff at time T as follows:

Payoff = $6,000,000(0.08 − 0.07)(91/360)DF = $14,866.37

DF in this equation is calculated according to equation (1) as equal to 0.9802.

If, on the other hand, interest rates fall to, for instance, 6 percent, a loss will be incurred on the long FRA. The settlement amount at time T is, in this case:

Payoff = $6,000,000(0.06 − 0.07)(91/360)DF = ms $14,940.68

where:

DF = 0.9851

The following observations can be made:

• By taking a long position in the FRA, the hedger/borrower guarantees a loan rate of exactly 7 percent on the $6,000,000 loan requirement. Firms protect themselves against unexpected movements in LIBOR rates by using FRAs.
• The problem with the hedging strategy is that the borrowing cost is stuck at 7 percent, even should the rates fall to 6 percent. In this case, the firm ends up at a disadvantage

compared to competitors who did not hedge. One solution to this problem is to hedge only a proportion, say 60 percent, of the loan amount.

• For a firm that trades FRAs, hedging is of the utmost importance, as after having sold an FRA, the firm is exposed to adverse changes in the interest rates.

• The example showed that if the LIBOR goes to 8 percent, a profit of $14,866.37 will be made on the FRA. Therefore, the borrower needs to borrow the sum of $6,000,000 − $14,866.37, or $5,985,133.63, in order to obtain a total of $6 million. Interest at 8 percent on this loan is $5,985,133.63(0.08)(91/360), or $121,032.70. The total repayment amount at the end of the loan period is, therefore, $6,106,166.33 and the effective rate of interest is (6,106,166.33 − 6,000,000.00)360/(6,000,000.00)91, or 6.9 percent.

• The 12-month forward on the 3-month LIBOR in our example is referred to in the market as a 12 × 15 FRA. (Note that 15 = 12 + 3.)

• In the case of most currencies, settlement takes place on the same day as the LIBOR is determined. Thus, $i_{m,T}$ of equation (2) is determined at time T and settlement also takes place on that date. However, in the case of US dollars there is a gap of two business days between the day on which the LIBOR is determined (the fixing date) and the settlement date. Thus, $i_{m,T}$ is actually established two business days before T.

• If the date when the notional loan starts falls on a Saturday or Sunday, the next Monday is taken, according to the *Modified Business Day convention*.

• The money-market day count convention, M, is 360 when dealing with the LIBOR related to dollars (as in our example), German marks or yen values; however, when dealing with pounds sterling, M is equal to 365.

If a bank agrees to sell an FRA at a contract rate k, how should it fix k? Assuming that market participants take advantage of arbitrage opportunities as they occur, k has to be fixed at a level that makes the forward contract a fair, or zero-value, contract. The fixed rate, k, that achieves this at time t (current time) is the time t forward LIBOR for m maturity loans, for delivery at $t + T$, which we denote as $f_{m,T}$. Because the actual derivation of the expression for $f_{m,T}$ is far beyond the scope of this text, we simply present the formula itself:

$$f_{m,T} = [i_{T+m}(T + m - t) - i_T(T - t)]/[1 + i_T(T - t)/M]N \qquad (4)$$

where:

$i_{T + m}$ = LIBOR for $T + m$ at time t
i_T = LIBOR for T at time t
and all other terms are as previously defined

Suppose, for example, that on May 15, the LIBOR for 6 months is 7.0525 percent and the LIBOR for 3 months is 6.8025 percent. What is the forward rate for a 3 × 6 month FRA? To elucidate the use of equation (4), we note that the relevant time periods and interest rates in our example are:

t	T	$T + m$
May 15	August 15	November 17

<----------- 92 days -------------------><---------------94 days-------------------->
           6.8025%

<------------------------------------186 days ------------------------------------>
                         7.0525%

Thus, the number of days of the forward loan is 94 days from August 15 to November 17 since November 15 and 16 fall on a Saturday and Sunday. With the help of equation (4), we compute the forward rate as follows:

$$f_{m,T} = [7.0525\%(186) - 6.8025\%(92)]/[1 + 6.8025\%(92/360)]94 = 7.1725\%.$$

This forward rate can now be used to establish the value of the 3×6 month FRA with equation (5), which represents the value of an FRA at time t.

$$\text{Value of FRA}_t = P[(f_{m,T} - k)N/M]DF \qquad (5)$$

where all symbols are as defined above.

Suppose that $P = \$6,000,000$ and $k = 6$ percent. With the help of equation (1) we determine:

$$DF = 1/[1 + 7.0525\%(94/360)] = 0.98073.$$

Thus, the value of our FRA is:

$$\$6,000,000[(0.071725 - 0.06)(94/360)0.98073 = \$18,015.19.$$

SWAPS

A *swap* is an agreement between two parties to exchange debt service payment streams. The exchange can be a floating-rate payment for a fixed-rate payment, an *interest rate swap*, or an exchange of currency of denomination of payment, a *currency swap*. Chapter 3 discusses interest rate and currency swaps. It is noted here that the relatively easy access provided by the interest rate swap to different interest rate structures enables firms to reposition their financial obligations as their expectations on the movements of interest rates change. For instance, a firm that has been paying floating rates while interest rates have been falling has enjoyed a reduction in debt service expense. If the firm believes that interest rates have fallen as far as they are going to, it can swap from floating to fixed rate at little cost. A floating- to fixed-rate swap allows the firm to lock in fixed interest rates at levels the firm's financial managers believe to be in its best interest.

The interest rate and currency swap markets act together to offer the firm with current debt service payments of fixed or floating rates in one currency the ability, with little associated transaction cost, to redenominate both the interest rate payment structure and currency of denomination. It is, therefore, not surprising that the swap markets have grown astronomically in size during the last 15 years.

The purchase of a swap option—a *swaption*—gives the firm the right but not the obligation to enter into a swap on a predetermined notional principal at some defined future date at a specified strike rate. A firm's treasurer would typically purchase a *payer's swaption*, giving the treasurer the right to enter a swap in which they pay the fixed rate and receive the floating rate. He would exercise this option if rates had risen above the strike level of the swaption; otherwise he would allow the option to expire and take advantage of the lower rate environment. A firm may sell a swaption, called a *receiver's swaption*, struck at an acceptable fixed rate, giving the buyer the right to receive the fixed rate from the firm. The buyer would exercise this option if rates decline below the strike level.

INTEREST RATE FUTURES

An *interest rate futures* contract is a futures contract on an asset whose price is dependent solely on the level of interest rates. Treasury bond (T-bond) futures contracts traded on the Chicago Board of Trade (CBOT) are the most popular long-term interest rate futures. In these contracts, any government bond with more than 15 years to maturity on the first day of the delivery month and not callable within 15 years from that day can be delivered. T-bond prices and futures prices are quoted in dollars and 32nds of a dollar. A T-bond normally has a face value of $100,000. Thus, a quote of 90–05 means that the price for a bond with a face value of $100,000 is $90,156.25, where $156.25 = 5(1/32)(1,000)$. The quoted price is not the same as the cash price paid by the purchaser because the accrued interest since the last coupon date is added to the quoted price in order to arrive at the cash price.

In the T-bond futures contract there is a provision for the party with the short position to choose to deliver any bond with a maturity over 15 years and not callable within 15 years. When a bond is delivered, a parameter known as its *conversion factor* defines the price received by the party with the short position. The quoted price applicable to the delivery is the product of the conversion factor and the quoted futures price. Taking accrued interest into account, the cash received by the party with the short position equals the product of the quoted futures price and the conversion factor for the delivered bond plus the accrued interest on the bond. Suppose, for instance, that the quoted futures price is 90–05, the conversion factor for the bond delivered is 1.5705, and the accrued interest on this bond at the time of delivery is $3.50 per $100.00 face value. The cash received by the party with the short position upon delivery of the bond is $(90,156.25 \times 1.5705) + \$3,500.00 = \$145,090.39$.

The conversion factor for a bond is equal to the value of the bond on the first day of the delivery month on the assumption that the interest rate for all maturities equals 8 percent per year (with semiannual compounding). In order to enable CBOT to produce comprehensive tables and assist with calculation, the bond maturity and the times to the coupon payment dates are rounded to the nearest three months. If, after rounding, the bond lasts for an exact number of half years, the first coupon is assumed to be paid in six months. If, after rounding, the bond does not last for an exact number of six-month periods (i.e., there is an extra three months), the first coupon is assumed to be paid after three months and accrued interest is subtracted. The following example elucidates the procedure.

Let us calculate the conversion factor of a 14 percent coupon bond with 18 years, four months to maturity. To simplify the calculation, it is first carried out for each $100 face value of the bond. In view of the rounding procedure, the bond is assumed to have exactly 18 years, three months to maturity. Discounting all the payments back to a point in time three months from today gives a value of (see Appendix 2):

$$\text{pwf}(i = 4\%, n = 36) \times \$7.00 + \text{sppwf}(i = 4\%, n = 36) \times \$100.00$$
$$= \$163.74$$

where:

$$\text{pwf}(i = 4\%, n = 36) = \text{the series present worth factor for a discount rate,}$$
$$i, \text{ equal to 4 percent and for 36 half-year periods}$$
$$\text{sppwf}(i = 4\%, n = 36) = \text{the single payment present worth factor for a}$$
$$\text{discount rate, } i, \text{ equal to 4 percent and for 36}$$
$$\text{half-year periods}$$

The interest rate for a three-months period is 1.98 percent. Discounting back to the present gives the bond's value at $163.74/1.0198 = $160.56, and after subtracting the accrued interest of $3.50, we get $157.06. Since the calculation was carried out for each $100 face value of the bond, we divide by 100 to arrive at a conversion factor of 1.5706. Note that 4 percent mentioned in the above present worth factors is based on half the 8 percent mentioned in the definition of the conversion factor and that the accrued interest of $3.50 is equal to $(3/12) \times \$14.00$.

At any time, there are about 30 bonds that can be delivered in the CBOT T-bond futures contracts. These vary as far as coupon and maturity are concerned. The party with the short position can choose which of the available bonds is "cheapest" to deliver. For example, suppose a party with a short position has decided to deliver and is trying to choose between three bonds with the quoted prices, conversion factors, and the current quoted futures price (93–08, or 93.25), as given in the second, third and fourth columns of Table 8.1. To compute which of the three bonds is cheapest to deliver, the party computes the cost of

Table 8.1
Example of Deliverable Bonds

Bond	Quoted Price	Conversion factor	Quoted Futures Price	Cost of Delivering
1	98.50	1.0380	93.25	1.71
2	142.50	1.5177	93.25	0.97
3	117.75	1.2515	93.25	1.05

delivering each of the bonds. This is done by first multiplying the current quoted futures price by the conversion factor of each bond. Next, the party computes the cost of delivering each bond as the difference between the quoted price and the result of the aforementioned multiplication. The results of these computations, as shown in the last column of Table 8.1, indicate that the *cheapest-to-deliver bond* is bond 2. Note that the figure of 1.71 in the last column of Table 8.1 is the result of $98.50 - (1.0380 \times 93.25)$. The other amounts in the last column are obtained in a similar manner.

Interest rate futures are often used to immunize a portfolio against interest rate risks. In order to show how this is done, we introduce the following information:

F = contract price for the interest rate futures contract
V = value of the portfolio being hedged
D_F = duration of the portfolio underlying the futures contract
D_V = duration of the portfolio being hedged
ΔV = change in the value of the portfolio being hedged
Δy = change in the yield
N = optimal number of contracts to short when hedging the portfolio

It can be shown that the percentage change in a bond price equals its duration multiplied by the size of the parallel shift in the yield curve. Similarly, the percentage change in the value of a bond portfolio is equal to the bond portfolio's duration times the parallel shift in the yield curve, where the bond portfolio's duration is defined as the weighted average of the durations of the individual bonds in the portfolio (with the weights being proportional to the bond prices).

The movement in prices can be described as:

$$\Delta V/V = (-D_V)(\Delta y)$$

For a futures contract:

$$\Delta F/F = (-D_F)(\Delta y)$$

We can construct a new portfolio consisting of the original portfolio plus a short position in N futures contracts, whose value will fluctuate as:

$$\Delta V - N(\Delta F) = (- D_V)(V)(\Delta y) - N[- D_F(F)]\Delta y = [N(D_F)(F) - D_V(V)]\Delta y$$
$$= (\text{exposure})(\Delta y)$$

The portfolio will be immunized against interest rate risks by setting the exposure equal to zero, or choosing:

$$N = V(D_V)/F(D_F)$$

The above expression is called the *duration-based hedge ratio*. It is sometimes also called the *price-sensitivity ratio*.

To enhance our understanding of the duration-based hedge ratio, we consider the following example. Suppose a company wishes to hedge a $10,000,000 portfolio invested in US government bonds using T-bond futures. The current futures price is 93–04, or 93.13, with a face value of $100,000. The duration of the cheapest-to-deliver bond in the T-bond contract is 9.1 years. The portfolio duration is 6.7 years. Thus, $V = \$10,000,000$, $F = \$93.13$, $D_F = 9.1$ and $D_V = 6.7$. The value of N is obtained with the expression of the duration-based hedge ratio:

$$N = \$10,000,000(6.7)/\$93.13(9.1) = 79.06$$

Consequently, the number of contracts to sell short is 79.

Consider the following observations about this example:

• The company will hedge the value of its portfolio if there is concern that interest rates will be highly volatile over, for instance, the next three months. For example, if this occurred in the beginning of August, the company would use a December T-bond futures contract to hedge the value of its portfolio.

• If interest rates decrease, a loss will be made on the short position, but there will be a gain on the bond portfolio. If interest rates increase, a gain will be made on the short futures position and a loss will be made on the portfolio.

• The company determines the cheapest-to-deliver bond in a manner similar to the example pertaining to Table 8.1.

INTEREST RATE CAPS, FLOORS AND COLLARS

An *interest rate cap* is an option to fix a ceiling or maximum short-term interest rate payment. The contract is written so the buyer of the cap will receive a cash payment equal to the difference between the actual market interest rate and the cap strike rate on the notional principal, if the market rate rises above the strike rate. As with any option, the buyer of the cap pays a premium up front. An *interest rate floor* gives the buyer the right to receive the compensating payment when the reference interest rate falls below the strike rate of the floor. In other words, interest rate caps are basically call options on an interest rate and interest rate floors are put options on an interest rate.

It is noted that with interest rate caps and floors, it is not the total maturity that is the only important item, but also the number of interest *resets* involved. For instance, a common interest rate cap would be two years on three-month LIBOR, meaning that the total cap agreement will last for two years, in which there will be seven three-month LIBOR interest rate reset dates, or *fixings*. There are two principal types of interest rate caps:

- *Interest Rate Guarantee*, which provides protection to the buyer for a single period only. Protection is provided to the borrower in the event of a single major variable rate refunding or reinvestment.
- *Interest Rate Cap*, which provides protection for an extended period of time (two to ten years) on some interest rate reset. The subperiod reset (e.g., three- or six-month LIBOR) is called the cap's *tenor*. This protection is for the interest rate put into effect on a reset date and not just any day over the period in which the actual market rate may creep up over the strike rate.

An example of an interest rate guarantee is a *caplet*, which is an option to enter a long FRA. Let us consider a caplet with a maturity of six months; the underlying loan has a maturity of six months, so the final maturity is in 12 months' time. The underlying loan has a notional principal of $10,000,000. We call this a notional principal, since with an FRA, no loan principal changes hands; however, the interest payments are determined by the size of the underlying principal, P. The option pays the difference between the six-month $LIBOR and a strike rate of 7 percent discounted to time T. The option premium, which is usually paid up front on the spot date, is 30 basis points, or $(0.30)(0.01)(\$10,000,000) = \$30,000$, since one basis point is equal to 0.01 percent. Assume that the spot date of the option contract is June 10. Thus, the settlement day is December 10 and the loan maturity date is 12 months from June 10. It is noted that the next business day (Monday) is used if the settlement and the loan maturity dates fall on either Saturday or Sunday. In the example, we assume that this is not the case.

The payoff of the caplet depends on the underlying interest rate in six-months' time. If it is higher than the strike rate of 7 percent, the option will be exercised and the firm will receive a payoff from the option, but if it is lower than 7 percent, no payoff will be received. Ignoring, for the time being, the premium that has to be paid, the payoffs are:

$$(i - k)P(N/M)\text{DF} \tag{6}$$

where:

i = LIBOR
N = number of days between interest reset dates (182 in the example)
M = the money market day count convention (360 for $LIBOR)
DF = discount factor = $1/[1 + i(N/M)]$
k and P are as previously defined

Let us determine the payoffs to the firm if $LIBOR turns out to be 5, 6, 7, 8 or 9 percent. There is no need to compute the payoff for 5, 6 or 7 percent, since it is always zero (the option is not exercised). Thus, we compute DF for 8 and 9 percent. For 8 percent, it is:

$$DF = 1/[1 + 0.08(182/360)] = 0.9611$$

For 9 percent, it is:

$$DF = 1/[1 + 0.09(182/360)] = 0.9565$$

Next, we calculate the payoffs with the help of equation (6). For 8 percent, it is:

$$(0.08 - 0.07)(\$10,000,000)(182/360)(0.9611) = \$48,588.94$$

For 9 percent, it is:

$$(0.09 - 0.07)(\$10,000,000)(182/360)(0.9565) = \$96,712.78$$

In order to compare the premium of $30,000 payable on the spot date with the payoffs listed here we need to compound it at the current $LIBOR for six months, which we assume to be 7.05 percent for the example. The compounded premium amounts to $30,000[1 + 0.0705(182/360)] = $31,069.25. The net profits/losses can now be determined as the difference of the option payoff and the compounded premium. They are as follows:

5 percent: −$31,069.25
6 percent: −$31,069.25
7 percent: −$31,069.25
8 percent: $48,588.94 − $31,069.25 = $17,519.69
9 percent: $96,712.78 − $31,069.25 = $65,643.53

The net profit/loss made on the caplet changes the amount the borrower has to borrow at time T. For instance, if $LIBOR turns out to be 9 percent, the net profit of $65,643.53 made on the option reduces the required loan to $9,934,356.47. Interest on this loan at 9 percent is $452,013.22, leaving a repayment at the loan maturity date of $10,386,369.69. The effective rate on a $LIBOR basis is then:

$$3.86\%(360/182) = 7.64\%$$

We could also compute the break-even LIBOR at which a zero net profit is made. To do so, we equate the compounded premium with the payoff, where LIBOR is i percent or:

$$\$31,069.25 = (i - 7\%)(182/360)(\$10,000,000)\{1/[1 + i(N/M)]\}$$

From the above equation we determine that the break-even rate is about 7.6 percent. The reader is encouraged to analyze a *floorlet* in the same manner as done here for a caplet. A floorlet is defined as an option to enter a short FRA.

A typical interest rate cap written over the counter by a bank for a firm looks like the following:

- maturity: 2 years
- strike rate: 6.00%
- reference rate: 3-month US dollar LIBOR
- total periods: 8 (4 per year for 2 years)
- notional principal: $10,000,000
- premium: 80 basis points (0.80%)
- fixed borrowing rate: 7.00%

This agreement establishes a cap on all quarterly reset dates for two years. The cap rate is 6.00 percent per annum and all interest payments are calculated on the basis of a notional principal of $10,000,000. The up-front cost of the cap, the premium, is 80 basis points. If the firm were to borrow at fixed interest rate it would pay 7.00 percent. To illustrate how the cap would work in practice we assume that the three-month LIBOR on the reset date has risen above the strike rate of 6.00 percent to 6.50 percent. We compute (a) the actual three-month interest payment, (b) the amount of the cap payment to the cap buyer if the reference rate rises above the cap rate and (c) the annualized cost of the cap.

Interest rate payment. Regardless of whether the cap is activated, the buyer of the cap is responsible for making the normal interest payment. The firm owes a payment of three-month US dollar LIBOR of 6.5 percent on a three-month period of actual 90 days on a notional principal of $10,000,000:

$$\$10,000,000 \times 0.065 \times 90/360 = \$162,500.$$

Cap payment. If the three-month LIBOR has risen above the cap rate on the reset date, the cap is activated and the buyer of the cap receives a cash payment from the cap seller equal to the difference between the actual three-month LIBOR of 6.50 percent and the cap rate of 6.00 percent:

$$\$10,000,000 \times [(0.0650 - 0.0600) \times 90/360] = \$12,500.$$

Amortized cap premium. The cap premium of 0.80 percent is a single lump sum payment made at the beginning of the three-month period; therefore, it must be annualized in order to calculate the cost of the capped payment. The fixed rate of interest at which the firm could borrow is 7.00 percent and this is, therefore, the rate of interest used in the amortization of the cap premium over 8 reset periods. The amortized premium, for 8 periods, discounted at a rate of 7.00 percent per year (1.75% per quarter) is obtained with the standard amortization formula used in computing mortgage payments:

$$\text{quarterly payment} = 0.80\%/[1/0.0175 - 1/\{0.0175 \times (1.0175)^8\}] = 0.09684\%$$

This is 0.09684 percent on a quarterly basis, or 0.38737 percent on an annual basis. Consequently, the resulting total cost of the capped interest payment is 6.38737 percent or a maximum of $159,684 every three months as shown below:

Cap component	Annualized interest cost	Quarterly cash flows
Interest payment outflow	6.5000%	$162,500
Cap cash payment inflow	6.0000–6.5000%	– 12,500
Cap premium payment outflow	0.38737%	+ 9,684
Total cost	6.38737%	$159,684

If the three-month LIBOR is below the cap rate of 6.00 percent on the next reset date, the firm's total cost would be the actual LIBOR payment plus its quarterly premium payment of 0.38737 percent. The premium payment will be made for the life of the cap regardless of whether the gap is exercised or not.

An interest rate floor guarantees the buyer of the floor a minimum interest rate to be received for a specified reinvestment period or series of periods. For instance, if a firm expects a cash inflow in three months, which it must invest, it will want to invest at the highest possible rate. The firm may wish to purchase a floor if it fears interest rates will fall by that time. The pricing and valuation of an interest rate floor is similar to that of the interest rate cap. Let us, for instance, consider the following specifications of the floor:

- maturity: 2 years
- strike rate: 6.00%
- reference rate: 6-month US dollar LIBOR

- total periods: 4 (semiannually for 2 years)
- notional principal: $5,000,000
- floor premium: 108 basis points (1.08%)
- fixed investment rate: 6.50%

Let us assume that at the end of a six-month period, the six-month LIBOR has fallen to 5.70 percent (below the floor rate of 6.00%). The valuation of the floor consists of the same three elements as the cap.

Interest rate payment. Regardless of whether the floor is activated, the firm that bought the floor will invest its funds at the market rate of interest. Thus, the firm will earn 5.70 percent, the six-month LIBOR, on a notional principal of $5,000,000:

$$\$5,000,000 \times 0.0570 \times 180/360 = \$142,500.$$

Floor cash receipt. The floor is activated since the reference rate has fallen below the floor strike rate. The buyer of the floor receives the difference between the floor rate and the reference rate:

$$\$5,000,000 \times [(0.0600 - 0.0570) \times 180/360] = \$7,500.$$

Amortized floor premium. Regardless of whether the floor is activated, the firm must pay for the floor option. The single lump sum payment of 1.08 percent made up front is amortized over the two-year period of six-month reset periods. We use the fixed rate of interest available to the firm at the beginning of the period for the amortization, in this case 6.50 percent. Thus, the premium expense per semiannual period is:

$$\text{semiannual premium} = 1.08\%/[1/0.0325 - 1/\{0.0325 \times (1.0325)^4\}]$$
$$= 0.2923\%$$

This is 0.2923 percent on a semiannual basis or 0.5846 percent per annum. As shown below, the total yield of the floor-covered instrument is 5.4154 percent per annum, or a minimum return of $135,385 each six months on a notional principal of $5,000,000 for the two-year period:

Floor component	Amortized interest yield	Quarterly cash flows
Interest payment inflow	5.7000%	$142,500
Floor cash payment inflow	6.0000–5.7000%	7,500
Floor premium payment outflow	0.5846%	− 14,615
Total yield	5.4154%	$135,385

An *interest rate collar* is the simultaneous purchase (sale) of a cap and sale (purchase) of a floor. The firm constructing the collar earns a premium from the sale of one side to cover in part or in full the premium expense of purchasing the other side of the collar. The position is called a *zero-premium collar* if the two premiums are equal. Interest rate collars enable a firm to retain some of the benefit of declining rates while removing the unpleasantness of paying an up-front premium for the cap. This unpleasantness is completely eliminated in the case of the zero-premium collar. Appendix 8 provides information about second-generation currency risk management products.

INTEREST RATE OPTIONS

Options may be considered a form of insurance against adverse movements in asset prices. For example, if a corporation needs to sell bonds at a future date to raise capital, a put option on a bond gives it the right to sell the bond at a fixed price. The premium one pays for the option is like a premium one has to pay for an insurance policy.

Let us consider the following put option on a bond. An MNC buys an option to sell a six-month, zero coupon bond with a face value of $10,000,000 in three months' time at a strike price of $0.97; the premium is $25,000. The spot date of the contract is June 10, and the maturity is 92 days. Thus, the underlying asset is a bond that will have a maturity of 182 days, 92 days after June 10. The strike price at which the option may be exercised is $0.97 per $1.00 of principal.

The payoff of the option depends on the bond's price in 3 months' time. If, for instance, the price falls to $0.96, the option will be exercised and a profit is made. Since the option is to sell at $0.97, the bonds can be bought at $0.96 and sold for $0.97, yielding a profit of $0.01 per bond. However, if the bond price rises, say, to $0.98, the bonds would have to be bought for more than the strike price; consequently, the option is not exercised and the payoff is zero. The payoffs for the two cases, excluding the option premium, are as follows:

(strike price − bond price)principal amount = payoff

If the price falls:

($0.97 − $0.96)10,000,000 = $100,000

If the price rises:

($0.97 − $0.98)10,000,000 = $0

The option premium is usually paid up front at the date of the contract (June 10). The net profit of the option position should take into account the interest on the premium. Suppose the interest rate is 7 percent. Thus, the interest is $0.07(92/365)\$25,000 = \$441.10$. This makes the respective profit and loss after paying the premium:

> gross payoff − compounded premium = net profit from put option.
> Case 1: $100,000 − $25,441.10 = $74,558.90.
> Case 2: $0.00 − $25,441.10 = −$25,441.10.

For this example, the position of a hedger who needs to sell $10 million of zero coupon bonds and buys the put option in order to provide protection against a fall in the market price is as follows. Before accounting for the premium, the hedger receives:

> cash from sales of bonds + gross payoff from put option = sales proceeds.
> Case 1: $9,600,000 + $100,000 = $ 9,700,000.
> Case 2: $9,800,000 + $0.00 = $9,800,000.

In other words, the hedger is guaranteed a sale proceeds of $9,700,000; however, if the price rises to more than $0.97, the hedger can sell for the market price ($0.98) and the proceeds will amount to $9,800,000. After paying the premium, the net position for the hedger is as follows:

> cash from sales of bonds + net profit from the put option = net sales proceeds.
> Case 1: $9,600,000 + $74,558.90 = $9,674,558.90.
> Case 2: $9,800,000 − $25,441.10 = $9,774,558.90.

This shows that the hedger guarantees minimum sales proceeds of $9,674,558.90 and more if the market price goes above $0.97.

The earlier described caplet may be considered as a special case of an interest rate option.

SUGGESTIONS FOR FURTHER READING

Arak, M., A. Estrella, L. Goodman, and A. Silver. "Interest Rate Swaps: An Alternative Explanation." *Financial Management* 17 (Summer 1988): 12–18.

Brown, K. C., and D. J. Smith. "Forward Swaps, Swap Options, and the Management of Callable Debt." *Journal of Applied Corporate Finance* 2 (Winter 1990): 59–71.

Marshall, J. F., and K. R. Kapner. *Understanding Swap Finance*. Cincinnati, OH: South-Western Publishing, 1990.

Stokes, Houston H., and H. M. Neuburger. *New Methods in Financial Modeling*. Westport, CT: Quorum Books, 1998.

Turnbull, S. M. "Swaps: A Zero Sum Game?" *Financial Management* 16 (Spring 1987): 15–21.

Appendix 1

Water Supply Project
(Case Study)

PURPOSE

The purpose of this case study is to become familiar with the outline term sheet and project-finance issues related to security, completion guarantee, escrow account, limited recourse and insurance.

PROJECT SUMMARY

The Republic of Rasanesia (the "Host Government") through the Municipality of Wanang (the "Municipality") has granted an exclusive mandate to the Eastern Water Company and the Western Water Company (together the "Project Sponsors") to implement a water supply project. The Project involves the design, construction and supervision of a dam located in a different municipality, water treatment plant, two pump stations and a pipeline.

The implementation of the Project is governed by the terms of a Concession Agreement entered into between the Municipality and the Project Sponsors. This agreement stipulates that the Project will be realized on a Build-Operate-Transfer (BOT) basis, implying that the Project is to be constructed and operated by a private-sector, special purpose company (the "Water Supply Company") established by the Project Sponsors, which will be transferred back to the Municipality at the end of a specified concession period. During this period the water produced by the Project is to be supplied to the Municipality under a *take-or-pay* contract. The Municipality's payment obligations under this contract are to be guaranteed by Rasanesia and payable in local currency, the rupiah.

It is noted that take-or-pay and *take-and-pay* contracts are long-term contracts guaranteeing periodic payments, in certain minimum amounts, for the supply of services or goods. The expressions are often used interchangeably; however, in a true take-or-pay contract, the obligation is unconditional and, therefore, payment must be made whether or not the services are actually rendered or the goods actually delivered. In a take-and-pay contract, payment is only made when the service is actually rendered or the goods are actually delivered.

The People's Bank has been approached by the Project Sponsors to arrange a syndicated project facility in favor of the Water Supply Company. The Project Sponsors have agreed to contribute $5 million toward the Project by way of an equity investment in the Borrower (i.e., the Water Supply Company).

A summary of the Project costs and funding is as follows:

Project Costs (US $ million)		Project Funding (US $ million)	
Construction:	15.2	Equity:	5.0
Supervision:	2.5	Local bank loan:	3.0
Capitalization of interest:	0.8	Export credit guaranteed	
General contingencies:	0.5	Loan:	12.0
Pre-operating costs	1.0		
Total:	20.0	Total:	20.0

Prior to the Term Sheet being agreed, heated discussions were held between the Project Sponsors and the People's Bank regarding guarantees from the Eastern Water Company and the Western Water Company for the loan facility. The net result was that these two companies agreed that the Project would be completed by December 31, 2001 without any further debt having to be raised. People's Bank then set out what it believed was the appropriate format for this Completion Guarantee in the Term Sheet.

On the basis of the requirements imposed by the Project Sponsors, People's Bank put together the Term Sheet given after the "Examination" section.

EXAMINATION

We are asked to examine the nature of the financing and, in particular, the security structure of the Project, the allocation of the Project risks and insurance arrangements. We will focus on the following issues:

- the issues in relation to the taking/sharing of security,
- the assets over which security should be taken,
- the purpose of the Completion Guarantee and how it can be improved as set out in the Term Sheet,
- the purpose of the Escrow Account and, in particular, how the provision for the Escrow Account set out in the Term Sheet could be expanded on and improved,
- the meaning of limited recourse, and
- the insurance arrangements, that is, what risk should be insured against, which insurers

should be used, who should insure, on-shore versus off-shore insurance and the application of the insurance proceeds in *reinstatement* or *repayment*.

Term Sheet

Borrower: The Water Supply Company.

Project: The construction and operation of a dam, water treatment plant, two pump stations and trunk main to supply the municipality of Wanang.

Project Sponsors: Eastern Water Company and Western Water Company.

Arranger: People's Bank.

Lenders: A syndicate of international banks including the Arranger ("the Banks").

Agent: People's Bank.

Amount: $12 million.

Facility: Term Loan with Export Credit Agency guarantee.

Purpose: To finance: (a) capital expenditure on the Project, (b) operating costs associated with the Project, (c) interest and other financing charges and (d) professional and other fees and expenses.

Availability Period: The period from the date of the Facility Agreement until the earlier of (a) the Completion Date and (b) December 31, 2001.

Final Maturity: The sixth anniversary of the date of the Facility Agreement or five years from the Completion Date, whichever is the earlier.

Interest: The rate of interest shall be the aggregate of the London Interbank Offered Rate (LIBOR) for each interest period and the appropriate Margin.
  Margin: (a) Prior to Completion: 125 basis points (bp); (b) Post-Completion: 135 bp.
  Payment: Interest will be paid at the end of each interest period.
  Calculation: Calculated on the basis of the actual number of days elapsed and a year of 360 days.

Interest Period: Shall be 3 or 6 months as selected by the Borrower.

Commitment Fee: 50 bp p.a., payable on the undrawn and uncancelled portion of the facility from the date of signing of the Facility Agreement to the end of the Availability Period.

Arrangement Fee: 50 bp flat on the amount of the facility payable on the earlier of the first drawdown or 14 days from the date of the Facility Agreement.

Agency Fee: $6,000 p.a. payable annually in advance.

Reduction/Repayment: Repayments will be made in ten semiannual installments commencing six months after the end of the Availability Period.

Cancellation: Undrawn amounts of the facility may be canceled without premium or penalty during the Availability Period (in amounts and multiples to be agreed) if the Banks are satisfied that the Borrower will have sufficient funds to complete the Project.

Prepayment: The facility may be prepaid in full at any time in which event any amount remaining undrawn will be canceled. Partial prepayments will be permitted at any time after the Availability Period in minimum amounts and multiples to be agreed.

Security: To include security as follows: (a) Fixed and floating charge over the Borrower's interest in the Project facilities; (b) Assignment on interest of the Borrower's interest in Project Agreements; (c) Assignment of Insurances; and (d) Mortgage over the Escrow Account.

Escrow Account: The Borrower shall open and maintain with a first class bank acceptable to the Banks, an interest-bearing account (the "Escrow Account") into which all funds received by the Borrower will be paid.

Project Forecasts: Procedures will be put in place for the delivery of Project forecasts (each a "Project Forecast") to the Banks in order to, inter alia, ascertain the Total Debt Cover Ratio.

Total Debt Cover Ratio: The Project Forecast will be used to calculate the "Total Debt Cover Ratio," which will be the ratio of the net present value of cash flow to total debt.

Completion Date: The Project shall be deemed complete on the date when the Banks are satisfied that the dam, water treatment plant, pumping stations, trunk main and all related facilities have been constructed to the plan and designs provided for in the construction contract relating thereto.

Completion Guarantee: Eastern Water Company and Western Water Company will undertake with the Banks that: (a) the Completion Date will occur no later than December 31, 2001; and (b) neither will dispose of its shareholding in the Borrower during the term of the Facility Agreement.

Conditions Precedent to First Drawdown: To include:

(a) Acceptance by a majority by value of the Banks of the initial Project Forecast.

(b) Eastern Water Company and Western Water Company have subscribed, and paid for, ordinary shares in the Borrower having a par value of not less than $5m.

(c) Completion of all Facility Documents.

(d) All Project Documents executed and in full force and effect, including: (i) Concession Agreement; (ii) Construction Contract; (iii) Operation and Maintenance Contract; (iv) Water Utilization Agreement; (v) Dam Establishment Agreement; (vi) Water Off-take Agreement.

(e) No material adverse change in the financial condition of the Borrower, the Project Sponsors or in the Project.

(f) Due authorization and incorporation of the Borrower.

(g) Satisfactory evidence of all approvals, authorizations, consents, agreements, licenses and exemptions required for the Project.

(h) Local Bank Loan Facility of the rupiah equivalent of $3.0m to have been executed and fully available for drawing.

(i) Guarantee of Rasanesia to Export Credit Agency and all other conditions of the Export Credit Agency cover satisfied.

Conditions Precedent to all Drawdowns: The Borrower shall be entitled to make additional drawings under the Facility in accordance with the Purpose clause provided the following conditions are met: (a) five business days notice; and (b) repetition of representations and absence of actual or potential event of default.

Covenants: The Borrower will provide covenants customary for a transaction of this nature.

Events of Default: The events of default will include, but not be limited to, the following: (a) Nonpayment; (b) Breach of a covenant under the Facility Documents; (c) Any representation or warranty made by the Borrower in the Facility Documents being untrue in any material respect; (d) Any bankruptcy, liquidation or insolvency event affecting the Borrower or either of the Project Sponsors; (e) Completion Date not occurring by December 31, 2001; and (f) Abandonment/destruction of the Project.

Taxes: All amounts payable under the Facility Documents will be made free and clear of all present and future taxes, or any other deductions whatsoever. The Borrower shall be liable for all taxes other than taxes on the overall net income of any commercial bank lender.

Transferability: The commitments and outstandings of the Banks will be fully transferable subject to the Borrower's consent (not to be unreasonably withheld or delayed).

Costs and Expenses: The Borrower will pay all costs and expenses (including legal fees) incurred by the Agent and the Arranger in connection with the preparation, negotiation and execution of all loan documentation and the completion of the transactions therein contemplated.

Other Terms: All other standard terms for facilities of this nature including provisions relating to market disruption, confidentiality, increased costs, indemnities and illegality will be included.

Governing Law: Laws of England.

Jurisdiction: Courts of England.

Clear Market: Neither the Borrower nor either of the Project Sponsors will enter into any negotiations with any other financial institutions for the raising of any finance without the prior consent of the Arranger.

PROJECT DISCUSSION

Arranger Bank

The arranger is the bank that has arranged the financing and syndication of the lending. It will normally take the lead role in negotiating the loan conditions and security documentation.

Agent Bank

The agent bank is responsible for coordinating drawdowns and dealing with communications between the parties to the finance documentation. It is not responsible for the credit decisions of the lenders entering into the transaction. The arranger and agent banks do not have to be the same bank (as in the case study).

Security

As with other project financing schemes, lenders normally take security over the Project assets if allowed under the laws of the country where the assets are located. The Banks want to secure all assets financed by them and the Project

Sponsors (e.g., tangible assets, contracts, etc). It is important that the Banks' lawyers work closely with local lawyers at an early stage. The local lawyers must also advise on the enforcement procedures in their jurisdiction.

The type of security to be taken needs to be analyzed with the local lawyers. For instance, the *floating charge* (British) provides a convenient means of taking a security interest in all existing project assets and all project assets to be acquired during the construction and operation phases. However, this procedure is not available in many civil law jurisdictions.

The Banks may be asked to share their security with another financial institution involved in the Project financing and/or an Export Credit Agency. In this case the following potential issues should be addressed:

- Should the security be held by a trustee (who holds it *on trust* for the Banks and other secured Lenders)?
- What to do if one lender will insist on being entitled to require the enforcement of security and other lenders do not wish to enforce.
- How to allocate the proceeds of enforcement if all lenders do not share equally in all of the security (for instance, some but not all lenders are to receive the benefit of a host government guarantee).
- What to do if lenders disagree on the satisfaction of the conditions precedent to the drawdowns.

Different lenders may have different views on the above issues, since a commercial bank may have other priorities than an export credit agency, a regional development bank or a multilateral agency.

The assignment of the benefit of the off-take agreement will form the most valuable part of the security package since (a) it contains a take-or-pay obligation and (b) the Municipality's payment obligations are guaranteed by Rasanesia. The Banks should explicitly address the currency (rupiah) convertibility, availability and repatriation risks in the Rasanesian guarantee.

Security should also be taken over the Concession Agreement itself. Support from the host government may be required in relation to the government undertaking to or setting out the conditions upon which it would give its consent to granting security over the concession. Issues to be discussed under the government's support are:

- If the Host Government agrees to notify the Banks of alleged breaches, does it give them the opportunity to remedy the breaches (for instance, appoint a new operator).
- If the Host Government agrees to grant a replacement concession, what are the terms of repayment by the new Concessionaire?
- Does the Host Government give a form of financial commitment in respect of outstanding indebtedness?
- Does the Host Government agree to postpone termination until the Banks have had an opportunity to recoup themselves from production?

The assignment of, or joint interest in, the insurance taken out over the Project's assets is another important element of the security package. To protect their interests, the Banks should insist that the insurance policies contain a "loss payee and notice of cancellation clause" requiring the insurers to pay any claims directly to the Banks and to advise them of any changes, cancellations or non-renewals.

Finally, the Banks should take a first priority mortgage over the Escrow Account and take security over specific tangible assets. In the context of a large project finance, such as the Water Supply Project, it is unlikely that the realizable value of the tangible assets are significant in relation to the overall debt. The real value of such security is often the fact that it prevents the project company from granting, and third parties from otherwise acquiring, the Banks' rights as secured creditors.

Completion Guarantee

The Term Sheet should focus more on when completion will have occurred rather than merely stating the completion of the actual physical facilities (dam, water treatment plant, pumping stations and pipelines). It would be more prudent to include in the Completion Test an express reference to the treatment and supply of a specific number of cubic meters of water. The test may also require a certificate from an independent technical expert.

Another shortcoming of the Completion Guarantee as set out in the Term Sheet is that no sanction is provided in the event that the completion does not take place by December 31, 2001. Such sanction requires the evaluation of actual financial loss due to the failure to complete on time which can be a difficult and lengthy process. As an alternative, the Banks could require that the Project Sponsors repay the loan facility if completion does not occur by December 31, 2001. To further enhance the Banks' position, it is recommended to specify that the Completion Guarantee be issued on a joint and several basis so that each Sponsor is liable along with the other Sponsor and is also liable alone and individually.

Escrow Account

The Project Sponsors will put $5m in the Water Supply Company. The Banks may want to ensure that this money will be applied toward the Project. This can be achieved by requiring that the money be paid into an Escrow Account where its application will be controlled in the sense that it will only be capable of being used toward the Project.

The Term Sheet is not very specific with regard to the Escrow Account. It merely states that the Borrower shall "open and maintain with a first-class bank acceptable to the Banks, an interest-bearing escrow account into which all funds received by the Borrower will be paid." Specifically, the Term Sheet should also address the following issues:

• What should be paid into the Escrow Account (e.g., drawings under the Facility Agreement, equity contributions the Borrower receives from the Eastern Water Company and the Western Water Company, and income earned by the Borrower in supplying water to the Municipality).

• The Escrow Account cannot be used to fund any debt service reserve the Borrower is obliged to maintain or any shareholder distributions.

• The Term Sheet should distinguish between what may come out prior to the Completion Date and what may come out after it (the Banks wish to ensure that the Borrower also fulfills its commitments after the Completion Date with regard to the payment of interest, commitment commission, agency fees, and so on).

• It is also recommended to establish a priority for drawdowns from the Escrow Account after the Completion Date, such that essential operating expenditures are paid out first and next principal and interest due under the facility.

• In the event of a default, the Banks should require that the Escrow Account be "blocked."

• To cover the risk of not being able to convert local currency, the Banks may want to ensure that (a) the Host Government guarantees the availability of foreign currency and/or an off-shore debt service account is opened.

Limited Recourse

The issue to be resolved is what are the assets/revenues to which the Banks will look for repayment. In project finance it is a sine qua non that the risks of the project being financed are to be allocated between the Borrower and the Banks. In the context of a company which has assets in addition to those comprising the project being financed, the Banks may, therefore, be asked to limit their right of recovery to the cash flows which will be generated by the Project and their security to the facilities used to generate the same. In other words, "limited recourse" is recourse which is limited to the Project's cash flows and assets. Note that in the Term Sheet all the security is project specific (it relates only to the various project assets identified therein).

Insurance

Review of the insurance arrangements is a key part of the structure of the financing terms. Mechanisms for the payment of claims need to be considered to ensure that the insurance proceeds will go to the appropriate recipients. The possibility and length of delay between the occurrence of the loss and receipt of the insurance proceeds, as well as the determination of how the Project may be financed in the interim, need to be considered.

During the construction phase the Banks should, as a minimum, ensure that the insurance is in place against (a) physical damage to project facilities and other assets such as machinery, (b) third-party liability, (c) environmental liability and (d) delay in start-up. During the operating phase the Banks should ensure that insurance is in place against items (a) through (c) and business interruption.

The Project may be insured by a specific tailor-made policy with an independent third-party insurer, which is the preferred way, or as an addition to the block policy/policies of the Project Company or Project Sponsors. A *block policy* covers both the Project and other unconnected activities and raises the problem of verifying cover, particularly if the Project Sponsors refuse inspection of their block policy terms on confidentiality grounds. A block policy is, therefore, not recommended.

During both the construction and the operating phases of the Project, the Water Supply Company should take out the necessary insurance policies. In other words, it is not advisable to have contractors and subcontractors take out insurance policies since this will result in the Water Supply Company losing control of the insurance proceeds. In addition, it could result in an increase in the cost of premiums if multiple approaches to the insurance market are made by various contractors and subcontractors.

The Banks will want to ensure that insurance is taken out in the currency of their debt (dollars). It is, therefore, preferable that foreign currency insurance is to be effected offshore; however, local insurance laws may prohibit this. If local laws require insurance to be effected onshore, the Banks could enter into negotiations with the Rasanesian government or reinsurance could be effected offshore with the Banks given direct access to the reinsurance proceeds.

The Water Supply Company, Rasanesia and the Municipality prefer an automatic right to apply insurance proceeds in reinstatement. The Banks may, however, require insurance proceeds to be applied in repayment of their debt rather than reinstatement, particularly if delay and increased interest and other costs of reinstatement may render a continuation of the Project financially no more viable. In any case, the Banks want to control the application of insurance proceeds to reinstatement themselves rather than have the proceeds paid to the Water Supply Company (or Rasanesia or the Municipality) for application toward reinstatement; this could be accomplished by providing for the insurance proceeds to be paid to a specified account with withdrawals only allowed for reinstatement on terms approved by the Banks.

Appendix 2

Interest Tables for Discrete Compounding

A given sum of money now is normally worth more than an equal sum at some future date. The concept "money has a time value" is the basic assumption of discounting and compounding. Frequently one considers time in discrete units of one year.

We introduce the following definitions:

P = an amount of money at the present time
F = an amount of money at the end of n periods in the future
A = a constant amount paid or received at the end of each of n periods in the future ("uniform series")
n = the number of periods or times at which interest is calculated
i = the interest rate used for calculations of interest in any one of the n periods mentioned above

The definitions refer to "periods of time," which are normally years. However, "period of time" rather than "year" is preferred to eliminate redefining the symbols when other units of time are considered.

Table A2.1 presents six interest factors to use when specific data is given:

spcaf   when P is given and F is to be obtained
sppwf   when F is given and P is to be obtained
caf   when A is given and F is to be obtained
sff   when F is given and A is to be obtained
pwf   when A is given and P is to be obtained
crf   when P is given and A is to be obtained

The interpretation of the above acronyms is as follows:

spcaf = single payment compound amount factor
sppwf = single payment present worth factor
caf   = (series) compound amount factor
sff   = sinking fund factor
pwf   = (series) present worth factor
crf   = capital recovery factor

Table A2.1
Interest Factors for Discrete Discounting and Compounding

Find Given	P	F	A
P	1	$spcaf = (1+i)^n$	$crf = [1-(1+i)^{-n}]^{-1}i$
F	$sppwf = (1+i)^{-n}$	1	$sff = [(1+i)^n-1]^{-1}i$
A	$pwf = [1-(1+i)^{-n}]i^{-1}$	$caf = [(1+i)^n-1]i^{-1}$	1

The first of these six factors, spcaf, allows us to determine the value n periods hence of a present amount P if the interest rate is i. Thus, given P, i and n it allows for the computation of F. Consider the following simple, arithmetic example of the use of spcaf.

Suppose it is desired to find the sum to which $1,000.00 would grow over three years when the appropriate annual interest rate is 10%. From the spcaf formula of Table A2.1 we compute as follows:

$$
\begin{aligned}
F &= P(\text{given } P, \text{find } F, i=10\%, n=3) \\
&= P.\text{spcaf } (i=10\%, n=3) \\
&= P(1 + i)^n \text{ for } i=10\% \text{ and } n=3 \\
&= \$1,000(1 + 0.10)^3 = \$1,000(1 + 0.10)(1 + 0.10)(1 + 0.10) \\
&= \$1,000(1.331) = \$1,331.00
\end{aligned}
$$

The single payment present worth factor (sppwf) permits us to answer questions about the present value of capital available at some time in the future. Given F, i, and n, the P may be calculated from:

$$P = F.\text{sppwf} = F(1 + i)^{-n}$$

where the expression $(1 + i)^{-n}$ is a convenient way of writing $1/(1 + i)^n$.

Suppose it is desired to know the present value of a sum of $150.00 arising two years hence when the appropriate annual interest rate is 10%. Using the sppwf formula we compute:

$$P = F \text{ (given } F, \text{ find } P, i=10\%, n=2)$$
$$= F.\text{sppwf } (i=10\%, n=2)$$
$$= F(1 + i)^{-n} \text{ for } i=10\%, \text{ and } n=2$$
$$= \$150(1 + 0.10)^{-2} = \$150(0.8264)$$
$$= \$123.96$$

The (series) present worth factor or pwf enables us to calculate the present value of a uniform series A. Let us consider the following problem to illustrate the application of the pwf formula.

A firm is offered the choice of a 5-year lease on a machine:

Alternative (a) \$10,000.00 down and \$3,000.00 per annum for 5 years.
Alternative (b) \$13,000.00 down and \$2,150.00 per annum for 5 years.

Annual payments are to be made at the year end, the relevant interest rate is 7%, while problems of risk, inflation, tax, etc., are ignored. Alternative (b) requires the firm to pay down \$3,000.00 more at the beginning of the lease than alternative (a), but results in an annual end-year saving of \$850.00 for 5 years. From the pwf formula the present values of alternatives (a) and (b) are:

(a) $P = \$10,000 + \$3,000[1 - (1 + i)^{-n}]i^{-1}$
$\quad\quad = \$10,000 + \$3,000(4.100)$
$\quad\quad = \$22,300.00$
(b) $P = \$13,000 + \$2,150[1 - (1 + i)^{-n}]i^{-1}$
$\quad\quad = \$13,000 + \$2,150(4.100)$
$\quad\quad = \$21,815.00$

There is a gain of net present value by taking alternative (b) equal to:

$$\$22,300.00 - \$21,815.00 = \$485.00$$

and this alternative is, therefore, preferred.

A perpetual annuity or perpetuity is a perpetual series of annual constant cash flows. An example of a perpetuity is a consol, which is an interest-bearing bond issued by the British government having no maturity date. When a regular annual series is expected to go on perpetually or $n \to \infty$ (the symbol for n tending to infinity), then the pwf formula becomes simply $P = A.i^{-1}$. This is so, since $(1 + i)^{-n}$ tends to zero when $n \to \infty$.

The (series) compound amount factor or caf permits the calculation of a future sum F given that an amount A is invested at $i\%$ at the end of each of n equal intervals. The series of constant annual cash flows is known as an annuity.

Suppose an investor has an annuity in which a payment of $500.00 is made at the end of each year. If interest is 6% compounded annually, what is the amount after 20 years? From the caf formula this amount is as follows:

$$
\begin{aligned}
F &= A.caf(i=6\%, n=20) \\
&= \$500[(1 + 0.06)^{20} - 1](0.06)^{-1} \\
&= \$500(36.786) = \$18,393.00
\end{aligned}
$$

Note that the expression $(0.06)^{-1}$ is again a convenient way of writing $1/(0.06)$.

The reciprocal of the caf is the sinking fund factor or sff, which allows us to calculate the constant amount A which must be invested at the end of each period to yield an amount F at the end of the n-th period. In financial terminology, the terminal value of a constant annual investment or annuity is usually referred to as a "sinking fund". This is a fund to which periodic payments are made and then invested to accumulate to a given amount by a certain date. This is often done for the purpose of replacing a machine at the end of its expected life or the redeeming of a loan.

Consider as an example involving the use of sff, an asset with a value of $5,000.00, a service life of 5 years, and a salvage value of $1,000.00. Using the sinking-fund depreciation method we are asked to compute the required year-end sinking fund deposits if the interest rate is 6%. Using the sff formula of Table A2.1 we compute as follows:

$$
\begin{aligned}
A &= F.sff(i=6\%, n=5) \\
&= \$4,000i[(1 + i)^n - 1]^{-1} \\
&= \$4,000(0.1774) = \$709.60
\end{aligned}
$$

Note that for F a value of $4,000.00 rather than $5,000.00 is used. This is so, since the asset has a salvage value of $1,000.00. Table A2.2 shows the yearly depreciation charge, the total depreciation charge to the end of a year together with the undepreciated balance at the end of a year. According to the sinking-fund depreciation method the amount by which the asset is depreciated is the sum of (1) the amount deposited into the sinking fund at the end of the year, and (2) the amount of interest earned on the sum already in deposit in the sinking fund.

The capital recovery factor or crf permits us to calculate the equal end of period payment A for n periods which is equivalent to a present sum P. The following example illustrates the use of pwf, sppwf, and crf.

Table A2.2
Example of the Sinking-Fund Depreciation Method

Year	Deposit A	Interest Earned during Year	Yearly Depreciation Charge	Total Depreciation Charge to End of Year	Undepreciated Balance at End of Year
0	$ 0.00	$0.00	$ 0.00	$ 0.00	$5,000.00
1	709.60	0.00	709.60	709.60	4,290.40
2	709.60	.06(709.60)	752.18	1,461.78	3,538.22
3	709.60	.06(1,461.78)	797.31	2,259.09	2,740.91
4	709.60	.06(2,259.09)	845.15	3,104.24	1,895.76
5	709.60	.06(3,104.24)	895.85	4,000.00	1,000.00

Note: Asset's value = $5,000.00   Salvage value = $1,000.00
Service life = 5 years   i = 6%

A young economist has estimated that his annual earnings should average $20,000.00, $30,000.00, and $40,000.00 per year in succeeding decades after graduation. He hopes to graduate next month and wants an idea of the value of all his years of studying. Assuming an annual interest rate of 6%, he, therefore, decides to determine (a) the present worth (at graduation) in cash of the 30 years' earning, and (b) the equivalent uniform annual value of the 30 years' estimated income.

His present worth is:

$[\$20,000.\text{pwf}(i=6\%, n=10)] + [\$30,000.\text{pwf}(i=6\%, n=10).\text{sppwf}(i=6\%, n=10)] + [\$40,000.\text{pwf}(i=6\%, n=10).\text{sppwf}(i=6\%, n=20)] = \$20,000$ $(7.360) + \$30,000(7.360)(0.5584) + \$40,000(7.360)(0.3118) = \$147,200 +$ $\$123,294 + \$91,791 = \$362,288$

The equivalent uniform annual value of the 30 years' estimated income is:

$\$362,288.\text{crf}(i=6\%, n=30) = \$362,288(0.07265) = \$26,320$

Heretofore we have adopted the convention of discounting for an annual period. Now to analyze the discounting for periods of less than a year, we introduce these following definitions:

m = the total number of years
k = the number of compounding or conversion periods per year
j = the nominal yearly interest rate to be converted n times per year

Thus, $i = j/k$ and $n = m.k$, where i and n are as defined previously.

Suppose you want to determine the amount to which $10,000.00 would grow in one year at 8% interest compounded semiannually. Thus, the nominal yearly interest rate, sometimes simply called the nominal rate, is equal to $j = 8\%$ and $n = 2$, since the interest is calculated twice a year. Consequently, the interest rate per conversion period is $i = j/k = 8\%/2 = 4\%$ and the amount F to which $10,000.00 will grow in one year at $j = 8\%$ is:

$$
\begin{aligned}
F &= \$10,000(1 + i)^2 = \$10,000(1.04)^2 \\
&= \$10,000 \text{ spcaf } (i=4\%, n=2) \\
&= \$10,820.00
\end{aligned}
$$

In other words, the $10,000.00 increased to $10,820.00 or by 8.2%. Thus the interest rate used for calculations of interest or i is 4%, the nominal yearly interest rate is 8.0%, and the effective yearly interest rate is 8.2%.

Tables A2.3 through A2.6 give values for spcaf, sppwf, pwf, and caf of Table A2.1 for given values of i and n. The crf and sff are not included since their values may be obtained by taking the reciprocal of the values for pwf and caf, respectively.

Table A2.3
Given P, Find F (spcaf)

Period	1%	2%	3%	4%	5%	6%	7%	8%	10%	12%	15%	20%
1	1.0100	1.0200	1.0300	1.0400	1.0500	1.0600	1.0700	1.0800	1.1000	1.1200	1.1500	1.2000
2	1.0201	1.0404	1.0609	1.0816	1.1025	1.1236	1.1449	1.1664	1.2100	1.2544	1.3225	1.4400
3	1.0303	1.0612	1.0927	1.1249	1.1576	1.1910	1.2250	1.2597	1.3310	1.4049	1.5209	1.7280
4	1.0406	1.0824	1.1255	1.1699	1.2155	1.2625	1.3108	1.3605	1.4641	1.5735	1.7490	2.0736
5	1.0510	1.1041	1.1593	1.2167	1.2763	1.3382	1.4026	1.4693	1.6105	1.7623	2.0114	2.4883
6	1.0615	1.1262	1.1941	1.2653	1.3401	1.4185	1.5007	1.5869	1.7716	1.9738	2.3131	2.9860
7	1.0721	1.1487	1.2299	1.3159	1.4071	1.5036	1.6058	1.7138	1.9487	2.2107	2.6600	3.5832
8	1.0829	1.1717	1.2668	1.3686	1.4775	1.5938	1.7182	1.8509	2.1436	2.4760	3.0590	4.2998
9	1.0937	1.1951	1.3048	1.4233	1.5513	1.6895	1.8385	1.9990	2.3579	2.7731	3.5179	5.1598
10	1.1046	1.2190	1.3439	1.4802	1.6289	1.7908	1.9672	2.1589	2.5937	3.1058	4.0456	6.1917
11	1.1157	1.2434	1.3842	1.5395	1.7103	1.8983	2.1049	2.3316	2.8531	3.4785	4.6524	7.4301
12	1.1268	1.2682	1.4258	1.6010	1.7959	2.0122	2.2522	2.5182	3.1384	3.8960	5.3503	8.9161
13	1.1381	1.2936	1.4685	1.6651	1.8856	2.1329	2.4098	2.7196	3.4523	4.3635	6.1528	10.699
14	1.1495	1.3195	1.5126	1.7317	1.9799	2.2609	2.5785	2.9372	3.7975	4.8871	7.0757	12.839
15	1.1610	1.3459	1.5580	1.8009	2.0789	2.3966	2.7590	3.1722	4.1772	5.4736	8.1371	15.407
16	1.1726	1.3728	1.6047	1.8730	2.1829	2.5404	2.9522	3.4259	4.5950	6.1304	9.3576	18.488
17	1.1843	1.4002	1.6528	1.9479	2.2920	2.6928	3.1588	3.7000	5.0545	6.8660	10.761	22.186
18	1.1961	1.4282	1.7024	2.0258	2.4066	2.8543	3.3799	3.9960	5.5599	7.6900	12.375	26.623
19	1.2081	1.4568	1.7535	2.1068	2.5270	3.0256	3.6165	4.3157	6.1159	8.6128	14.232	31.948
20	1.2202	1.4859	1.8061	2.1911	2.6533	3.2071	3.8697	4.6610	6.7275	9.6463	16.367	38.338
21	1.2324	1.5157	1.8603	2.2788	2.7860	3.3996	4.1406	5.0338	7.4002	10.804	18.822	46.005
22	1.2447	1.5460	1.9161	2.3699	2.9253	3.6035	4.4304	5.4365	8.1403	12.100	21.645	55.206
23	1.2572	1.5769	1.9736	2.4647	3.0715	3.8197	4.7405	5.8715	8.9543	13.552	24.891	66.247
24	1.2697	1.6084	2.0328	2.5633	3.2251	4.0489	5.0724	6.3412	9.8497	15.179	28.625	79.497
25	1.2824	1.6406	2.0938	2.6658	3.3864	4.2919	5.4274	6.8485	10.835	17.000	32.919	95.396
26	1.2953	1.6734	2.1566	2.7725	3.5557	4.5494	5.8074	7.3964	11.918	19.040	37.857	114.48
27	1.3082	1.7069	2.2213	2.8834	3.7335	4.8223	6.2139	7.9881	13.110	21.325	43.535	137.37
28	1.3213	1.7410	2.2879	2.9987	3.9201	5.1117	6.6488	8.6271	14.421	23.884	50.066	164.84
29	1.3345	1.7758	2.3566	3.1187	4.1161	5.4184	7.1143	9.3173	15.863	26.750	57.575	197.81
30	1.3478	1.8114	2.4273	3.2434	4.3219	5.7435	7.6123	10.063	17.449	29.960	66.212	237.38
35	1.4166	1.9999	2.8139	3.9461	5.5160	7.6861	10.677	14.785	28.102	52.800	133.18	590.67
40	1.4889	2.2080	3.2620	4.8010	7.0400	10.286	14.974	21.725	45.259	93.051	267.86	1469.8
45	1.5648	2.4379	3.7816	5.8412	8.9850	13.765	21.002	31.920	72.890	163.99	538.77	3657.3
50	1.6446	2.6916	4.3839	7.1067	11.467	18.420	29.457	46.902	117.39	289.00	1083.7	9100.4
55	1.7285	2.9717	5.0821	8.6464	14.636	24.650	41.315	68.914	189.06	509.32	2179.6	22645
60	1.8167	3.2810	5.8916	10.520	18.679	32.988	57.946	101.26	304.48	897.60	4384.0	56348

Table A2.4
Given F, Find P (sppwf)

Period	1%	2%	3%	4%	5%	6%	7%	8%	10%	12%	15%	20%
1	.9901	.9804	.9709	.9615	.9524	.9434	.9346	.9259	.9091	.8929	.8696	.8333
2	.9803	.9612	.9426	.9246	.9070	.8900	.8734	.8573	.8264	.7972	.7561	.6944
3	.9706	.9423	.9151	.8890	.8638	.8396	.8163	.7938	.7513	.7118	.6575	.5787
4	.9610	.9238	.8885	.8548	.8227	.7921	.7629	.7350	.6830	.6355	.5718	.4823
5	.9515	.9057	.8626	.8219	.7835	.7473	.7130	.6806	.6209	.5674	.4972	.4019
6	.9420	.8880	.8375	.7903	.7462	.7050	.6663	.6302	.5645	.5066	.4323	.3349
7	.9327	.8706	.8131	.7599	.7107	.6651	.6227	.5835	.5132	.4523	.3759	.2791
8	.9235	.8535	.7894	.7307	.6768	.6274	.5820	.5403	.4665	.4039	.3269	.2326
9	.9143	.8368	.7664	.7026	.6446	.5919	.5439	.5002	.4241	.3606	.2843	.1938
10	.9053	.8203	.7441	.6756	.6139	.5584	.5083	.4632	.3855	.3220	.2472	.1615
11	.8963	.8043	.7224	.6496	.5847	.5268	.4751	.4289	.3505	.2875	.2149	.1346
12	.8874	.7885	.7014	.6246	.5568	.4970	.4440	.3971	.3186	.2567	.1869	.1122
13	.8787	.7730	.6810	.6006	.5303	.4688	.4150	.3677	.2897	.2292	.1625	.0935
14	.8700	.7579	.6611	.5775	.5051	.4423	.3878	.3405	.2633	.2046	.1413	.0779
15	.8613	.7430	.6419	.5553	.4810	.4173	.3624	.3152	.2394	.1827	.1229	.0649
16	.8528	.7284	.6232	.5339	.4581	.3936	.3387	.2919	.2176	.1631	.1069	.0541
17	.8444	.7142	.6050	.5134	.4363	.3714	.3166	.2703	.1978	.1456	.0929	.0451
18	.8360	.7002	.5874	.4936	.4155	.3503	.2959	.2502	.1799	.1300	.0808	.0376
19	.8277	.6864	.5703	.4746	.3957	.3305	.2765	.2317	.1635	.1161	.0703	.0313
20	.8195	.6730	.5537	.4564	.3769	.3118	.2584	.2145	.1486	.1037	.0611	.0261
21	.8114	.6598	.5375	.4388	.3589	.2942	.2415	.1987	.1351	.0926	.0531	.0217
22	.8034	.6468	.5219	.4220	.3418	.2775	.2257	.1839	.1228	.0826	.0462	.0181
23	.7954	.6342	.5067	.4057	.3256	.2618	.2109	.1703	.1117	.0738	.0402	.0151
24	.7876	.6217	.4919	.3901	.3101	.2470	.1971	.1577	.1015	.0659	.0349	.0126
25	.7798	.6095	.4776	.3751	.2953	.2330	.1842	.1460	.0923	.0588	.0304	.0105
26	.7720	.5976	.4637	.3607	.2812	.2198	.1722	.1352	.0839	.0525	.0264	.0087
27	.7644	.5859	.4502	.3468	.2678	.2074	.1609	.1252	.0763	.0469	.0230	.0073
28	.7568	.5744	.4371	.3335	.2551	.1956	.1504	.1159	.0693	.0419	.0200	.0061
29	.7493	.5631	.4243	.3207	.2429	.1846	.1406	.1073	.0630	.0374	.0174	.0051
30	.7419	.5521	.4120	.3083	.2314	.1741	.1314	.0994	.0573	.0334	.0151	.0042
35	.7059	.5000	.3554	.2534	.1813	.1301	.0937	.0676	.0356	.0189	.0075	.0017
40	.6717	.4529	.3066	.2083	.1420	.0972	.0668	.0460	.0221	.0107	.0037	.0007
45	.6391	.4102	.2644	.1712	.1113	.0727	.0476	.0313	.0137	.0061	.0019	.0003
50	.6080	.3715	.2281	.1407	.0872	.0543	.0339	.0213	.0085	.0035	.0009	.0001
55	.5785	.3365	.1968	.1157	.0683	.0406	.0242	.0145	.0053	.0020	.0005	.0000
60	.5504	.3048	.1697	.0951	.0535	.0303	.0173	.0099	.0033	.0011	.0002	.0000

226

Table A2.5
Given *A*, Find *P* (pwf)

Period	1%	2%	3%	4%	5%	6%	7%	8%	10%	12%	15%	20%
1	0.9901	0.9804	0.9709	0.9615	0.9524	0.9434	0.9346	0.9259	0.9091	0.8929	0.8696	0.8333
2	1.9704	1.9416	1.9135	1.8861	1.8594	1.8334	1.8080	1.7833	1.7355	1.6901	1.6257	1.5278
3	2.9410	2.8839	2.8286	2.7751	2.7232	2.6730	2.6243	2.5771	2.4869	2.4018	2.2832	2.1065
4	3.9020	3.8077	3.7171	3.6299	3.5460	3.4651	3.3872	3.3121	3.1699	3.0373	2.8550	2.5887
5	4.8534	4.7135	4.5797	4.4518	4.3295	4.2124	4.1002	3.9927	3.7908	3.6048	3.3522	2.9906
6	5.7955	5.6014	5.4172	5.2421	5.0757	4.9173	4.7665	4.6229	4.3553	4.1114	3.7845	3.3255
7	6.7282	6.4720	6.2303	6.0021	5.7864	5.5824	5.3893	5.2064	4.8684	4.5638	4.1604	3.6046
8	7.6517	7.3255	7.0197	6.7327	6.4632	6.2098	5.9713	5.7466	5.3349	4.9676	4.4873	3.8372
9	8.5660	8.1622	7.7861	7.4353	7.1078	6.8017	6.5152	6.2469	5.7590	5.3282	4.7716	4.0310
10	9.4713	8.9826	8.5302	8.1109	7.7217	7.3601	7.0236	6.7101	6.1446	5.6502	5.0188	4.1925
11	10.368	9.7868	9.2526	8.7605	8.3064	7.8869	7.4987	7.1390	6.4951	5.9377	5.2337	4.3271
12	11.255	10.575	9.9540	9.3851	8.8633	8.3838	7.9427	7.5361	6.8137	6.1944	5.4206	4.4392
13	12.134	11.348	10.635	9.9856	9.3936	8.8527	8.3577	7.9038	7.1034	6.4235	5.5831	4.5327
14	13.004	12.106	11.296	10.563	9.8986	9.2950	8.7455	8.2442	7.3667	6.6282	5.7245	4.6106
15	13.865	12.849	11.938	11.118	10.380	9.7122	9.1079	8.5595	7.6061	6.8109	5.8474	4.6755
16	14.718	13.578	12.561	11.652	10.838	10.106	9.4466	8.8514	7.8237	6.9740	5.9542	4.7296
17	15.562	14.292	13.166	12.166	11.274	10.477	9.7632	9.1216	8.0216	7.1196	6.0472	4.7746
18	16.398	14.992	13.754	12.659	11.690	10.828	10.059	9.3719	8.2014	7.2497	6.1280	4.8122
19	17.226	15.678	14.324	13.134	12.085	11.158	10.336	9.6036	8.3649	7.3658	6.1982	4.8435
20	18.046	16.351	14.877	13.590	12.462	11.470	10.594	9.8181	8.5136	7.4694	6.2593	4.8696
21	18.857	17.011	15.415	14.029	12.821	11.764	10.836	10.017	8.6487	7.5620	6.3125	4.8913
22	19.660	17.658	15.937	14.451	13.163	12.042	11.061	10.201	8.7715	7.6446	6.3587	4.9094
23	20.456	18.292	16.444	14.857	13.489	12.303	11.272	10.371	8.8832	7.7184	6.3988	4.9245
24	21.243	18.914	16.936	15.247	13.799	12.550	11.469	10.529	8.9847	7.7843	6.4338	4.9371
25	22.023	19.523	17.413	15.622	14.094	12.783	11.654	10.675	9.0770	7.8431	6.4641	4.9476
26	22.795	20.121	17.877	15.983	14.375	13.003	11.826	10.810	9.1609	7.8957	6.4906	4.9563
27	23.560	20.707	18.327	16.330	14.643	13.211	11.987	10.935	9.2372	7.9426	6.5135	4.9636
28	24.316	21.281	18.764	16.663	14.898	13.406	12.137	11.051	9.3066	7.9844	6.5335	4.9697
29	25.066	21.844	19.188	16.984	15.141	13.591	12.278	11.158	9.3696	8.0218	6.5509	4.9747
30	25.808	22.396	19.600	17.292	15.372	13.765	12.409	11.258	9.4269	8.0552	6.5660	4.9789
35	29.409	24.999	21.487	18.665	16.374	14.498	12.948	11.655	9.6442	8.1755	6.6166	4.9915
40	32.835	27.355	23.115	19.793	17.159	15.046	13.332	11.925	9.7791	8.2438	6.6418	4.9966
45	36.095	29.490	24.519	20.720	17.774	15.456	13.606	12.108	9.8628	8.2825	6.6543	4.9986
50	39.196	31.424	25.730	21.482	18.256	15.762	13.801	12.233	9.9148	8.3045	6.6605	4.9995
55	42.147	33.175	26.774	22.109	18.633	15.991	13.940	12.319	9.9471	8.3170	6.6636	4.9998
60	44.955	34.761	27.676	22.623	18.929	16.161	14.039	12.377	9.9672	8.3240	6.6651	4.9999

Table A2.6
Given *A*, Find *F* (caf)

Period	1%	2%	3%	4%	5%	6%	7%	8%	10%	12%	15%	20%
1	1.0000	1.0000	1.0000	1.0000	1.0000	1.0000	1.0000	1.0000	1.0000	1.0000	1.0000	1.0000
2	2.0100	2.0200	2.0300	2.0400	2.0500	2.0600	2.0700	2.0800	2.1000	2.1200	2.1500	2.2000
3	3.0301	3.0604	3.0909	3.1216	3.1525	3.1836	3.2149	3.2464	3.3100	3.3744	3.4725	3.6400
4	4.0604	4.1216	4.1836	4.2465	4.3101	4.3746	4.4399	4.5061	4.6410	4.7793	4.9934	5.3680
5	5.1010	5.2040	5.3091	5.4163	5.5256	5.6371	5.7507	5.8666	6.1051	6.3528	6.7424	7.4416
6	6.1520	6.3081	6.4684	6.6330	6.8019	6.9753	7.1533	7.3359	7.7156	8.1152	8.7537	9.9299
7	7.2135	7.4343	7.6625	7.8983	8.1420	8.3938	8.6540	8.9228	9.4872	10.089	11.067	12.916
8	8.2857	8.5830	8.8923	9.2142	9.5491	9.8975	10.260	10.637	11.436	12.300	13.727	16.499
9	9.3685	9.7546	10.159	10.583	11.027	11.491	11.978	12.488	13.579	14.776	16.786	20.799
10	10.462	10.950	11.464	12.006	12.578	13.181	13.816	14.487	15.937	17.549	20.304	25.958
11	11.567	12.169	12.808	13.486	14.207	14.972	15.784	16.645	18.531	20.655	24.349	32.150
12	12.683	13.412	14.192	15.026	15.917	16.870	17.888	18.977	21.384	24.133	29.002	39.581
13	13.809	14.680	15.618	16.627	17.713	18.882	20.141	21.495	24.523	28.029	34.352	48.497
14	14.947	15.974	17.086	18.292	19.599	21.015	22.550	24.215	27.975	32.393	40.505	59.196
15	16.097	17.293	18.599	20.024	21.579	23.276	25.129	27.152	31.772	37.280	47.580	72.035
16	17.258	18.639	20.157	21.825	23.657	25.673	27.888	30.324	35.950	42.753	55.717	87.442
17	18.430	20.012	21.762	23.698	25.840	28.213	30.840	33.750	40.545	48.884	65.075	105.93
18	19.615	21.412	23.414	25.645	28.132	30.906	33.999	37.450	45.599	55.750	75.836	128.12
19	20.811	22.841	25.117	27.671	30.539	33.760	37.379	41.446	51.159	63.440	88.212	154.74
20	22.019	24.297	26.870	29.778	33.066	36.786	40.995	45.762	57.275	72.052	102.44	186.69
21	23.239	25.783	28.676	31.969	35.719	39.993	44.865	50.423	64.002	81.699	118.81	225.03
22	24.472	27.299	30.537	34.248	38.505	43.392	49.006	55.457	71.403	92.503	137.63	271.03
23	25.716	28.845	32.453	36.618	41.430	46.996	53.436	60.893	79.543	104.60	159.28	326.24
24	26.973	30.422	34.426	39.083	44.502	50.816	58.177	66.765	88.497	118.16	184.17	392.48
25	28.243	32.030	36.459	41.646	47.727	54.865	63.249	73.106	98.347	133.33	212.79	471.98
26	29.526	33.671	38.553	44.312	51.113	59.156	68.676	79.954	109.18	150.33	245.71	567.38
27	30.821	35.344	40.710	47.084	54.669	63.706	74.484	87.351	121.10	169.37	283.57	681.85
28	32.129	37.051	42.931	49.968	58.403	68.528	80.698	95.339	134.21	190.70	327.10	819.22
29	33.450	38.792	45.219	52.966	62.323	73.640	87.347	103.97	148.63	214.58	377.17	984.07
30	34.785	40.568	47.575	56.085	66.439	79.058	94.461	113.28	164.49	241.33	434.75	1181.9
35	41.660	49.994	60.462	73.652	90.320	111.43	138.24	172.32	271.02	431.66	881.17	2948.3
40	48.886	60.402	75.401	95.026	120.80	154.76	199.64	259.06	442.59	767.09	1779.1	7343.9
45	56.481	71.893	92.720	121.03	159.70	212.74	285.75	386.51	718.90	1358.2	3585.1	18281
50	64.463	84.579	112.80	152.67	209.35	290.34	406.53	573.77	1163.9	2400.0	7217.7	45497
55	72.852	98.587	136.07	191.16	272.71	394.17	575.93	848.92	1880.6	4236.0	14524.	113219
60	81.670	114.05	163.05	237.99	353.58	533.13	813.52	1253.2	3034.8	7471.6	29220.	281733

Appendix 3

Arcadian Telecom (Case Study)

PURPOSE

The purpose of this case study is the establishment of the value of a company, factors affecting this value, the application of the capital asset–pricing model (CAPM) and options of privatization.

PROJECT SUMMARY

In 1880, Arcadia was discovered by an English explorer, Sir H. L. Lost. Over the next 70 years it was colonized by the British, the Germans and the Spanish. In 1955 the country eventually achieved independence and during the last 20 years it has experienced a large degree of stability and prosperity due to its extensive mineral resources. The currency of Arcadia is the Arcadian dollar which is freely exchangeable outside Arcadia and has the same value as the US dollar.

The Arcadian Post Office (PO) was the largest organization in the country. It had assets of $4.5 billion, annual revenues of over $1.5 billion and a payroll for about 40,000 employees. Under the direction of the Postmaster General, the PO had three business functions: Telecommunications, Postal Agency and Postal Banking.

In January 1995, an internal PO review commented that (a) the organization was not working as well as it should and (b) its structure was very old-fashioned for the fast-changing environment. The review argued that each business was distinctly different and of sufficient size to merit the attention of its own board of directors and management.

In addition to this review, Parliament had recently made well-publicized statements aimed at improving the efficiency of the government operations and state-owned enterprises and called for the implementation of systems to delegate responsibility, evaluate managers and ensure public accountability. The PO, therefore, planned the breakup of the businesses and thus formed the Telecom Establishment Board (TEB) which was empowered with the task of managing the transition to "corporatize" and take control of the Telecom of Arcadia (Telecom) beginning on March 1, 1996 (the target date).

It appeared that the Arcadian government did not want to "privatize," but rather "corporatize" these businesses so that under the direction of their own boards, they may raise their own financing, and pay taxes and dividends to the government. In other words, the aim was to get them off the budget and reduce the Arcadian public debt burden. At the same time, control was to be maintained by having all the shares held by the Ministry of Finance.

In November 1995, as proposals were floated regarding the reorganization of the telecom service in Arcadia, the TEB asked the US consulting firm World Telecom (WT) to help in three areas: (a) advise on the impact of different strategies, (b) determine the valuation of Telecom, and (c) develop investment and project evaluation criteria and techniques. TEB also asked Smith & Co., a respected local merchant bank, to assist Telecom in the evaluation study. On the other hand, the government had International Telecom (IT), a US consulting firm, advising them in the preparation for the negotiations.

In initial negotiations with the government, TEB advanced a proposal regarding the future operating environment of Telecom. This proposal had four points, each of which was crucial to the assessment of the company's valuation: (1) freedom to set prices without government intervention, (2) flexibility in personnel policies, (3) ability to arrange commercial finance, and (4) no competition in basic network services. These points (if agreed to) would allow Telecom to operate in a manner comparable with other businesses not owned by the government and to ensure that there were no special impediments imposed on it.

Aside from the discussions about the future operating environment, there were other important differences to be resolved in the discount rate, level of capital expenditures needed by Telecom and the perpetuity value of its future cash flow. As for the environment, the government would not guarantee a monopoly for Telecom, but rather any move toward deregulation would be considered in the light of Telecom's financial viability.

With regards to the discount rate, it was agreed that the capital asset-pricing model was appropriate for evaluation; however, there were differences as follows:

Parameter	Telecom's Estimate	Government's Estimate
Market risk	8.5%	7.0%
Debt credit risk	0.7%	0.5%
Beta	1.0	0.7
D/E ratio	30:70	40:60

Later on, it was agreed that the proper debt-equity ratio would be 30:70, and Beta = .80, and while the Treasury raised its market risk estimate to 7.5 percent, there still existed a gap in both risk percentages.

As for capital expenditures, the government argued that WT's estimate was too high. In response, WT pointed out that further reductions in expenditures would result in lost revenues as follows:

Reduction in Capital Expenditures (%)	Lost Revenue over 10 Years (%)	(billion Arcadian $)
10	4	1,000
20	6	1,500
30	12	3,200

As the negotiations wore on, it was apparent that it would be unwise for Telecom to be overvalued as well as undervalued. Smith & Co. estimated that the prospective Price-Earnings ratio of listed Arcadian companies was approximately 7.80. They argued that Telecom could not be priced too high because it would conflict with overseas equity markets where similar companies trade at a 10–25 percent discount on the applicable market average P-E. In any case, the opening balance sheet would be practically financed by the government, which would own all the shares. Since Telecom was expected to be profitable, it would pay interest, taxes and dividends to the government.

With the talks exceeding the March 1 deadline, it was important to get the evaluation completed because it was taking a great amount of management time. In addition, several major operating decisions regarding strategy and investments were delayed because of this delay in establishing a value for Telecom.

EXAMINATION

We are asked to discuss the following questions:

1. What would you expect to be the key drivers of value for a telecommunications company?
2. What are the specific business risks associated with operating Telecom?
3. How would you estimate the demand for the services offered by Telecom?

Table A3.1
Comparable Statistics Based on December 20, 1995 Value Line

Parameter	Ameritech	Bell Atl.	Bell S.	Nynex	US West	AllTel	Contel
Recent Price ($/Sh.)	92	71	61	68	57	46	32
P/E Ratio	11.4	11.8	11.5	11.0	11.1	12.8	10.1
Dividend Yield (%)	5.4	5.3	5.3	5.4	5.5	4.4	5.9
Beta	0.90	0.85	1.10	0.95	0.85	0.80	0.75
Unleveraged Beta	0.71	0.66	0.86	0.70	0.65	0.50	0.50
Market Value of Equity ($ Mil.)	13,211	14,129	19,392	13,784	10,796	998	2,454
Total Debt ($ Mil.)	4,768	5,419	6,599	5,876	5,103	642	2,146
Debt Due within One Year ($ Mil.)	228	635	932	9	447	32	112
Shares (Mil.)	144	199	318	203	189	22	77
Preferred ($ Mil.)	0	0	0	0	0	48	30
Access Lines (Mil.)	15	15	15	14	11	1	2
Employees ('000)	75	77	93	94	70	6	22
Lines per Employee	196	201	161	147	159	161	91
Est. Plant Age (yrs)	12	NA	NA	NA	14	14	12
Revenues ($ Mil.)	9,360	9,810	11,500	11,210	8,360	700	3,060
Net Profit ($ Mil.)	1,130	1,180	1,640	1,230	930	80	235
Earnings/Net Worth (%)	15	14	15	14	13	13	15
Capital Spending	2,051	2,497	2,594	1,998	1,857	166	568
Capital Spending/Share	14	13	8	10	10	8	7
As % of Revenues	0.22	0.25	0.23	0.18	0.22	0.24	0.19

4. How confident are you that the Capital Asset Pricing Model yields the appropriate discount rate, commensurate with Telecom's business and financial risks?

5. What additional steps, if any, should the Arcadian government take?

6. What options for private investment does the Arcadian government have?

7. What are the alternative approaches to issuing telecommunications franchises?

In your discussion you may wish to use some of the statistics of Table A3.1.

DISCUSSION

Value of a Telecommunications Company

The value of a telecommunications firm depends heavily on the regulatory regime, the degree of competition engendered in the tender, the level of debt, potential demand for services, as well as the number of people employed. This value should be established with a discounted cash flow analysis, based on full modeling, using various regulatory and other assumptions. The model includes parameters such as population growth, per capita GDP, long-term inflation rate, price elasticity, number of employees and salary growth. Existing models normally use a discount rate based on the Capital Asset–Pricing Model.

The value obtained with the aforementioned model can be compared with (a) various measures of quoted telcos and (b) various measures of previous telco transactions. The measures may include enterprise value (EV) per line, EV per population, EV/revenue and EV/EBIT. Comparison (a) provides a rough estimate of the value attributed to a telecom operator. It is, however, imperfect since the performance of telcos is heavily influenced by local market conditions, specific regulatory regime and growth prospects.

Comparison with previous telco transactions may give an indication of the premium strategic investors would be willing to pay, in consideration for a degree of control, and the consequent influence they can bring to the future growth prospects. However, one has to be careful since particular circumstances may have prevailed in the previous transactions. For instance, the privatization of a Brazilian telecom operator was very competitive, as bidders felt it was most important to get a foothold in Brazil ahead of the restructuring of the whole telecoms sector, with a view to possibly influencing government decisions. The price paid by the investor for Telefonica del Peru took into account a very beneficial management contract.

Demand for Telecommunication Services

Macroeconomic indicators may be used to estimate future demand for telecommunication services. Examples of such indicators are (a) the relationship between GDP and teledensity, (b) the relationship between per capita income and teledensity and (c) expenditure on telecoms is between 1 percent and 4 percent of GDP.

Consideration of Conflicting Objectives

Presumably, the primary purpose of reform is to get consumers more, better, new and less costly services. Pressures from interest groups (incumbents who want ongoing protection, new entrants seeking special deals, treasury officials expecting to use sale revenues to reduce deficits, financial advisers earning success fees tied to transition prices) can steer reform off this track. Sales strategies that drive up the prices paid for existing companies or new licenses can hold down growth, reduce the funding available to invest in these companies or result in high tariffs.

In Brazil, the consortium that won the cellular license in Sao Paulo in 1997 with a US$2.5 billion bid (four times the government's asking price and 60%

more than the second-highest bid) is likely to pass on the cost to consumers through much higher tariffs than those proposed by rival bidders. By contrast, the Bolivian government privatized ENTEL in 1996 by issuing new shares for which the winning bidder paid US$600 million, immediately available for investment in the company.

Incremental Reform

International experience suggests that a step-by-step approach is essential where divestiture is involved. Ideally, divestiture should be preceded by (a) a restructuring process in which the state-owned carrier is commercialized, and (b) separation of the government's regulatory responsibilities from its policy-making and operational roles and placement in a separate organization. In addition, initially selling only the minimum number of government shares needed for the effective transfer control to the new owners (20 to 30%) allows a government to float the balance later and obtain higher prices, once the company appreciates under private management.

Telecommunications is now a multi-product sector with alternative service delivery mechanisms that permit competition in service provision. For instance, a high-capacity digital wireless network costing about US$2 billion could replace the wire-based network covering the whole of Britain and initially costing several times more than the wireless network. However, competition has not eliminated the need for regulation. Regulators are the gatekeepers of the transformation of the telecommunications market. They have influence or control over pricing, standards, market entry and interconnection arrangements. The focus of the regulatory agenda has shifted from minimizing the price of subscribing to local telephone service or maintaining cross-subsidy to managing the transition to a new environment. Managing this transition requires addressing the following:

- Determining whether entry in different market segments should be limited or open and setting the terms of entry and thus creating market forces.

- Adopting processes for the award of licenses to service providers (these may include bidding processes in which the evaluation criteria are clear and easily measured, as in price bids, or "beauty contests," in which the bid evaluation criteria are subjective and the selection process is less transparent).

- Resolving network interconnection issues and managing numbering plans to promote the emergence of a multi-operator environment.

- Authorizing rate rebalancing (whereby prices are moved closer to costs by reducing prices for international and long-distance services and increasing them for local services) in order to reduce cross-subsidies.

- Applying new approaches to cross-subsidies, such as improved targeting of beneficiaries, bidding for minimum subsidies, and the administration of subsidies in a way that does not favor one operator over another.

• Responding to the increased need to manage radio spectrum due to the wireless revolution reflected in the rapid growth of cellular telephony (this involves allocating portions of the radio spectrum to different uses, assigning frequencies and authorizing transmission power levels to transmitters at specified locations, maintaining standards to ensure that transmitters make optimum use of the radio spectrum and implementing measures to control unauthorized use).

In the absence of competitive markets, regulators adopt price control rules. A "fair and reasonable rate" standard is designed to ensure that the operator obtains a reasonable return on its investment but without exploiting its monopoly position in the market. This standard usually covers the costs of services over the medium to long term.

The price an operator is allowed to charge its customers is the most important determinant of profitability and ability to finance growth. Tariffs observed in competitive markets probably offer the best guidance on efficient prices. Although some cost elements (labor, land, taxes) vary considerably among countries, the main costs (equipment, capital) are determined in global markets and thus international benchmarks are relevant. As the market becomes more competitive, pricing can be increasingly left to the operators. Since telecommunications networks exhibit scale economies in some cases, the technical efficiency of the network may be frustrated if carriers serving adjacent territory can refuse interconnection. In addition, where competing carriers are licensed, the public may benefit by having nondiscriminatory access to the networks of all carriers.

Options for Private Investment

Divestiture of a state-owned carrier may involve the sale, total or partial, of the state's ownership in the dominant telecommunications operator through a series of public share offerings (UK, Japan, Malaysia). Alternatively, a strategic stake in the operator may be sold by competitive tender to a prequalified group of bidders (as in Mexico, New Zealand and Australia), following which the bidder or the government may sell additional shares in the company.

In low- and middle-income countries with less than two lines per hundred people, divestiture of the state-owned carrier will only partly solve the shortfall of supply. The demand is simply too great and the current base of telephone lines too small. In these countries new entry and other "bottom-up" measures for private-sector participation have become important and, in the future, may become the prevalent means of closing the gap between demand and supply. They may take several forms: competitive franchises granted to independent telephone companies in designated areas; refranchising of unserved or underserved areas of the country; capital provided by public companies (including municipalities) or the private sector through a build-transfer (B-T) scheme, or a joint venture. The service provider may be a stand-alone company or a subcontractor for an existing licensee; the scope of service may be limited to local exchange services or may extend to interchange offerings. "Bottom-up" private development, like divestiture, will not be effective, however, if it is not supported by appropriate regulatory commitments.

Build-transfer schemes are usually specified as build-operate-transfer, in which the investors or B-T company maintain ownership of the project assets for a period of years, or as build-transfer-operate, in which case ownership of project assets is transferred to a public administration or state-owned company immediately upon commissioning, with the B-T company remaining in place to operate and manage the new facilities for a period of years. In these schemes, the flow of revenues to the B-T company (e.g., an agreed share of operating revenues generated by the project) is broadly comparable to lease payments.

Telecommunications Franchises

Franchises or licenses for the provision of public telecommunications services, whether conventional local or long distance, or cellular telephone service, can be issued in different ways: (a) direct assignment, (b) lottery, or (c) competitive bidding. Although direct assignment is a common approach, it has the clear disadvantage of not providing for the systematic review of alternative applicants and proposals. As a result, important opportunities for optimizing sector performance or franchise revenues to the government may be missed.

The best-known use of a lottery approach was for the allocation of radio frequencies for the provision of cellular telephone service in the United States in the 1980s. In that case, in each cellular franchise area in the country, one license was issued to a local wireline carrier, and a second one was issued by lottery. The approach recognized that the regulator would not be able to make a meaningful distinction, based on merit, between many applicants. On the other hand, many licenses were in fact issued to companies that had neither the intention nor the capability to provide service, and were quickly sold. As a result, the scarcity value of the licenses went to the lottery winners.

The award of a license on the basis of competitive bidding with respect to well-defined criteria is, in most circumstances, the best approach. The selection criteria must ultimately depend on government objectives. Nevertheless, many economists favor franchise fee bidding by prequalified applicants. This approach involves the most transparent process and thereby gives legitimacy to the franchise award. It will also tend to select the applicant that can create the most value in providing the franchised service. In addition, since this approach involves paying the government for the franchise, it not only may result in substantial payments to the government, but also creates an incentive for the franchiser to invest quickly to provide service. Critics of the franchise bidding process argue that it increases the cost of service. However, to the extent that expected bid prices are considered too high, governments can consider issuing more licenses to reduce the scarcity value of each franchise, thereby increasing competition in the provision of franchised services.

Appendix 4

Credit Rating Agencies

Credit rating agencies such as Standard & Poor's Corporation and Moody's Investors Services, Inc. base their ratings largely on an analysis of the level and trend of some of the issuer's financial ratios. The key ratios used to evaluate "safety" are the following:

- *Debt management ratios* such as:

    times-interest-earned ratio = earnings before interest and taxes (EBIT) divided by interest charges;

    fixed-charge coverage ratio = the ratio of (EBIT + lease payments) to (interest charges + lease payments + sinking fund payments divided by [1 − tax rate]);

    > Note that since sinking fund payments are paid with after-tax dollars and interest and lease payments are paid with pre-tax dollars, the sinking fund payments must be divided by (1 − tax rate) to find the before-tax income required to pay taxes and still have enough left to make the sinking fund payment;

    net worth ratio = the ratio of long-term debt to net worth;

    > *net worth* = common and preferred share capital + earned surplus + surplus reserves or total assets of a company less third-party claims on those assets; and

    net tangible assets ratio = the ratio of long-term debt to the sum of net worth and long-term debt.

- *Liquidity ratios* such as:

    current ratio = the ratio of current assets to current liabilities;

    > *current assets* = cash, marketable securities, accounts receivable and inventories, and

    > *current liabilities* = accounts payable, short-term notes payable, current matur-

ities on long-term debt, accrued income taxes and other accrued expenses (e.g., wages); and

quick ratio = the ratio of current assets minus inventories to current liabilities.

* *Profitability ratios* such as:

  return on assets = EBIT divided by total assets;

  operating margin of profit = operating profit divided by sales; and

  cash flow-to-debt ratio = the ratio of total cash flow to outstanding debt.

* *Asset management ratios* such as:

  inventory turnover ratio = sales divided by accounts receivable;

  fixed assets turnover ratio = the ratio of sales to net fixed assets; and

  days sales outstanding ratio = average daily sales divided by accounts receivable.

* *Market value ratios* such as:

  price/earnings ratio (P/E) = the ratio of price per share to earnings per share; and

  market/book ratio (M/B) = the ratio of market price per share to the book value per share.

Note that:

* debt management ratios tell us whether a company earns more on investments financed with borrowed funds than it pays interest, or give us information about owner-supplied funds to provide a safety margin;
* liquidity ratios measure the firm's ability to pay off its short-term obligations with available cash, cash currently being collected and cash to be easily obtained with the sale of marketable securities (and inventories);
* profitability ratios indicate the effects of liquidity, debt management and asset management on operating results, or the firm's overall financial health;
* asset management ratios measure how effectively a company is managing its assets; and
* market value ratios give a company's management an indication of what investors think of its past performance and its future prospects.

It is important to:

* analyze trends in ratios as well as their absolute values, because trends give insight into whether the financial situation is improving or deteriorating;
* realize that each of the data-supplying organizations (Dun and Bradstreet, Robert Morris Associates, US Commerce Department, and so on) may use a somewhat different set of ratios and/or different definitions designed for its own purposes; and
* balance the tax advantages of writing down fixed assets as fast as possible against the disadvantage of reducing the company's ability to raise money as cheaply as possible.

Moody's and S&P use primarily the debt management ratios, liquidity ratios and profitability ratios. S&P periodically computes median values of selected ratios for several rating classes. Of course, ratios must be evaluated in the context of industry standards. For instance, successful firms such as computer software firms achieve high rates of return on their assets, while a typical railroad company has a low rate of return on assets. Nevertheless, the following median financial ratios for the period 1991–1993 demonstrate the tendency of ratios to improve with the firms' rating class.

Rating Category	Fixed-charge coverage ratio	Cash flow to total debt	Return on capital (%)	Long-term debt/capital
AAA	6.34	0.49	24.2	11.7
AA	4.48	0.32	18.4	19.1
A	2.93	0.17	13.5	29.4
BBB	1.82	0.04	9.7	39.5
BB	1.33	0.01	9.1	51.1
B	0.78	(0.02)	6.3	61.8

The definitions of the bond ratings are as follows:

	Very high quality	High quality	Speculative			Very poor	
Standard & Poor's	AAA AA	A BBB	BB	B	CCC	D
Moody's	Aaa Aa	A Baa	Ba	B	Caa	C

At times both Moody's and Standard & Poor's have used adjustments to these ratings: S&P uses plus and minus signs: A+ is the strongest A rating and A– the weakest. Moody's uses a 1, 2 or 3 designation, with 1 indicating the strongest.

Moody's	S&P	
Aaa	AAA	Debt rated Aaa and AAA has the highest rating. Capacity to pay interest and principal is extremely strong.
Aa	AA	Debt rated Aa and AA has a very strong capacity to pay interest and principal. Together with the highest rating, this group comprises the high-grade bond class.
A	A	Debt rated A has strong capacity to pay interest and principal, although it is somewhat more susceptible to the adverse effects of changes in circumstances and economic conditions than debt in higher-rated categories.
Baa	BBB	Debt rated Baa and BBB is regarded as having an adequate capacity to pay interest and principal. Whereas it normally exhibits adequate protection parameters, adverse economic conditions or changing circumstances are more likely to lead to a weakened capacity to pay interest and principal for debt in this category than in higher-rated categories. These bonds are medium-grade obligations.
Ba	BB	Debt rated in these categories is regarded, on balance, as
B	B	predominantly speculative with respect to capacity to pay
Caa	CCC	interest and principal in accordance with the terms of the
Ca	CC	obligations. Ba and BB indicate the lowest degree of speculation, and Ca and CC the highest degree of speculation. Although such debt will likely have some quality protective characteristics, these are outweighed by large uncertainties or major risk exposures to adverse conditions. Some issues may be in default.
C	C	This rating is reserved for income bonds on which no interest is being paid.
D	D	Debt rated D is in default and payment of interest and/or principal is in arrears.

Cash Flow Analysis (Case Study)

PURPOSE

The purpose of this case study is to become familiar with the establishment of cash flows, the modified internal rate of return (MIRR), the treatment of inflation and tax issues and the type of sensitivity analysis to be carried out. Amelectro manufactures customized integrated circuits for use in cars, computers and robots. Korelectro has been Amelectro's wholly owned *distribution* affiliate in Korea for five years. Consideration is now being given to making Korelectro a *manufacturing* affiliate; its products would be sold in Korea and the sales would be in Korean won.

COMPANY AND COUNTRY DATA

Korelectro will pay a license fee of 2 percent of sales revenue to Amelectro. The fee is tax deductible in Korea; however, it provides taxable income to Amelectro.

Korea has no withholding tax on dividends, interest or fees paid to foreign residents. Its corporate income tax rate is 30 percent as compared to 34 percent in the United States.

The weighted average cost of capital used by Amelectro is the same as the one used by Korean companies of comparable risk and amounts to 20 percent.

Korelectro needs gross working capital (i.e., cash, receivables and inventory) equal to 20 percent of sales. Half of this can be financed by local accruals and accounts payable; the other half is to be considered as an investment in working capital.

Korelectro will pay 65 percent of accounting net income to Amelectro as an annual cash dividend. They estimate that over a period of five years the other 35 percent of net income must be reinvested to finance working capital growth.

Components sold by Amelectro to Korelectro have a direct cost to Amelectro equal to 97.5 percent of their sales price.

Plant and equipment will be depreciated on a straight-line basis for both accounting and tax purposes over an expected life of ten years.

Sales in the first year are forecast to be Won44,000 million and are expected to grow at 8 percent per annum during the foreseeable future.

The effect of inflation on prices is estimated as follows:

US general price level: +3% per year

Korean general price level: +6% per year

Korelectro average sales price: +6% per year

Korean raw material costs: +1% per year

Korean labor costs: +7% per year

The exchange rate is Won1,200 to the dollar in the year in which the initial investment takes place. Amelectro expects the won to depreciate relative to the dollar at 3 percent per year. Thus, year-end exchange rates are forecast as follows:

Year	Calculation	Won/dollar
0	(given)	1,200
1	1,200 x 1.03 =	1,236
2	1,236 x 1.03 =	1,273
3	1,273 x 1.03 =	1,311
4	1,311 x 1.03 =	1,351
5	1,351 x 1.03 =	1,392

Korelectro will be financed by Amelectro with an $18,000,000 purchase of Won21,600,000,000 common stock, all to be owned by Amelectro.

ASSUMPTIONS

In order to establish the cash flow projections, we make the following assumptions:

- In the first year of operations, sales revenue is estimated at Won44,000 million. In subsequent years sales revenue will increase annually at 8 percent because of physical growth and at an additional 6 percent due to price increases. Therefore, sales revenue will grow at (1.08) (1.06) = 1.1448, or 14.48 percent per annum.

- Costs of Korean raw materials in the first year are budgeted at Won6,000 million and

Table A5.1
Korelectro's Beginning Balance Sheet (Year 0)

	Millions of won	Thousands of dollars
Assets		
(1) Cash balance	1,500	1,251
(2) Accounts receivable	0	0
(3) Inventory	2,500	2,083
(4) Net plant and equipment	19,000	15,833
(5) Total	23,000	19,167
Liabilities and Net Worth		
(6) Accounts payable	1,400	1,167
(7) Common stock equity	21,600	18,000
Total	23,000	19,167

are expected to increase at 8 percent per annum because of the physical growth, and at an additional 1 percent because of price increases. Thus, raw material costs will grow at (1.08) (1.01) = 1.0908, or 9.08 percent per annum.

- Direct labor costs in the first year are budgeted at Won8,000 million and are expected to increase at 8 percent per annum because of physical growth, and at an additional 7 percent per annum because of increases in Korean wage rates. Consequently, Korean direct labor costs will increase at (1.08) (1.07) = 1.1556, or 15.56 percent per annum.

- Parent-supplied component costs in the first year are budgeted at Won16,000 million. These costs are estimated to increase at 8 percent per annum because of physical growth, plus an additional 3 percent because of US inflation, plus another 3 percent in won terms because of the expected deterioration of the won relative to the dollar. Consequently, the won cost of parent-supplied imports will increase at (1.08) (1.03) (1.03) = 1.1458, or 14.58 per annum.

- Overhead (general and administrative expenses) is budgeted at Won10,000 million in the first year of operation. Overhead is expected to increase at 1 percent annually as Korelectro expands production and sales.

- At the end of five years the project (including working capital) is expected to be sold on a going-concern basis to Korean investors for Won23,664 million, or $17,000,000 at the expected exchange rate of Won1,392/$. This sales price is free of all Korean and US taxes, and will be used as the terminal value for capital budgeting purposes.

BEGINNING BALANCE SHEET

Table A5.1 presents the beginning balance sheet. Won accounts are translated in year 0 at the current exchange rate of Won1,200 per dollar.

Table A5.2
Revenue and Cost Data for Korelectro (millions of won)

Item (by year)	1	2	3	4	5
(1) Total sales revenue	44,000	50,372	57,664	66,014	75,574
(2) Korean raw material	6,000	6,545	7,139	7,787	8,494
(3) Parent purchased comp.	16,000	18,332	21,004	24,066	27,574
(4) Korean labor	8,000	9,245	10,683	12,346	14,267
(5) Total variable costs [(2) + (3) + (4)]	30,000	34,122	38,826	44,199	50,335
(6) Gross profit	14,000	16,250	18,838	21,815	25,239
(7) License fee [2% of (1)]	880	1,007	1,153	1,320	1,511
(8) Overhead	10,000	10,100	10,201	10,303	10,406
(9) Depreciation	1,900	1,900	1,900	1,900	1,900
(10) EBIT [(6) − {(7) + (8) + (9)}]	1,220	3,243	5,584	8,292	11,422
(11) Korean income taxes (30%)	366	973	1,675	2,488	3,427
(12) Net income	854	2,270	3,909	5,804	7,995
(13) Cash dividend [65% of (12)]	555	1,476	2,541	3,773	5,197

PROJECTED REVENUES AND COSTS

Table A5.2 presents revenue and cost projections for Korelectro over the expected five-year life of the project.

WORKING CAPITAL

Table A5.3 shows how the annual increase in working capital investment is computed. According to the given data, half of the working capital can be financed by local accruals and accounts payable, and the other half represents an additional required capital investment.

KORELECTRO'S FORECAST PROJECT CASH FLOWS

Table A5.4 shows forecast cash flows from the viewpoint of Korelectro. Due to a high terminal value, the project has a positive net present value (NPV) of Won497 million and a modified internal rate of return (MIRR) greater than the 20 percent Korean cost of capital for projects of similar risk. Note that line (3) of Table A5.4 equals line (12) of Table A5.2 since Korelectro has no long-term debt, and thus no interest expense. If Korelectro had interest expense, line 12 of Table A5.2 would have been calculated after deducting interest, whereas line (3) of Table A5.4 would have been before interest expense. The MIRR concept is explained at the end of this appendix.

The above positive NPV and MIRR greater than 20 percent are necessary but

Table A5.3
Working Capital Calculation for Korelectro (millions of won)

Item (by year)	1	2	3	4	5
(1) Total revenue	44,000	50,372	57,664	66,014	75,574
(2) Net working capital needs at year end [20% of (1)]	8,800	10,074	11,533	13,203	15,115
(3) Less year-beginning working capital	4,000	8,800	10,074	11,533	13,202
(4) Required addition to working capital	4,800	1,274	1,459	1,670	1,913
(5) Less working capital financed in Korea by accruals and accounts payable	2,400	637	730	835	957
(6) Net new investment in working capital	2,400	637	730	835	957

Table A5.4
Korelectro's Cash Flows, All-Equity Basis (millions of won)

Item (by year)	0	1	2	3	4	5
(1) EBIT [Table A5.2 (10)]		1,220	3,243	5,584	8,292	11,422
(2) Korean income taxes		(366)	(973)	(1,675)	(2,488)	(3,427)
(3) Net income, all equity basis		854	2,270	3,909	5,804	7,995
(4) Depreciation		1,900	1,900	1,900	1,900	1,900
(5) Terminal value						23,644
(6) Half of addition to working capital		(2,400)	(637)	(730)	(835)	(957)
(7) Cost of Project	(21,600)					
(8) Net cash flow	(21,600)	345	3,533	5,079	6,869	32,602
(9) Present value factor	1.000	0.833	0.694	0.579	0.482	0.402
(10) NPV each year	(21,600)	287	2,452	2,941	3,311	13,106
(11) Cumulative NPV	(21,600)	(21,313)	(18,861)	(15,920)	(12,609)	497
(12) MIRR = 20.5%						

not sufficient requirements. That is, Korelectro must pass a second test which shows that from Amelectro's viewpoint the cumulative NPV is positive and the MIRR is at least the 20 percent USA's cost of capital. Table A5.5 presents the calculation for expected after-tax dividends from Korelectro to be received by Amelectro.

Table A5.5
After-Tax Dividend Received by Amelectro from Korelectro

Item (by year)	0	1	2	3	4	5
In Millions of Won						
(1) Cash dividend paid [Table A5.2, (13)]		555	1,476	2,541	3,773	5,197
(2) 65% of Korean income tax [Table A5.2, (11)]		238	632	1,089	1,617	2,228
(3) Grossed-up dividend		793	2,108	3,630	5,390	7,425
(4) Exchange rate (won/$)	1,200	1,236	1,273	1,311	1,351	1,392
In Thousands of Dollars						
(5) Grossed-up dividend [(3)/(4) x 1,000]		642	1,656	2,769	3,990	5,334
(6) US tax (34%)		218	563	941	1,357	1,814
(7) Credit for Korean tax [(2)/(4) x 1,000]		193	496	831	1,197	1,601
(8) Additional US tax due [(6) − (7), if (6) is larger]		25	67	110	160	213
(9) Excess US tax credit [(7) − (6), if (7) is larger]		0	0	0	0	0
(10) Dividend received by Amelectro, after all taxes [(1)/(4) x 1,000 − (8)]		424	1,092	1,828	2,633	3,520

Amelectro must pay regular US corporate income taxes (34 percent rate) on dividends received from Korelectro; however, the US tax law allows Amelectro to claim a tax credit for income taxes paid to Korea on the Korean income that generated the dividend. The process of computing the original income in Korea, which is called "grossing up," is shown in lines (1), (2) and (3) of Table A5.5. The imputed Korean won income is converted from won to dollars in lines (4) and (5). US income tax (34 percent) is calculated in line (6) and a tax credit is given for Korean income taxes paid as shown in line (7). Line (8) gives the net additional US tax due, and line (10) shows the net dividend received by Amelectro after the additional US tax is paid.

Finally, Table A5.6 computes the cumulative NPV and MIRR on cash flows from Korelectro from the viewpoint of Amelectro. In this case Korelectro does not pass the test because it has a negative NPV and an MIRR of 17 percent, insufficient for the 20 percent rate of return required by Amelectro.

Table A5.6
Net Present Value to Amelectro of Cash Flows from Korelectro

Item (by year)	0	1	2	3	4	5
In Millions of Won						
(1) License fee from Korelectro [Table A5.2, (7)]		880	1,007	1,153	1,320	1,511
(2) Margin on exports to Korelectro [2.5% of (3) in Table A5.2]		400	459	525	602	690
(3) Total receipts		1,280	1,466	1,678	1,922	2,201
(4) Exchange rate (won/$)	1,200	1,236	1,273	1,311	1,351	1,392
In Thousands of Dollars						
(5) Pretax receipts [(3)/(4) x 1,000]		1,036	1,152	1,280	1,423	1,581
(6) US taxes (34%)		(352)	(392)	(435)	(484)	(538)
(7) License fee and export profit, after tax		684	760	827	939	1,043
(8) After-tax dividend [Table A5.5, (10)]		424	1,092	1,828	2,633	3,520
(9) Project cost	(18,000)					
(10) Terminal value						17,000
(11) Net cash flow	(18,000)	1,108	1,852	2,655	3,572	21,563
(12) PV factor (20%)	1.000	0.833	0.694	0.579	0.482	0.402
(13) NPV each year	(18,000)	923	1,285	1,537	1,722	8,668
(14) Cumulative NPV	(18,000)	(17,077)	(15,792)	(14,255)	(12,533)	(3,865)
(15) MIRR = 17%						

SENSITIVITY ANALYSIS

The above analysis was carried out with a set of "most likely" assumptions to forecast NPVs and MIRRs. The sensitivity to foreign exchange and/or political risks can be tested by simulating what would happen to NPV and MIRR under a variety of "what if" scenarios. For instance, the analysis can be repeated by assuming that the Korean won would depreciate at a 6 percent annual rate as opposed to the 3 percent initially assumed. With reference to political risk, one could ask, "what if Korea should impose controls on the payment of dividends or license fees to Amelectro?" The impact of blocked funds on the NPV from Amelectro's viewpoint would depend on when the blockage occurs, when the blocked funds would eventually be released (if ever) and what reinvestment opportunities exist in Korea for the blocked funds. In case of expropriation the value of future cash flows forgone is the key to establishing its effect. With reference to tables A5.4 and A5.6, the project's NPV and MIRR would also be sensitive to a change in the assumed terminal value, the size of the initial project cost, the amount of working capital financed locally and the tax rates in Korea and the United States. It is possible that the project would qualify at the 20 percent required rate of return if some of the variables which are within control of Amelectro could be changed. For instance, it may be possible for Amelectro to reduce the initial investment, to raise license fees and to increase the margin on exports to Korelectro from Amelectro.

THE MODIFIED INTERNAL RATE OF RETURN (MIRR)

This rate of return is a modification of the *internal rate of return*, which is defined as the rate of return that equates the present values of capital outlays and their resultant cash flows. The internal rate of return is a rough indicator of relative profitability since it ignores a company's cost of capital, which depends on the prevailing borrowing rate of corporations and the return equity shareholders expect. In other words, the internal rate of return assumes that net receipts or cash flows from a project are reinvested at the project's rate of return, which is not realistic since future investments will most likely have a different rate of return. In still other words, it would be preferred to assume that all net receipts from a project are reinvested at a company's cost of capital.

To overcome the above-mentioned shortcoming of the internal rate of return, we introduce the modified internal rate of return. The computation of the MIRR can best be explained by way of an example. Let us consider an investment of \$2,000 which results in a cash flow of \$1,000, \$800, \$600 and \$200 at the end of the first, second, third and fourth year, respectively. Thus, we have:

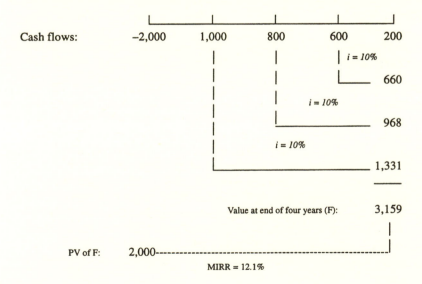

Note that in the above example, we first compute the values of $1,000, $800, $600 at the end of the fourth year assuming a cost of capital of 10 percent and using the discount tables of Appendix 2. Next, we add the four values at the end of the fourth year ($200, $660, $968 and $1,331). Finally, we compute the interest rate which transforms the present value of $2,000 into a value of $3,159 at the end of the fourth year; this gives a MIRR of 12.1 percent.

Probability of a Value of $Z = [P - E(P)]/\sigma$ Being Smaller than (or Equal to) the Values Tabulated in the Margins

z	.00	.01	.02	.03	.04	.05	.06	.07	.08	.09
.0	.5000	.4960	.4920	.4880	.4840	.4801	.4761	.4721	.4681	.4641
.1	.4602	.4562	.4522	.4483	.4443	.4404	.4364	.4325	.4286	.4247
.2	.4207	.4168	.4129	.4090	.4052	.4013	.3974	.3936	.3897	.3859
.3	.3821	.3783	.3745	.3707	.3669	.3632	.3594	.3557	.3520	.3483
.4	.3446	.3409	.3372	.3336	.3300	.3264	.3228	.3192	.3156	.3121
.5	.3085	.3050	.3015	.2981	.2946	.2912	.2877	.2843	.2810	.2776
.6	.2743	.2709	.2676	.2643	.2611	.2578	.2546	.2514	.2483	.2451
.7	.2420	.2389	.2358	.2327	.2296	.2266	.2236	.2206	.2177	.2148
.8	.2119	.2090	.2061	.2033	.2005	.1977	.1949	.1922	.1894	.1867
.9	.1841	.1814	.1788	.1762	.1736	.1711	.1685	.1660	.1635	.1611
1.0	.1587	.1562	.1539	.1515	.1492	.1469	.1446	.1423	.1401	.1379
1.1	.1357	.1335	.1314	.1292	.1271	.1251	.1230	.1210	.1190	.1170
1.2	.1151	.1131	.1112	.1093	.1075	.1056	.1038	.1020	.1003	.0985
1.3	.0968	.0951	.0934	.0918	.0901	.0885	.0869	.0853	.0838	.0823
1.4	.0808	.0793	.0778	.0764	.0749	.0735	.0721	.0708	.0694	.0681
1.5	.0668	.0655	.0643	.0630	.0648	.0606	.0594	.0582	.0571	.0559
1.6	.0548	.0537	.0526	.0516	.0505	.0495	.0485	.0475	.0465	.0455
1.7	.0446	.0436	.0427	.0418	.0409	.0401	.0392	.0384	.0375	.0367
1.8	.0359	.0351	.0344	.0336	.0329	.0322	.0314	.0307	.0301	.0294
1.9	.0287	.0281	.0274	.0268	.0262	.0256	.0250	.0244	.0239	.0233
2.0	.0228	.0222	.0217	.0212	.0207	.0202	.0197	.0192	.0188	.0183
2.1	.0179	.0174	.0170	.0166	.0162	.0158	.0154	.0150	.0146	.0143
2.2	.0139	.0136	.0132	.0129	.0125	.0122	.0119	.0116	.0113	.0110
2.3	.0107	.0104	.0102	.0099	.0096	.0094	.0091	.0089	.0087	.0084
2.4	.0082	.0080	.0078	.0075	.0073	.0071	.0069	.0068	.0066	.0064
2.5	.0062	.0060	.0059	.0057	.0055	.0054	.0052	.0051	.0049	.0048
2.6	.0047	.0045	.0044	.0043	.0041	.0040	.0039	.0038	.0037	.0036
2.7	.0035	.0034	.0033	.0032	.0031	.0030	.0029	.0028	.0027	.0026
2.8	.0026	.0025	.0024	.0023	.0023	.0022	.0021	.0021	.0020	.0019
2.9	.0019	.0018	.0018	.0017	.0016	.0016	.0015	.0015	.0014	.0014
3.0	.0013	.0013	.0013	.0012	.0012	.0011	.0011	.0011	.0010	.0010
3.1	.0010	.0009	.0009	.0009	.0008	.0008	.0008	.0008	.0007	.0007
3.2	.0007	.0007	.0006	.0006	.0006	.0006	.0006	.0005	.0005	.0005
3.3	.0005	.0005	.0005	.0004	.0004	.0004	.0004	.0004	.0004	.0003
3.4	.0003	.0003	.0003	.0003	.0003	.0003	.0003	.0003	.0003	.0002
3.6	.0002	.0002	.0001	.0001	.0001	.0001	.0001	.0001	.0001	.0001
3.9	.0000									

Appendix 7

Development of a New Subsidiary (Case Study)

PURPOSE

The purpose of this case study is to demonstrate a capital budgeting analysis which starts with simplifying assumptions. Next, we relax some of these simplifying assumptions to show the potential complexity of capital budgeting analysis.

PROJECT SUMMARY

About half a year ago a US-based manufacturer of high-quality roller skates, Rolling Ahead Inc., considered the export of roller skates to Switzerland. It has not yet made a decision, since it anticipates that the Swiss government plans to prohibit these exports in retaliation for recent trade restrictions placed by the US government on Swiss exports of watches and high precision railway equipment. Rolling Ahead is, therefore, considering the development of a subsidiary in Switzerland that could manufacture and sell the roller skates locally. The following information has been collected from various departments of Rolling Ahead and meetings between its executives and Swiss government officials:

- *Initial investment*. It is estimated that 30 million Swiss francs (SF) are needed for the project (including funds to support working capital). With the existing spot exchange rate of $0.50 per Swiss franc, this implies a $15 million initial investment by the parent company.
- *Project life*. The host government of Switzerland has promised to make a payment to the parent company in order to purchase the plant after four years. Thus, the project has an expected life of four years.

- *Salvage value.* The Swiss government will pay the parent SF18 million to assume ownership of the subsidiary at the end of four years. There is no capital gain tax on the sale of the subsidiary.

- *Exchange rates.* Rolling Ahead is using the spot exchange rate as its best forecast of the exchange rates in the future. Thus, the forecast exchange rate for all future periods is $0.50.

- *Costs.* The expense of leasing extra office space is SF1.5 million per year; other annual overhead expenses are estimated at SF1.5 million. The variable costs (labor, materials, etc.) per unit are estimated at SF300 during the first and second year, SF375 during the third year and SF390 during the fourth year.

- *Price and demand.* The estimated price and demand during the next four years are estimated as follows:

Year	Price per Roller Skate	Demand in Switzerland ('000 units)
1	SF525	60
2	SF525	60
3	SF540	100
4	SF570	100

- *Swiss taxes on income earned.* The Swiss government will impose a 20 percent tax rate on income earned by the subsidiary.

- *US government taxes on income earned by the subsidiary.* The US government will allow a tax credit on taxes paid in Switzerland. Earnings remitted by the parent will not, therefore, be taxed in the United States.

- *Cash flows from subsidiary to parent.* At the end of each year, the subsidiary plans to send all net cash flows received to the parent. There are no restrictions on the cash flows to be send to the parent; however, the Swiss government imposes a 10 percent withholding tax on any funds sent to the parent.

- *Depreciation.* The Swiss government will allow the subsidiary of Rolling Ahead to depreciate the cost of the plant and equipment at a maximum rate of SF3 million per year.

- *Required rate of return.* Rolling Ahead requires a 15 percent return on this project.

EXAMINATION

We will examine the effect of (a) exchange rate fluctuations, (b) inflation, (c) financing arrangements, (d) blocked funds and (e) uncertain salvage value by answering the following questions:

1. What is the net present value (NPV) of the proposed Swiss subsidiary, from the parent's perspective?

2. Rolling Ahead is using the Swiss franc's current spot rate ($0.50) as a forecast for all future periods of concern. Please carry out a sensitivity analysis under weak-franc and strong-franc scenarios.

3. What is the impact of inflation on the NPV of the proposed subsidiary? Would this impact be different if the subsidiary would be in a developing country with a high inflation rate?

4. Rolling Ahead has the possibility to borrow SF15 million to purchase the offices in Switzerland instead of leasing them. The annual interest payments on this loan amount to SF1.5 million and the principal will be paid at the end of Year 4, when the project is terminated. The offices are expected to have a market value of SF15 million at the end of Year 4, at which time they will be sold. Would you recommend the leasing or purchasing option?

5. Rolling Ahead also wants to consider using its own funds to purchase the offices. Thus, the initial investment is $22.5 million, consisting of the original $15 million investment explained earlier, plus an additional $7.5 million to purchase the offices. Would you recommend this option?

6. In some cases, the host country may block funds that the subsidiary attempts to send to the parent. How would the NPV of the proposed subsidiary be affected if earnings generated by it had to be reinvested locally until it is sold at the end of Year 4? Rolling Ahead decided that these funds will be used to purchase marketable securities that are expected to yield 5 percent annually, after taxes.

7. The salvage value of a project can have a significant impact on its NPV. You are, therefore, asked to determine the break-even salvage value or the salvage value necessary to achieve a zero NPV for the proposed subsidiary.

8. Assuming that Rolling Ahead's export business to Switzerland would generate annual net cash flows of $1.5 million over the next four years, would the proposed subsidiary still be feasible if the exporting business to Switzerland could be continued (i.e., Switzerland does not impose trade restrictions on imported roller skates)?

PROJECT DISCUSSION

Table A7.1 shows the computations necessary to arrive at the project's accumulative NPV at the end of the last year. Provided the discount rate of 15 percent fully accounts for the project's risk, Rolling Ahead may accept it since the NPV is positive ($3,344,000).

Table A7.2 presents the results of a weak-franc and a strong-franc scenario. A strong franc is clearly beneficial as demonstrated by the increased dollar value of cash flows received. The large differences in cash flow received by the parent in the different scenarios illustrate the impact of exchange rate expectations on the feasibility of an international project.

Table A7.2 shows that the estimated NPV is highest if the franc is expected to strengthen and lowest if it is expected to weaken. The estimated NPV is negative for the weak-franc scenario and positive for the stable-franc and strong-franc scenarios. Provided data are available, the analysis could be further refined

Table A7.1
Capital Budgeting Analysis of Rolling Ahead Inc. ('000)

	Year 0	Year 1	Year 2	Year 3	Year 4
1. Demand		60	60	100	100
2. Price per unit		SF525	SF525	SF540	SF570
3. **Total revenue = (1) x (2)**		**SF31,500**	**SF31,500**	**SF54,000**	**SF57,000**
4. Variable cost per unit		SF0.30	SF0.30	SF0.375	SF0.39
5. Total variable cost = (1) x (4)		SF18,000	SF18,000	SF37,500	SF39,000
6. Lease expenses		SF1,500	SF1,500	SF1,500	SF1,500
7. Other overhead		SF1,500	SF1,500	SF1,500	SF1,500
8. Depreciation		SF3,000	SF3,000	SF3,000	SF3,000
9. **Total expenses = (5) + (6) + (7) + (8)**		**SF24,000**	**SF24,000**	**SF43,500**	**SF45,000**
10. Before-tax earnings = (3) − (9)		SF7,500	SF7,500	SF10,500	SF12,000
11. Swiss tax (20%)		SF1,500	SF1,500	SF2,100	SF2,400
12. After-tax earnings		SF6,000	SF6,000	SF8,400	SF9,600
13. **Net cash flow to subsidiary = (8) + (12)**		**SF9,000**	**SF9,000**	**SF11,400**	**SF12,600**
14. SF remitted by subsidiary (100% of CF)		SF9,000	SF9,000	SF11,400	SF12,600
15. Tax on remitted funds (10%)		SF900	SF900	SF1,140	SF1,260
16. **SF remitted after withholding tax**		**SF8,100**	**SF8,100**	**SF10,260**	**SF11,340**
17. Salvage value					SF18,000
18. Exchange rate $ per SF		$0.50	$0.50	$0.50	$0.50
19. Cash flow to parent		$4,050	$4,050	$5,130	$14,670
20. **PV of parent cash flows (15%)**		**$3,522**	**$3,062**	**$3,372**	**$8,388**
21. Initial investment by parent	$15,000				
22. Cumulative NPV		−$11,478	−$8,416	−$5,044	$3,344

Table A7.2
The Impact of Different Exchange Rates ('000)

	Year 0	Year 1	Year 2	Year 3	Year 4
SF remitted after withholding taxes (including salvage value)		SF8,100	SF8,100	SF10,260	SF29,340
Weak-franc Scenario					
Exchange rate of SF		$0.48	$0.45	$0.40	$0.36
Cash flows to parent		$3,888	$3,645	$4,104	$10,562
PV of cash flows (15%)		$3,381	$2,756	$2,698	$6,040
Initial investment by parent	$15,000				
Cumulative NPV		–$11,619	–$8,863	–$6,165	–$125
Strong-franc Scenario					
Exchange rate of SF		$0.53	$0.57	$0.60	$0.65
Cash flows to parent		$4,293	$4,617	$6,156	$19,071
PV of cash flows (15%)		$3,733	$3,491	$4,048	$10,905
Initial investment by parent	$15,000				
Cumulative NPV		–$11,267	–$7,776	–$3,728	$7,177

by introducing the probability distribution of these three scenarios for the franc during the project's life.

The case study takes inflation into account since the variable costs and the price of the roller skates increase over time. In some developing countries, inflation can be strong and, therefore, affect a project's net cash flows significantly. Although costs and revenues are affected in the same direction by inflation, their magnitudes can be quite different from each other. This may, for instance, be the case when a project involves importing partially manufactured components and selling the product locally. If the local economy's inflation is stronger than the inflation in the country from where the foreign components are imported, the impact of inflation will be more significant on revenues than on costs.

From the viewpoint of the parent, the joint impact of inflation and exchange rate fluctuations on a subsidiary's net cash flows may produce a partial offsetting effect since exchange rates of highly inflated countries tend to weaken over time. In other words, a subsidiary's inflated earnings are deflated when converted into the parent's home currency. There is, however, no guarantee that a currency will depreciate when the local inflation rate is high, since inflation is only one of the factors which influence exchange rates.

General inflation exists if all current prices increase at approximately the same rate both at home and abroad, or if domestic current prices increase at one rate and foreign current prices at another rate, but these differential rates of inflation are completely offset by exchange rates (which is not likely to happen). Thus, if domestic and foreign inflation is estimated at a rate of, say 8 percent per year, or if domestic and foreign inflation is expected at respective annual rates of 8 percent and 11 percent and domestic currency is estimated to appreciate at 3 percent per year, then all real project prices remain the same.

From the financial point of view there is no difference between borrowing SF 15 million to purchase the Swiss offices and to lease them since:

- the annual cash outflows in the purchase and lease options are the same (annual lease payments of SF1.5 million and annual interest payments of 1.5 million);
- the loan principal of SF15 million, which must be paid at the end of four years, is offset by the price at which the offices are expected to be sold (SF15 million) at the end of Year 4; and
- the subsidiary's maximum depreciation expense allowed by the Swiss government already has been taken before the subsidiary would own the offices (therefore, it cannot increase its annual depreciation expenses).

In order to examine the possibility of having Rolling Ahead use its own funds to purchase the offices in Switzerland, we have to introduce the following revisions:

- there will be no lease payments since the parent purchases the offices,
- the initial investment by the parent is $22.5 million instead of $15 million, and
- the savage value to be received by the parent is SF33 million instead of SF18 million because the offices are assumed to have a market value of SF15 million at the end of Year 4.

Table A7.3 shows the capital budgeting analysis for Rolling Ahead in which the parent finances the entire $22.5 million investment. The original, stable exchange rate of $0.50 per Swiss franc is used.

Comparing the results of Tables A7.1 and A7.3, we can see that leasing the offices in Switzerland is preferred to purchasing them with Rolling Ahead's funds, since in the former case the NPV is $3,344,000 and in the latter case the NPV amounts to $1,675,000. In addition, the purchasing option causes more exchange exposure to the parent because the parent provides the entire initial investment in dollars, the SF cash flows to be remitted to the parent are larger and the salvage value in SF to be remitted to the parent is larger.

Table A7.4 presents the capital budgeting analysis with blocked funds. Thus, Rolling Ahead is not allowed to remit the subsidiary's revenues to the United States until the end of Year 4 and, therefore, purchases marketable securities that are expected to yield 5 percent annually, after taxes. Note that the original stable exchange rate is used and that the withholding tax is not applied until the funds are remitted to the parent, which is in Year 4. The NPV of the proposed subsidiary is reduced from $3,344,000 to $1,702,000 since Rolling Ahead makes

Table A7.3

Analysis with Alternative Financing Arrangement: Rolling Ahead Inc. ('000)

	Year 0	Year 1	Year 2	Year 3	Year 4
1. Demand		60	60	100	100
2. Price per unit		SF525	SF525	SF540	SF570
3. **Total revenue =** (1) x (2)		**SF31,500**	**SF31,500**	**SF54,000**	**SF57,000**
4. Variable cost per unit		SF0.30	SF0.30	SF0.375	SF0.39
5. Total variable cost = (1) x (4)		SF18,000	SF18,000	SF37,500	SF39,000
6. Overhead		SF1,500	SF1,500	SF1,500	SF1,500
7. Depreciation		SF3,000	SF3,000	SF3,000	SF3,000
8. **Total expenses =** (5) + (6) + (7)		**SF22,500**	**SF22,500**	**SF42,000**	**SF43,500**
9. Before-tax earnings = (3) – (8)		SF9,000	SF9,000	SF12,000	SF13,500
10. Swiss tax (20%)		SF1,800	SF1,800	SF2,400	SF2,700
11. After-tax earnings		SF7,200	SF7,200	SF9,600	SF10,800
12. **Net cash flow to subsidiary =** (7) + (11)		**SF10,200**	**SF10,200**	**SF12,600**	**SF13,800**
13. SF remitted by subsidiary (100% of CF)		SF10,200	SF10,200	SF12,600	SF13,800
14. Tax on remitted funds (10%)		SF1,020	SF1,020	SF1,260	SF1,380
15. **SF remitted after withholding tax**		**SF9,180**	**SF9,180**	**SF11,340**	**SF12,420**
16. Salvage value					SF33,000
17. Exchange rate $ per SF		$0.50	$0.50	$0.50	$0.50
18. Cash flow to parent		$4,590	$4,590	$5,670	$22,710
19. **PV of parent cash flows (15%)**		**$3,991**	**$3,470**	**$3,728**	**$12,986**
20. Initial investment by parent	$22,500				
21. Cumulative NPV		–$18,509	–$15,039	–$11,311	$1,675

Table A7.4
Capital Budgeting with Blocked Funds: Rolling Ahead Inc. ('000)

	Year 0	Year 1	Year 2	Year 3	Year 4
SF to be remitted by subsidiary (line 14 of Table A7.1)		SF9,000	SF9,000	SF11,400	SF12,600
					SF11,970
SF accumulated by reinvesting funds to be remitted					SF 9,923
					SF10,418
					SF44,911
Withholding tax (10%)					SF 4,491
SF remitted after withholding tax					SF40,420
Salvage value					SF18,000
Exchange rate					$0.50
Cash flows to parent					$29,210
PV of parent cash flows (15%)					$16,702
Initial investment by parent	$15,000				
Cumulative NPV		–$15,000	–$15,000	–$15,000	$ 1,702

only 5 percent return with the marketable securities, which is low compared with its required 15 percent return on the proposed project. In addition, the risk of the project is greater because all parent cash flows depend on the exchange rate four years from now.

Typically, the salvage value of a project like the proposed subsidiary has a significant impact on its NPV. When the salvage value is uncertain, the parent may desire to incorporate various possible outcomes for the salvage value and reestimate the NPV based on each possible outcome. Under these circumstances, it is also recommended to determine the break-even salvage value or the salvage value which is necessary to achieve a zero NPV. We first compute the present value of parent cash flows (all calculations in '000 US dollars):

$$\text{PV of parent cash flows} = 0.8696(\$4,050) + 0.7561(\$4,050)$$
$$+ 0.6575(\$5,130) + 0.5718(\$5,670) = \$13,199$$

Given the present value of the cash flows and the estimated initial investment, the break-even salvage value (SV) is determined as follows:

$$SV = 1.7490(\$15,000 - \$13,199) = \$3,150$$

Table A7.5
Capital Budgeting When Prevailing Cash Flows Are Affected: Rolling Ahead Inc.
('000)

	Year 0	Year 1	Year 2	Year 3	Year 4
Original cash flows to parent (Table 1, line 19)		$4,050	$4,050	$5,130	$14,670
Impact of exports on prevailing cash flows		−$1,500	−$1,500	−$1,500	−$1,500
Cash flows to parent after above impact		$2,550	$2,550	$3,630	$13,170
PV of cash flows to parent (15%)		$2,217	$1,928	$2,387	$7,531
Initial investment	$15,000				
Cumulative NPV		−$12,783	−$10,855	−$8,468	−$937

Since all calculations were in '000 US dollars, we conclude that (given the original information of Table A7.1) Rolling Ahead would accept the project only if the salvage were estimated to be at least $3,150,000. Assuming the forecast exchange rate of $0.50 per Swiss franc, the project must sell for more than SF2(3,150,000) = SF6,300,000 to result in a positive NPV (assuming no taxes are paid on this amount). The Swiss government's offer to purchase the plant after four years for SF18 million is not a bad one! If Rolling Ahead did not have this offer, it could assess the probability that the subsidiary would sell for more than the break-even salvage value and then incorporate this evaluation in its decision to accept or reject the project.

Table A7.5 shows the capital budgeting analysis for the situation where (a) there is no concern about the Swiss government's imposing trade restrictions on imported roller skates, (b) Rolling Ahead still considers the establishment of a subsidiary in Switzerland because Swiss production costs are expected to be lower than in the United States and (c) without a subsidiary, Rolling Ahead's export business to Switzerland is expected to generate net cash flows of $1.5 million over the next four years. The project's NPV is now negative as a result of the adverse effect on prevailing cash flows.

Appendix 8

Second-Generation Currency Risk Management Products

Let us consider a US-based firm which possesses a long DM1,000,000 exposure—an account receivable (A/R)—to be settled in 90 days. At a forward rate of $0.5220/DM, the proceeds of the forward contract in 90 days will yield $522,000. A second alternative for the firm would be to construct a *synthetic forward* using options. The synthetic forward combines three different elements:

- long position in DM (A/R of DM1,000,000);
- buy a put option on DM at a strike price of $0.5220/DM, paying a premium of $0.0050/DM; and
- sell a call option on DM at a strike price of $0.5220/DM, earning a premium of $0.0050/DM.

Note that the purchase of the put option requires a premium payment whereas the sale of the call option earns the premium payment. If both options are struck at the forward rate, the premiums should be the same and the net premium payment should have a value of zero.

The outcome of the combined options can be easily confirmed by tracing what would happen at all exchange rates to the left of $0.5220/DM, and what would happen to the right of $0.5220/DM.

At all exchange rates to the left of $0.5220/DM:

- the firm would receive DM1,000,000 in 90 days;
- the call option on DM sold by the firm would expire out-of-the-money; and
- the firm would exercise the put option on DM to sell the DM received at $0.5220/DM.

At all exchange rates below \$0.5220/DM, the US-based firm would earn
\$522,000 from the receivable. At all exchange rates to the right of \$0.5220/DM:

- the firm would receive DM1,000,000 in 90 days;
- the put option on DM purchased by the firm would expire out-of-the-money; and
- the firm would turn over the DM1,000,000 received to the buyer of the call who now exercises the call option against the firm. The firm receives \$0.5220 from the call option buyer.

Thus, at all exchange rates above or below \$0.5220, the US-based firm nets
\$522,000 in domestic currency. The combined spot-option position has behaved
identically to that of a forward contract.

A firm with the exact opposite position, a DM1,000,000 payable in 90 days,
can construct a synthetic forward in the following way:

- the firm would pay DM1,000,000 in 90 days;
- buy a call option on German marks at a strike price of \$0.5220/DM; and
- sell a put option on German marks at a strike price of \$0.5220/DM.

Why would a firm undertake the above relatively complex position in order
to simply create a forward contract? The answer is obtained by considering the
option premiums earned and paid. We have assumed that the option prices used
were precisely the forward rate and the resulting option premiums paid and
earned were exactly equal. This need not be the case. If the option strike prices,
which must be identical for both options, are not the same as the forward rate,
the two premiums may differ by a slight amount. The net premium position
may then end up as a net premium earning or a net premium payment.

An additional possibility is that the firm finds, for the moment at which the
position is taken, that the call premium earned may actually slightly exceed or
be lower than the put option premium paid. This means the options market is
temporarily out of equilibrium. Such occurrence is possible given the judgment
required in the pricing of options (different banks pricing options do not necessarily use the identical volatilities at all times) and the inherent decentralized
structure of the currency and currency option markets.

Many firms consider the main "problem" with the use of options for risk
management the up-front premium payment. Although it is only a portion of
the total payoff profile of the hedge, many firms view the expenditure for the
purchase of a financial derivative as prohibitively expensive. In comparison, the
forward contract that eliminates currency risk requires no out-of-pocket expenditure by the firm and requires no real specification of expectations regarding
exchange rate movements. To overcome the aforementioned problem, *zero-
premium option* products have been introduced.

Zero-premium option products are designed to require no out-of-pocket premium payment at the initiation of the hedge and include the *range forward* and the *participating forward*. Both of these products (a) are priced on the basis of the forward rate, (b) are constructed to provide a zero-premium payment up front and (c) allow the hedger to take advantage of expectations of the direction of exchange movements. It is noted that if hedgers have no expectation of the direction of exchange movements (e.g., the German mark will strengthen in relation to the US dollar), they should buy a forward or do nothing at all.

THE RANGE FORWARD

The range forward is constructed by:

• buying a put option with a strike rate below the forward rate, for the full amount of the long currency exposure (100% coverage); and

• selling a call option with a strike rate above the forward rate, for the full amount of the long currency exposure (100% coverage).

The range forward has been marketed under a variety of other names: *flexible forward, option fence* or simply *fence, mini-max* or *zero-cost tunnel*.

The hedger chooses one side of the "range" or spread, normally the down side (put strike rate), which then dictates the strike rate at which the call option will be sold. The call option must be chosen at an equal distance from the forward rate as the put option strike price from the forward rate. If the hedger believes that there is a significant possibility the currency will move in the firm's favor, and by a sizable degree, the put floor rate may be set relatively low in order for the ceiling to be higher or further out from the forward rate and still enjoy a zero premium.

For instance, if the aforementioned US-based firm possessing a long DM1,000,000 believes that the exchange rate will move in its favor over the 90-day period, it could obtain a range forward by buying a put with a strike price of $0.5020/DM, paying a premium of $0.0047/DM, and selling a call option with a strike price of $0.5420/DM, earning a premium of $0.0052/DM. The hedger has bounded the range over which the firm's A/R value moves as an uncovered position, with a put option floor and a sold call option ceiling. It is noted that this forward range is not exactly a zero premium option since there is a small difference between the premium paid and the premium earned. However, these premiums are close enough to result in a near-zero net premium:

$$\text{Net premium} = (\$0.0047/\text{DM} - \$0.0052/\text{DM}) \times \text{DM1,000,000} = -\$500.$$

The benefits of the combined position are clear given that the put option premium alone amounts to $4,700.

If both strike prices are the same, the range forward becomes a synthetic forward as described above. If both strike prices chosen are equal to the actual forward rate, the synthetic equals the actual forward contract. The synthetic forward should have zero-net premium. If the strike rates of the options are selected independently of the desire for an exact zero-net premium up front (it must still bracket the forward rate), it is called an *option collar* or *cylinder option*.

THE PARTICIPATING FORWARD

The participating forward is constructed by:

- buying a put option with a strike price below the forward rate, for the full amount of the long currency exposure (100% coverage); and
- selling a call option with a strike price which is the same as the one of the put option, for a portion of the total currency exposure (<100% coverage).

It is an option combination that allows a hedger to take a position which will share in potential upside movements in the exchange rate, while providing option-based downside protection, all at a net-zero premium. The participating forward is sometimes referred to as the *zero-cost ratio option* or the *forward participation agreement*.

Similar to the range forward, the buyer of a participating forward will normally choose the put option strike rate first. Since the call option strike rate is the same as the one of the put, all that remains is to establish the participation rate of the proportion of the exposure sold as a call option. For instance, our US-based firm possessing a long DM1,000,000 wishes to choose the put option protection level at $0.5020/DM with a premium of $0.0047/DM. A call option sold with the same strike rate of $0.5020/DM would earn a premium of $0.0077/DM. The call premium is substantially higher than the put premium because the call option is already in-the-money (ITM).

The percentage cover for the call option is then determined so that call premium earnings exactly offset put premiums paid:

Put premium = Percent cover × Call premium, or
Percent cover = ($0.0047/DM)/($0.077/DM = 0.6104 = 61.04%

The firm must sell a call option of 0.6104 × DM1,000,000, or DM610,400, in order to achieve a net-zero premium.

The *participation rate* is the residual percentage of the exposure that is not covered by the sale of the call option. For example, if the percent cover is 61.04 percent, the participation rate would be 1 − the percent cover, or 38.96 percent. This means that for all favorable exchange rate movements, those above $0.5020/DM, the hedger would "participate" or enjoy 38.96 percent of the differential. However, like all option-based hedges, downside exposure is bound by the put option strike rate. The expectations of the buyer are similar to the range forward; only the degree of foreign currency bullishness is greater. The participating forward will be superior in outcome to the range forward if the exchange rate moves further in the favorable direction than for the range forward.

Index

About the Author

HENRI L. BEENHAKKER teaches courses in finance, risk management, investment analysis, and enterprise evaluation at the New York Institute of Finance and the International Institute of USDA's Graduate School. He has served as principal economist at the World Bank, chairman of the Department of Industrial Management at the University of Iowa, and adjunct professor at the School of Advanced Studies at Johns Hopkins University. Dr. Beenhakker is the author of more than 40 articles and seven books, including two previously published by Quorum: *Risk Management in Project Finance and Implementation* (1997) and *Investment Decision Making in the Private and Public Sectors* (1996).